Secret Agenda

SECRET AGENDA

The United States Government,
Nazi Scientists,
and Project Paperclip, 1945 to 1990

LINDA HUNT

St. Martin's Press
New York

Design by Glen M. Edelstein

Library of Congress Cataloging-in-Publication Data

Hunt, Linda.
    Secret agenda : the United States government, Nazi scientists, and project paperclip, 1945 to 1990.
        p. cm.
    Includes bibliographical references and index.
    ISBN 0-312-05510-2
    1. World War, 1939–1945—Technology.   2. Brain drain—Germany—History
—20th century.   3. Scientists—Germany—Recruiting—History—20th century.
4. Scientists—United States—Recruiting—History—20th century.   5. National
socialists—History—20th century.   6. War criminals—Germany—History—
20th century.   7. Research—United States—History—20th century.   8. German
Americans—History—20th century.   I. Title.
D810.S2H86   1991   353.0085'6'08931—dc20   90-49185

First Edition: May 1991
10 9 8 7 6 5 4 3 2 1

To My Parents

CONTENTS

ACKNOWLEDGMENTS

This book would not exist were it not for the Freedom of Information Act. I am grateful to attorney Elaine English, the Reporters Committee for Freedom of the Press, attorneys Lee Levine and Gregory Burton from the Washington, D.C., law firm of Ross, Dixon and Masback, and Robert Gellman of Congressman Glen English's Government Information Subcommittee for helping me with FOIA requests.

Government agencies' responses to my FOIA requests ranged from helpful to outright obstructionist. On the helpful side, NASA's Marshall Space Flight Center in Huntsville, Alabama, the FBI, and Army intelligence deserve the highest praise for upholding the spirit of the FOIA. The U.S. Army Intelligence and Security Command at Fort Meade, Maryland, was a major source of information; many INSCOM dossiers are cited in the endnotes. My research was helped immensely in 1986 when I won an FOIA appeal in which the Department of Army counsel ruled that I could receive INSCOM files of living Paperclip scientists because the public's right to know outweighed the scientists' privacy rights under the law. I thank FOIA director Robert J. Walsh, former FOIA director Tom Conley, Marcia Galbreath, and others at INSCOM for working so conscientiously on my requests through the years.

I am especially grateful to the archivists and declassifiers at the National Archives and Records Service in Washington and the Washington National Records Center in Suitland, Maryland, who helped me get thousands of Paperclip records declassified under the FOIA. John Taylor, the late John Mendelsohn, Ed Reese, Richard Boylan, George Wagner, William Lewis, Will Mahoney, Jo Ann Williamson, Terri Hammett, Harry Rilley, and Sally Marks generously shared their knowledge and their humor while helping me locate documents to piece together this story.

At the other end of the scale lies the U.S. Army Materiel Command. I obtained six thousand Edgewood Arsenal documents in 1987, but it took more than a year, two attorneys, and a threatened lawsuit to get the records. My FOIA request was filed in May 1986 for documents held in Army custody at the Washington National Records Center. A month later I was told that I could inspect the records. However, when I arrived at the WNRC, an Army employee showed me forms that indicated that seven boxes had been checked out to Edgewood's historian and twelve additional boxes were "missing." Then Army Materiel circled its wagons, denied that the records existed, and later tried to charge me $239,680 in "search fees." The Army counsel's answer to my formal appeal of those charges was as outrageous as the fee. "The Army's funds were appropriated for the national defense, not to aid aspiring authors," counsel Thomas F. Kranz replied. The documents were finally released after numerous meetings between attorneys on both sides. I am grateful to attorneys Lee Levine and Gregory Burton for helping me obtain the documents.

Other government agencies, archives, and libraries that provided assistance include the U.S. Justice Department's Office of Special Investigations, the Library of Congress, the Harry S. Truman Library, the Dwight D. Eisenhower Library, the Franklin Roosevelt Library, the Hoover Institute at Stanford University, the Center for Military History in Washington, D.C., the U.S. Army Military History Institute at Carlisle Barracks, Pennsylvania, the history offices at Brooks, Maxwell and Bolling Air Force bases, the Office of Naval History, the National Institutes of Health, the Inter-American Defense Board, the Department of Commerce, NASA's history office, and the Oregon Historical Society in Portland. Private organizations include the National Security Archives, the Anti-Defamation League of B'nai B'rith, and the Simon Wiesenthal Center.

I am especially appreciative of those who encouraged my research from the beginning: Michael Jennings for providing invaluable assistance with research and interviews; Len Ackland, editor of the *Bulletin of the Atomic Scientists*, for publishing my coverup story in 1985; the Investigative Reporters and Editors for honoring that story with its prestigious award; Yaffa Eliach and Brana Gurewitsch from the Center for Holocaust Studies in Brooklyn; Albert Arbor, Eddie Becker, Jerry Eisenberg, Benjamin Eisenstadt, Jack Eisner, Shirley Eisner, Samuel Indenbaum, Dennis King, Hanna Klein, Frank Kuznik, John Loftus, Abram Medow, the Memorial Foundation for Jewish Culture, Dan Moldea, Eli Rosenbaum, Martin Salinger, Julius Schatz, and Cheryl Spaulding; and Jerry Fitzhenry, my agent Leona Schecter, and my parents, Fred and Winifred Hunt, for their unwavering belief that the American public has a right to know this story.

Prologue

AMERICAN soldiers fighting in World War II had barely laid down their guns when hundreds of German and Austrian scientists, including a number implicated in Nazi war crimes, began immigrating to the United States. They were brought here under a secret intelligence project code-named "Paperclip." Ever since, the U.S. government has successfully promoted the lie that Paperclip was a short-term operation limited to a few postwar raids on Hitler's hoard of scientific talent. The General Accounting Office even claims that the project ended in 1947.[1]

All of which is sheer propaganda. For the first time ever, this book reveals that Paperclip was the biggest, longest-running operation involving Nazis in our country's history. The project continued nonstop until 1973—*decades* longer than was previously thought. And remnants of it are still in operation today.[2]

At least sixteen hundred scientific and research specialists and thousands of their dependents were brought to the U.S. under Operation Paperclip. Hundreds of others arrived under two other Paperclip-related projects and went to work for universities, defense contractors, and CIA fronts. The Paperclip operation eventually became such a juggernaut that in 1956 one American ambassador characterized it as "a continuing U.S. recruitment program which has no parallel in any other Allied country."[3]

The lie that Paperclip ended in the 1940s has conveniently

concealed some of the most damning information about the project—in particular the shocking revelation that one of the intelligence officers who ran it was a spy. U.S. Army Lieutenant Colonel William Henry Whalen was the highest-placed American military officer ever convicted of espionage. Despite the extensive publicity devoted to Whalen's trial in the 1960s, exactly what he did for the Joint Chiefs of Staff (JCS) was not disclosed. This book reveals that in 1959 and 1960 Whalen was at the helm of the Joint Intelligence Objectives Agency (JIOA)—which means he was running Paperclip at the same time he was selling America's defense secrets to Soviet intelligence agents.[4]

The full extent of the Soviet penetration of Paperclip remains unknown, since Whalen shredded thousands of documents. But this much is clear: justified as being run in the interest of national security, Paperclip instead posed a serious security threat. In addition to Whalen's activities, there is evidence that the Soviets had penetrated the project almost from the beginning. Almost anything was possible, given the JIOA officers' lax investigations of the foreign scientists' backgrounds.[5]

The legacy of Paperclip is said to be the moon rockets, jet planes, and other scientific achievements that were a product of postwar research in this country. This is true—as far as it goes. What the project's defenders fail to mention is that its legacy also includes the horrific psychochemical experiments conducted on American soldiers at Edgewood Arsenal, Maryland, the U.S. Army center for chemical warfare research. In this book you'll meet eight Paperclip scientists who worked at Edgewood between 1947 and 1966 developing nerve gas and psychochemicals such as LSD. But Edgewood's contribution to the Paperclip legacy could not have been made by the Germans alone. The disturbing truth is that American doctors were the ones who sifted through grim concentration camp reports and ultimately used Nazi science as a basis for Dachau-like experiments on over seven thousand U.S. soldiers.[6]

Paperclip's legacy has its roots in the cold war philosophy espoused by the intelligence officers who ran the operation. Their motives, schemes, and coverup efforts are a logical focus for this book, since those are what shaped Paperclip from the beginning. Moreover, the military's secret agenda was far different from the one foisted on the American public. At its heart was an unshakable conviction that the end justified the means. The officers who ran Paperclip were determined to use any means necessary to keep Nazi scientists out of Russian hands, even if that meant violating U.S. laws and foreign policy.

There may be no better example of the officers' brazen disregard for U.S. policies than the action they took in 1948. As first revealed in an article in the *Bulletin of the Atomic Scientists*, JIOA officers simply changed the records of those scientists they wanted, expunging evidence of war crimes and ardent nazism. Though this meant directly defying an order given by President Truman, JIOA Director Bosquet Wev excused the action by asserting that the government's concern over "picayune details" such as Nazi records would result in "the best interests of the United States [being] subjugated to the efforts expended in beating a dead Nazi horse."[7]

The repercussions of the JIOA officers' actions are still being felt today. One example is retired NASA rocket engineer Arthur Rudolph, who left this country in 1984 rather than face war crimes charges. His case has attracted a bizarre assortment of defenders bent on bringing him back to the United States —including a U.S. congressman with alleged organized crime connections. On May 14, 1990, Congressman James A. Traficant of Ohio told a group of Rudolph's friends in Huntsville, Alabama, that the rocket scientist's problems were caused by a "powerful Jewish lobby" and warned: "If tonight it's Rudolph, who is it tomorrow?" That question undoubtedly made several of Rudolph's colleagues in the audience uncomfortable, since their wartime Nazi activities are also being scrutinized by Justice Department prosecutors.[8]

Other activities covered in this book that have not been

examined up to now or that take on new significance in light of Paperclip's true history include:

- the expansion of JIOA's intelligence operation in 1948 to include Project National Interest, which brought a convicted Nazi war criminal, an ex-Nazi spy, and other ardent Nazis to the United States to work for universities and defense contractors;
- how the CIA used National Interest as a cover to slip covert CIA operatives overseas into the United States;
- how another JIOA project, called "63," signed up Nuremberg defendant Kurt Blome, convicted Nazi war criminal Eduard Houdremont, and other notorious individuals while the JIOA ran the operation out of a New York hotel;
- details of a scheme by U.S. Air Force General Robert L. Walsh, Director of Intelligence, European Command, to intervene in court decisions involving ex-Nazi intelligence officers working for postwar U.S. intelligence in Germany;
- details of another scheme by Walsh, who, as head of the Inter-American Defense Board, relocated notorious German General Walter Schreiber from the United States to Argentina;
- how Whalen's Paperclip recruits in 1959 included a former Wehrmacht soldier who was working as a dishwasher in Canada;
- how an alliance formed in 1985 between political extremist Lyndon LaRouche and former Paperclip scientists tried to shut down the Justice Department's Nazi-hunting unit;
- details of another scheme in 1986 to squelch the Justice Department's investigations of former Paperclip specialists Guenther Haukohl and Dieter Grau;
- how NASA publicly honored those same men in a 1987 ceremony commemorating Wernher von Braun;
- how Rudolph's friends tried to bring him back in 1990 to attend a NASA moon walk celebration, despite laws barring his entry into the United States.

In essence this book deals with a hauntingly familiar and contemporary subject: a small group of men in the Pentagon who decided that they alone knew what was best for the country. "And that, I think, is the real danger here," said former U.S. congresswoman Elizabeth Holtzman, who authored the 1978 immigration law that bars Nazis from our shores. "We have agencies that think that they are a law unto themselves, that regardless of what the law of the land is, regardless of what the president of the United States says, they'll do whatever they think is best for themselves. And that's very dangerous."[9]

The Beginning

O N May 19, 1945, a military transport plane with windows blackened to hide its notorious cargo dropped out of the steely gray skies over Washington, D.C., and lurched down the landing field. As the propellers slowed and finally stopped, three figures stepped out of the aircraft. The first was a middle-aged man with a scarred face whose slight build belied his importance.[1]

Herbert Wagner had been the chief missile design engineer for the Henschel Aircraft Company and, more importantly, the creator of the HS-293, the first German guided missile used in combat during World War II. As of that moment, he and his two assistants were setting another historical precedent: they were the first German scientists to set foot on American soil at the end of the war.[2]

Anxious to tap Wagner's expertise in the design of glider

6

bombs for use against Japan, a U.S. Navy team smuggled him into the United States and then kept him hidden from immigration authorities so as to avoid troubling questions about his Nazi past. And no wonder. Wagner was reported to be an ardent member of the *Sturmabteilung* (the brown-shirted storm troopers) as well as four other Nazi organizations.[3]

Wagner's surreptitious arrival marked the beginning of a massive immigration of Nazi scientists to the United States and a long, sordid chapter in postwar history. Had he been kept overseas, Wagner almost certainly would have been questioned closely about his Nazi past in a denazification court. Instead he and many of his colleagues were able to take advantage of Project Paperclip, which, in direct contravention of official U.S. policy, gave the Nazi scientists an opportunity to escape justice and start afresh in America.[4]

Wagner's arrival actually predated the formal creation of Paperclip, though the effort to exploit Germany's scientific talent and resources was well underway by the time of the fall of the Third Reich. As Allied troops pushed inland from the beaches of Normandy in 1944, teams of scientific investigators trailed in their wake, roaming the battlefields in search of research installations that would yield up Hitler's scientific achievements and brain trust.

The scientific teams were made up of U.S. Army, Navy, and Army Air Forces teams and Office of Strategic Services (OSS) intelligence agents attached to special military units called T-forces. At their peak the teams comprised more than ten thousand men scattered over the United Kingdom (where their command group, the Combined Intelligence Objectives Subcommittee [CIOS], was headquartered), France, Belgium, Holland, Luxembourg, and Nazi Germany. The teams' mission was to capture and interrogate Hitler's scientists, locate and microfilm documents, and confiscate all useful equipment found in laboratories and factories.[5]

According to a journal kept by civilian scientist John Harris, in May 1945 one of those teams located a carefully camouflaged I. G. Farben chemical plant on the outskirts of the

German town of Gendorf. The entrance to the plant was flanked by two large brick gateposts, which Harris estimated that a Sherman tank might squeeze through with six inches to spare. But there was no time for such niceties. The tank accompanying Harris's team simply smashed through the entrance, knocking over one of the gateposts and trailing yards of the wire fence that had surrounded the plant behind it.[6]

The spoils that Harris and his colleagues discovered at Gendorf included some of the greatest scientific minds in Hitler's chemical warfare industry. One was Walter Reppe, an I. G. Farben director and pharmaceutical research expert. Even more impressive was Otto Ambros, a well-known chemist and Farben director who had come to Gendorf to construct a rubber plant nearby. Harris and the other members of the scientific team found Ambros to be a witty, "remarkably clever" man with an extraordinary command of the English language and a charming, personable manner.[7]

It wasn't long, however, before they discovered another side to Ambros—one that was horrendously evil. He had overseen the use of concentration camp prisoners as slave labor when he was in charge of an I. G. Farben factory at Auschwitz concentration camp. It was a bitterly cruel irony, inasmuch as an I. G. Farben–dominated company manufactured the poison gas used to murder millions of Jews in the camps. By the time Ambros was shipped off to Munich for interrogation, he was already on the U.S. list of war criminals.[8]

That dark side of Nazi science was inextricably linked to whatever benefits Hitler's technical brain trust had to offer, but from the beginning it was ignored by American military officers intent on exploiting German expertise. Even as one arm of the U.S. military was working to bring Nazi war criminals to justice after the war, another arm was using whatever means necessary to protect Nazi scientists and give them a safe haven in America. Ultimately this country paid a heavy price for that moral indifference. The methods and philosophies that the Nazi scientists brought with them resulted in serious breaches of U.S. security and the unthinkable horror of American soldiers being used as research guinea pigs in the same way that concentration camp prisoners had been used during the war.

The idea behind the original exploitation project was basically sound. During the planning phase for the Normandy invasion it had become clear that ultimate victory depended on breaking the scientific, economic, and industrial structure of the Third Reich as well as defeating Hitler's troops in the field. German scientists had unleashed a technological war of a kind never seen before. Buzz bombs and V-2 rockets rained down on Great Britain, and in America the War Department was terrified at the thought that Hitler was close to developing an atomic bomb.[9]

The main goal of the exploitation effort was to use the scientific intelligence it garnered to win the war against Nazi Germany and Japan. A secondary objective was to help advance the U.S. military's own technology once the war ended. One phase of the project, code-named "Safehaven," was designed to prevent Germans from escaping to other countries, primarily in Latin America, to continue their wartime research. Finally, the project would rectify an old mistake. Germany had been allowed to rearm after World War I. This time Washington policymakers were determined that Germany would be stripped bare, once and for all, of any technical and scientific capability to rearm and wage another war.[10]

When the exploitation project began, there was no thought of bringing German scientists to America. Indeed, there is strong evidence that President Franklin Roosevelt would have rejected the idea had it been presented to him at the time. Roosevelt already had turned down OSS chief William Donovan's request that the United States offer postarmistice privileges to Germans working for America's fledgling intelligence agency, which had recruited *Schutzstaffel* (SS) officers, members of the German Foreign Office, and high-ranking Abwehr intelligence agents. On December 1, 1944, Donovan asked the president if the recruits could be given special privileges, including "permission for entry into the United States after the war, the placing of their earnings on deposit in an American bank and the like." He acknowledged that only the president had the authority to approve the plan and asked for an immediate answer.[11]

Roosevelt's blunt, one-paragraph answer would reverberate all the way into the 1980s, when revelations that U.S. intelligence had helped war criminals Klaus Barbie and Arthur Rudolph escape justice gave the president's words stinging irony. He wrote:

> I do not believe that we should offer any guarantees of protection in the post-hostilities period to Germans who are working for your organization. I think that the carrying out of any such guarantees would be difficult and probably be widely misunderstood both in this country and abroad. We may expect that the number of Germans who are anxious to save their skins and property will rapidly increase. Among them may be some who should properly be tried for war crimes or at least arrested for active participation in Nazi activities. Even with the necessary controls you mention I am not prepared to authorize the giving of guarantees.[12]

Yet even before the war with Nazi Germany ended, and long before official Paperclip policies were set, members of the scientific teams were making unauthorized promises and cutting deals with German scientists whose names had appeared on war crimes "wanted" lists. In effect, the scientific teams wore blinders. Dazzled by German technology that was in some cases years ahead of our own, they simply ignored its evil foundation — which sometimes meant stepping over and around piles of dead bodies — and pursued Nazi scientific knowledge like a forbidden fruit. The teams often included American scientists and military personnel who were familiar with the Germans' work and tended to view them as colleagues. Occasionally the Germans even became their friends.

The team whose mission it was to learn if Hitler's scientists had developed an atomic bomb was already in Europe looking for key nuclear physicists by the time the other scientific units arrived in 1944. Code-named "Alsos," the atomic bomb team was headed by U.S. Army Lieutenant Colonel Boris Pash, whose long and highly controversial career ran the gamut from volunteering to fight in the 1918 Russian Revolution to being accused of running a CIA "special operations" unit which, according to testimony before Congress, "was responsible for assassinations and kidnappings as well as other 'special operations.' " No evidence was presented at the hearing that the unit carried out assassinations while Pash was in charge. Pash was also security chief for the Manhattan Project during the development of the atomic bomb in the United States.[13]

By the time Pash and Alsos's chief scientist, an American named Samuel Goudsmit, reached Strasbourg, France, Goudsmit was certain that the Germans had not yet completed their work on the bomb. Only a handful of men — Carl von Weizsäcker, Werner Heisenberg, and a few others — even had the expertise to do the work. Moreover, in November 1944 Goudsmit found von Weizsäcker's papers, proving that America's bomb project was at least two years ahead of Nazi Germany's. Nevertheless, when the Alsos team located physicist Rudolph Fleishman he was sent to the United States for interrogation.[14]

Although best known for tracking down German physicists, Alsos also investigated biological and chemical warfare. The University of Strasbourg was a major biological warfare research base, and Pash stayed in the home of the university's biological warfare chief, Eugen von Haagen, who had fled the area before Alsos arrived. Haagen had lived in America in the 1930s, working for the Rockefeller Institute in New York while participating in pro-Nazi German-American Bund activities in his spare time. In 1946, he was arrested and used as a witness for the prosecution at the Nuremberg war crimes trials, where he admitted that several Natzweiler concentration camp prisoners had died after he deliberately had infected them with spotted fever. In 1948 Haagen was offered a job as head of the medical department at the Institute of Medicine and Biology in Berlin. Later arrested by the British and turned over to the French, Haagen was convicted in 1954 by a French court and sentenced to twenty years imprisonment for his crimes.[15]

Goudsmit quickly discovered that a number of Haagen's colleagues at the University of Strasbourg were equally culpable in murder. The university was a model Nazi institution where many of the faculty were SS members whose chemical or biological warfare research consisted of horrific experiments on humans. Chief among them was professor of anatomy August Hirt, the official SS representative at the university, who provided other professors with prisoners for mustard gas experiments. The university proudly displayed Hirt's collection of skulls, which he had amassed by collaborating with Adolf Eichmann to kill Jews and send their still-warm bodies to the university for display.[16]

Alsos also interrogated Kurt Blome, Hitler's overall head of biological warfare, soon after his arrest as a war crimes suspect. (Blome's sordid Nazi past and subsequent employment in a Paperclip-related project are detailed in chapter 11.) When Alsos caught up with him, Blome admitted he had built a biological warfare laboratory at the request of Reichsführer-SS Heinrich Himmler. Power hungry and independent, Himmler planned to use biological warfare on Allied troops without Hitler's approval. He ordered Blome to conduct experiments on concentration camp prisoners to determine how effective a biological warfare attack would be against advancing Allied troops. But before he could begin, Blome told Alsos, Russian troops captured his laboratory.[17]

While Hitler's atomic bomb project may have lagged behind America's, that wasn't the case with chemical warfare. Surprisingly, the exploitation project's valuable chemical warfare discoveries, and especially the Paperclip chemical warfare experts, have been ignored by historians, even though their discoveries were certainly equal to the scientific advancement of the V-2 rocket. Chemical Warfare Service teams investigated everything from nerve gas experiments to rifle ranges where shackled prisoners under the influence of mind-altering drugs staggered around with loaded guns looking for the target. The teams were shocked to discover that the Germans had invented three new nerve gases — Tabun, Sarin, and Soman — which were far more deadly than the mustard gases the Allies had at that time. The German gases were so superior that after the war Sarin became America's standard nerve gas, while the USSR chose Tabun.[18]

Formulas and samples of these gases were discovered by a team of nineteen U.S., British, and Canadian chemical warfare experts that had targeted major German chemical warfare installations in the Munsterlager area. The team was headed by Commander A. K. Mills of the British Ministry of Aircraft Production. Mills's group tracked down a Wehrmacht experimental station at Raubkammer, a gas defense laboratory, a Luftwaffe chemical warfare experimental station, and several Luftwaffe and Wehrmacht chemical munition plants. The group was able to determine from captured documents and interrogations of German chemical warfare personnel that Tabun was produced at the rate of 1,000 tons a month at a factory in Dyhernfurth that was captured by the Russians.[19]

Mills's team discovered that chemical warfare experiments had been conducted on both animals and humans in the captured facilities. At Raubkammer a main laboratory and nine annexes housed laboratory animals used in experiments, including dogs, cats, guinea pigs, apes, and horses. He also found four thousand photographs of mustard gas experiments conducted on men who appeared to be political prisoners from concentration camps. In some cases liquid mustard had been applied directly to the victims' skin, which resulted in oozing blisters, burns, and deep scars all over their bodies. At least six of them had died.[20]

The investigators also captured fourteen of Nazi Germany's major chemical warfare experts, including General Walter Hirsch, head of Wa Prüf 9, the Wehrmacht's main chemical warfare section. They were taken for interrogation to a detention camp where other chemical warfare experts were held, including SS Brigadier General Walter Schieber, who had overseen the chemical industry for Albert Speer's Armaments Ministry. Schieber would later work under Paperclip for a decade in West Germany, making nerve gas for the Chemical Division of European Command.[21]

In another part of Nazi Germany, U.S. Army Air Forces teams were tracking down the scientists who designed Germany's highly advanced jet aircraft, underground bomb-proof shelters, parachutes, and anything else having to do with air combat. Air Corps Colonel Donald Putt headed a team that located the Hermann Göring Aeronautical Research Institute in Brunswick. The forty-year-old officer was a friendly, adventuresome man with a weatherbeaten face and a masters degree in aeronautical engineering. A veteran test pilot, Putt had helped supervise the development of the B-29 bomber at Wright Field air base near Dayton, Ohio.[22]

Putt thought he knew all about aircraft, but he was stunned by what he found at Brunswick. "There was this plane with incredible swept-back wings," he recalled forty years later. "I'd never seen anything like it." What Putt had found was Adolf Busemann's swept-back wing aircraft, which became a prototype for the U.S. Air Force's swept-wing planes in later years.[23]

The institute was one of Germany's largest scientific complexes, with twelve hundred specialists, five wind tunnels, and numerous laboratories. The specialists ran the gamut, from jet aircraft design to jet fuel, parachutes, and nearly every imaginable aeronautical invention. Putt gathered the Germans together and, without approval from higher authorities in the War Department, promised them jobs at Wright Field if they would go with him to a holding center for captured personnel in Bad Kissingen. He also promised to send their families to the United States, then instructed the scientists to sell all of their belongings and to travel light.[24]

Other Army Air Forces teams were looking for Germany's leading experts in aero medicine. But some of the most significant information about their work was found when American troops "opened the gates of hell," in the words of the liberator of Dachau, Colonel Walter J. Fellenz, commanding officer of the 42d Infantry Division. The young American soldiers who broke through Dachau's iron gate found the reason they had been fighting the war when they saw the tortured faces of the half-starved crowd that cheered when they entered the camp.[25]

While Fellenz's troops tended to the survivors, U.S. Army Major Leo Alexander sifted through documents to obtain names of the camp administrators and Nazi doctors—evidence that would be used later at Nuremberg. Alexander was a Boston psychiatrist whose medical expertise played a key role in the Nuremberg war crimes trials. He was the chief medical investigator and expert witness for the Nuremberg war crimes prosecution staff.[26]

Dachau's Experimental Block number 5 was where Nazi scientists conducted medical experiments on the camp's defenseless prisoners. U.S. soldiers in the 363d Medical Battalion were overwhelmed by the stench when they walked into the building. Parts of human bodies—arms, legs, organs of every type—were lying everywhere. Hundreds of innocent people had been murdered there in the name of science. And some of the men who conducted these experiments were the same respected scientists, university professors, and doctors that the AAF teams would later hire to work under Paperclip.[27]

The experiments were ostensibly conducted to find ways to save the lives of Luftwaffe pilots who crashed at sea and were forced to live on seawater, or parachuted out of airplanes at high altitudes, or were exposed to extremely cold weather. Dachau inmates were deliberately infected with disease, force-fed seawater, or starved for oxygen in a chamber.[28]

In one experiment a group of Russian prisoners was frozen to death in vats of ice water in the camp yard during the winter. The prisoners endured excruciating pain before they died, as parts of their bodies slowly began to freeze. A Luftwaffe doctor, Sigmund Rascher, and University of Kiel Professor E. Holzlöhner were among those conducting the experiments. They wanted to know if frozen flyers' lives could be saved if their bodies were thawed out.[29]

While investigating this crime, one scientist whom Alexander talked with was Luftwaffe Colonel Hubertus Strughold, a Paperclip hire who today is touted as the "father of American space medicine." Strughold was wartime head of the Luftwaffe's Institute for Aviation Medicine in Berlin. Like von Haagen, Strughold also had lived in the United States, and his work in aviation physiology was widely known in American scientific and military circles. When Alexander asked him about the freezing experiments, Strughold said that he knew of them from a meeting he had attended in Nuremberg in 1942, and that he had heard a radio broadcast mentioning that Rascher was wanted in connection with the experiments. Other than that, Strughold said he knew nothing.[30]

As Alexander continued his investigation, Himmler's SS records were found in a cave. They were a treasure trove of information that included Himmler's correspondence with Rascher and other individuals concerning the medical experiments at Dachau. As Alexander pieced the evidence together, he realized that Strughold had lied. Siegfried Ruff, another Paperclip hire and coauthor of a book with Strughold, was named in connection with high-altitude experiments. Ruff was head of the Department for Aviation Medicine at the German Experimental Institute for Aviation, the DVL (Deutsche Versuchsanstalt für Luftfahrt). Holzlöhner was identified as conducting the freezing tests, and several other names cropped up whom Alexander knew to be Strughold's close colleagues.[31]

Alexander submitted two CIOS reports about the experiments to the Army's war crimes staff in which he noted his suspicion that Strughold had "covered up" the involvement "by his friend and co-worker Ruff, and by his colleague Holzlöhner" in the Dachau experiments. By the time Alexander's reports wended their way to Nuremberg, however, Strughold was already sheltered under the protective wing of the U.S. Army Air Forces.[32]

Significantly, a CIOS team investigating aviation medicine was unimpressed with the value of Strughold's wartime work. Their final report concluded that Strughold and other Germans had suffered considerably from their isolation during the war, "since scientific achievements which they presented as new and revolutionary were in most cases long since attained by the Allied investigators."[33]

Meanwhile, U.S. Army Colonel Holger Toftoy was in charge of five Army Ordnance technical intelligence teams scouring the battlefields for weapons, equipment, and Hitler's rocket team. Like Colonel Putt, Toftoy had long been intrigued by technical matters. Before graduating from high school he had built an automobile from an old gasoline engine and bicycle parts. Now the West Point graduate was looking for the brains behind the rockets that blitzed London.[34]

Key members of the group that had been at the Peenemünde rocket base surrendered to the U.S. Army in a well-known story of their capture. One ordnance team member, Major Robert Staver, recalled that he was jubilant when the Army caught up with the Nazi rocket scientists. The most brilliant among them was the chief scientist and designer, who was only thirty-two years old. But Wernher von Braun's rocket career dated back to the 1930s, when he was the protégé of Hermann Oberth, the father of German rocketry. Von Braun and four hundred other rocket experts were taken to Garmisch for interrogation by Toftoy and other members of the ordnance team.[35]

As always, there was a dark side to the rocket scientists, too. This time it surfaced when American troops found the remains of Dora concentration camp inmates who had been starved, beaten, hanged, and literally worked to death as slaves in the Mittelwerk underground V-2 rocket factory. Colonel James L. Collins was leading an infantry unit toward Nordhausen when his liaison officer called him over the radio. "Colonel," he said, "you'd better get up here and see what we've got. It's terrible." By this time scenes from hell had become part of Collins's daily routine. But his mind reeled with horror at what he found at Camp Dora.[36]

As Collins approached the huge, cavelike entrance to the factory on the hill, six thousand bodies covered the ground. As far as he could see, row upon row of skin-covered skeletons were frozen solid in grotesque shapes, bearing bruises and wounds from beatings. "They had been starved to death," Collins recalled. "Their arms were just little sticks, their legs had practically no flesh on them at all." As the soldiers moved through the choking stench of death, they found the smoldering furnaces of Dora's crematory. The doors were still open where the SS had been shoving bodies in and burning them up.[37]

Yves Beon, a member of the French Resistance, was one of the few who survived that hell. He had been arrested by the Gestapo in 1943, imprisoned at Dora, and forced to work on the V-2 rocket. "We worked in the center of the mountain with no air, and just had one small piece of bread and margarine to eat all day," Beon recalled. "It was horrible."[38]

The next day, as American troops tried to recover from the shock of their discovery, a soldier sat down on a filthy stoop and stared at a crumpled news report. A Dora survivor sitting next to him quietly reached out his thin hand and touched the tears streaming down his liberator's face. The soldier's commander in chief was dead. Franklin D. Roosevelt had guided the nation through an unprecedented four terms, from the Depression into the war. Now the burden of war passed to Harry S. Truman.[39]

Members of the ordnance technical intelligence team, including Toftoy's aid, Major James Hamill, and Staver, arrived at the scene around the same time as an army war crimes unit. U.S. Army Major Herschel Auerbach had been sent to the site to investigate the crimes committed against the prisoners. His unit went one way, interrogating individuals and searching for evidence against those responsible for the deaths of twenty thousand Dora prisoners, while Hamill and Staver went in a different direction, to load up the V-2 rockets found in the tunnels, track down technical documents, and search the hills for rocket scientists who had worked in the Mittelwerk factory.[40]

In the end, however, both groups ended up looking for the same men. Dora survivors told war crimes investigators that

Mittelwerk personnel as well as the SS had harmed them. Particularly notorious was Mittelwerk's technical director, Albin Sawatzki. After Army MPs had imprisoned Sawatzki in a makeshift pen in the camp yard, a Frenchman standing nearby became enraged upon seeing him. "That bastard nearly beat the life out of me a dozen times," the Frenchman yelled as he drew back his fist and smashed it into Sawatzki's face.[41]

Sawatzki identified key Mittelwerk personnel and SS officers by name, and even told investigators where he thought they could be found. Sawatzki identified Georg Rickhey as Mittelwerk's general manager and said the Production Director Arthur Rudolph was one of the men responsible for the number of hours the prisoners were forced to work. He admitted that the prisoners had died from bad conditions, including food, exposure, and impure air in the factory. Sawatzki also brazenly admitted that he had "kicked some of the workers from time to time."[42]

Once again, however, the mind-set, opinions, and goals of the technical and scientific teams were so self-serving that Germans who should have been arrested as war crimes suspects escaped justice. Rickhey was arrested once, but was released. U.S. Strategic Bombing Survey Colonel Peter Beasley located Rickhey, struck up a friendship with him, and even moved into his house. After all, Rickhey possessed something that the colonel badly wanted. He had forty-two boxes of Mittelwerk management records that included information about V-2 rockets and bomb-proof shelters. Ignoring the potential those records held for evidence of war crimes, Beasley packed them — and Rickhey — off to London.[43]

By the time Nazi Germany surrendered in May 1945, Army Ordnance, CIOS, and other scientific teams had assessed nearly every primary technical and scientific target. But jealous rivalries erupted between the teams and among the four Allied nations, which were competing for the same spoils of war. That competition, particularly with the Soviets, would heighten when Germany was divided into four occupied zones.[44]

As a result of that competition more than fifteen hundred

German scientists and technicians were forced to leave their homes, and in some cases their families, and move to the U.S.-controlled zone of Germany. Many were glass technicians from the Carl Zeiss factory in Jena, who were forcibly evacuated and interned in a camp for over a year. At least two members of Zeiss's group committed suicide over the ordeal. Ironically, while there was an outcry of protest after the war when Russian troops kidnapped scientists to work in the USSR, American authorities conveniently hid the fact that they had done virtually the same thing — and in violation of international law.[45]

One of the most disturbing cases of forced relocation occurred toward the end of the war, when the Naval Technical Mission in Europe decided it wanted to exploit the skills of Wilhelm Eitel, the wartime head of the Kaiser Wilhelm Institute's silicates department in Berlin. Even his colleagues considered Eitel an ardent Nazi who had won his position by collaborating with Wilhelm Frick to fire nine Jewish scientists in 1933, when Hitler banned Jews from positions in government and elsewhere. One of those scientists ended up in a concentration camp; the others were forced to flee Germany.[46]

Russian troops were closing in on Berlin when an army colonel, Ralph Osborne, told Eitel to leave the city. Osborne was in charge of the Field Information Agency, Technical (FIAT), which later helped coordinate Paperclip operations in Europe. Eitel packed his bags and fled, abandoning his wife and five children to face the fast-approaching Soviet troops. His wife hanged herself instead. After the war Berlin police kept her suicide case open for years when they learned that Eitel had married his wife's sister soon after the suicide. But by then Eitel was safe in the United States, working for the Navy.[47]

In addition to Eitel, the Navy team located torpedo and submarine experts and the staff of Peenemünde Aerodynamics Institute, including the institute's codirectors, Rudolf Hermann and Hermann Kurzweg, who worked in Kochel. The Peenemünde group had built two high-speed wind tunnels to test guided missiles and projectiles. The tunnels were a rare find. Both operated at more than twice the mach speed of any wind tunnel in America.[48]

In May the Navy team traveled to the Bavarian village of Oberammergau looking for their key target — Herbert Wagner. Just weeks after they found him, he was ensconced in a Washington, D.C., hotel, being debriefed and given a new life.[49]

It had taken the greatest war in history to put a stop to an unspeakable evil. And now the cutting edge of that nightmare was being transplanted to America.

2 Rules of the Game

I N the summer of 1945, as American troops coped with the chaos and ruin of what once had been Hitler's Third Reich, the scientific teams held thousands of German scientists captive in detention camps across Germany. The Hotel Wittelsbacher Hof in Bad Kissingen was no exception, though it looked more like the site of a big scientific convention than a holding center for Germans captured by the Army Air Forces. American jeeps arrived daily, bringing in scientists of all ages, their luggage containing only the few personal belongings they had hurriedly gathered together. These men, some 120 in number, were jet engine, wind tunnel, and rocket fuel experts under Colonel Putt's control.[1]

Putt viewed his captives not as former enemies but as scientists whose technical know-how could benefit the Air Corps. "The Germans were years ahead of us in aircraft design," Putt later recalled. Nazi Germany had barely surrendered when Putt began asking his superiors to formulate a policy to bring the scientists to America. He quickly gained the support of Major General Hugh Knerr, who soon would be named commanding officer of Wright Field air base. Both Putt and Knerr believed that the Germans' knowledge would advance the AAF's own jet design by a decade. Knerr sought War Department permission to send at least five Germans to Wright Field, including Theodor Zobel, a designer whose innovative methods included photographing airflow patterns around jet wings to help improve aircraft designs. Another was Germany's preeminent supersonics expert, Adolf Busemann.[2]

But American interrogators in Putt's group were opposed to Knerr's idea, since they believed that some of these Germans were ardent Nazis. One navy officer, H. M. Mott-Smith, had already dropped the former co-director of Peenemünde's Aerodynamics Institute, Rudolf Hermann, from a project involving the dismantling of the Kochel wind tunnel that was sent to White Oaks, Maryland. Mott-Smith had found Hermann to be "untrustworthy and in some respects incapable." Hermann's colleagues and other American officers in Putt's group also shared this opinion. Mott-Smith's complaints increased after he learned that the Navy planned to send Hermann to America. "Dr. Hermann was twice picked up by the CIC and investigated for Nazi activities, the second time on accusation by one of his former associates of having been instrumental in having the man sent to a concentration camp," he told his superiors. Hermann later was cleared, but U.S. Army Counter Intelligence Corps (CIC) agents then interned his wife as an ardent Nazi. Once again Mott-Smith complained that Hermann's "uncertain political sympathies, the proved Nazi sympathies of his wife, and the mistrust of him by his subordinates" easily could damage the Navy's project. The Navy agreed and dropped Hermann from its hiring list. Putt eventually brought him to Wright Field despite the damaging reports.[3]

Unaware of those controversies, War and State Department

officials had not made a decision on numerous proposals sitting on their desks. These came not only from Knerr and the Navy but also Colonel Toftoy and other Army Ordnance officers who wanted to bring Wernher von Braun's rocket group to America. All of those involved in discussions agreed that America should use the Germans' skills to win the war against Japan — if steps were taken to eliminate security risks. "These men are enemies and it must be assumed that they are capable of sabotaging our war effort," remarked Under Secretary of War Robert Patterson.[4]

On the other hand, U.S. immigration laws at the time prohibited members of fascist groups from entering the country. In addition, Joint Chiefs of Staff policy required that the commanding general in the European theater "exclude from further research activity any persons who previously held key positions in German war research." Ardent Nazis in charge of German universities and scientific institutes were supposed to be replaced by those less politically suspect. But now policymakers were being asked to approve proposals to bring some of those same Germans to the United States and put them to work.[5]

The idea also conflicted with JCS policies regarding the prosecution of Nazi war criminals and denazification of the general German population. When Justice Robert Jackson returned from Europe shortly after his appointment as chief of counsel for the prosecution of war crimes, he told President Truman, "I have assurances from the War Department that those likely to be accused as war criminals will be kept in close confinement and stern control." Even with Jackson's assurance, Under Secretary of War Patterson remained concerned that accused war criminals might be included in the ranks of those the U.S. military now wanted to bring to America.[6]

Ultimately the war against Japan proved to be the deciding factor. The JCS approved the project, code-named "Overcast," and sent the rules of the game to commanders in the European theater. The project's stated purpose was to temporarily exploit German and Austrian scientists to "assist in shortening the Japanese war." It was limited to those few "chosen, rare minds" whose skills could not be fully exploited in Europe. Once that exploitation was completed they were to be returned immediately to Germany. The JCS acknowledged Patterson's concerns by including a clause that specifically banned known or alleged war criminals, and this order: "If any specialists who are brought to this country are subsequently found to be listed as alleged war criminals, they should be returned to Europe for trial." It was an order that soon would be ignored.[7]

Once Project Overcast was approved, a War Department spokesman made a terse public announcement that "a number of carefully selected scientists and technologists are being brought to the United States." He informed the press, however, that there would be "no interviews, no itineraries, no pictures," and then refused to reveal any further information.[8]

Over the next few months, three military intelligence agencies formed a power base enabling them to control the project's course for the next two decades and to hide their dubious activities from the American public. These were the Joint Intelligence Committee (JIC), the Joint Intelligence Objectives Agency (JIOA), and the Exploitation Branch under Army intelligence (G-2) in the War Department General Staff (WDGS).

It is important to keep in mind that the project was run by intelligence officers. While the American public may have been told that the German scientists were considered valuable because of their scientific skills, the intelligence officers running the project had a far different agenda. They viewed the project as the *intelligence* exploitation of Germany, and along with that, the Soviet Union and France. The decisions they made—often in secret—reflected that view. Despite JCS policies, some of those brought to the United States under the project were a far cry from being "scientists" or even Germans or Austrians. The scientists who did arrive were interrogated about what they knew about the Soviet Union, and their mail was constantly screened for intelligence information.

The JIC was the intelligence arm of the Joint Chiefs of Staff, responsible for advising the JCS on the intelligence problems and policies and furnishing intelligence information to the JCS and the State Department. The JIC was composed of the Army's director of intelligence, the chief of naval intelligence, the assistant chief of Air Staff – 2, and a representative of the State Department. They considered policy questions regarding the German scientist project and recommended procedural changes to the JCS. The Army's director of intelligence always played a key role in the project, since the policy made Army intelligence (G-2) administratively responsible for many aspects of the program, including background investigations. Lieutenant General Hoyt Vandenberg served in that position until June 1946, when President Truman appointed him director of the Central Intelligence Group, which became the Central Intelligence Agency in 1947.[9]

The JIOA was established as a subcommittee of the JIC specifically to assume direct responsibility for running the German scientist program until the JIOA was disbanded in 1962. The agency was comprised of a JIOA Governing Committee, made up of one representative of each member agency of the JIC, and an operational staff of military intelligence officers from the different services. Army Colonel E. W. Gruhn was the first JIOA director, a position that generally rotated annually among the agency's military officers. JIOA's duties included administering the project's policies and procedures, compiling dossiers, and serving as liaison to British intelligence officers running a similar project in Great Britain. In addition, JIOA took over many of CIOS's activities when that agency was dissolved shortly after Nazi Germany's surrender. JIOA was responsible for collecting, declassifying, and distributing CIOS and other technical intelligence reports on German science and industry.[10]

Finally, the Exploitation Branch under G-2, WDGS, was the implementing agency for the project. The chief of this branch represented the Army's director of intelligence on the JIOA Governing Committee. This secret unit, which changed names several times, was part of the Military Intelligence Division and had carried out many intriguing missions, a history that did not change once it became involved with German scientists. First called Prisoner of War (POW) Branch and then Captured Personnel and Material (CPM) Branch, the agency was responsible for directing "escape and evasion" activities that included interrogating enemy prisoners of war and helping individuals friendly to the Allies escape from behind enemy lines.[11]

Lieutenant Colonel Monroe Hagood was head of the unit when Overcast was approved in 1945. He was overwhelmed with work and frustrated that his small staff of interrogators received little support for numerous ongoing projects. Two months after the JCS approved the policy, Assistant Secretary of War Robert A. Lovett furiously accused G-2 of ineptitude when he learned that none of the German scientists had arrived. Hagood took the brunt of that criticism and later complained that while his staff was expected to be responsible for half the work needed to initiate Overcast, the War Department gave him no funds to accomplish the task.[12]

Hagood's biggest problem, however, was that his CPM Branch interrogation staff was too small to take on yet another group of Nazis. They already were helping officers who smuggled former intelligence experts, members of the German High Command, and high-ranking German naval intelligence officers into Washington, where they were hidden from public view and interrogated about the USSR.

On one side of Washington, Hitler's spy chief and Soviet expert General Reinhard Gehlen and other members of his wartime intelligence staff were cloistered behind high fences in Fort Hunt, Virginia. Under the direction of Major General Edwin Sibert, Army intelligence chief in Germany, Gehlen and the others were interrogated, put in a room with hidden listening devices, and left to talk among themselves as intelligence officers listened in. Along with Gehlen's group, Fort Hunt also housed a combined CPM Branch and Navy project to interrogate four German admirals, including Hitler's naval intelligence chief, Rear Admiral Otto Schulz, and sixteen other German Navy specialists on the USSR, including Norbert von Baumbach, the former naval attaché in Moscow. The commanding officer of Fort Hunt, Lieutenant Colonel Montie Cone, later was involved in Paperclip for over a decade.[13]

On the other side of the capital in Camp Ritchie, Maryland, a group of German High Command officers were interrogated and helped translate important captured German documents. One of these men was a notorious Nazi—Major General Gustav Hilger—who was on a U.S. Army war crimes wanted list while living at the camp. Hilger had been Nazi Foreign Minister Joachim Ribbentrop's informant on the operation of *Einsatzgruppen*, the SS killing units that massacred hundreds of thousands of Jews. While Ribbentrop was hanged as a war criminal after the war, Hilger returned to Washington in 1948 under State Department auspices, living openly, with his name listed in the telephone directory. Others in the Washington area with Hilger in 1945 were: Kurt Zinneman, who headed the Russian section of the German War Economy Branch; General August Koestring, military attaché in Moscow; and Nazi historian Peter-Heinz Seraphim, whose research on Jews was used avidly by Hitler's propaganda chief.[14]

Hagood's overworked interrogators in CPM Branch were not the only source of delays. A British project called "Backfire" lasted through the summer. It was supposed to be a major effort to study the Germans' V-2 rocket launching techniques, but it soon turned into a fiasco tying up several of the main rocket experts. Hundreds of Allied officers and nearly a thousand Germans, including von Braun and Arthur Rudolph, gathered at an isolated area off the Dutch coast known as Cuxhaven. Entire units of officers spent months scouring an area from Paris to Berlin, digging up fields and rummaging through factories to find enough V-2 parts to reassemble rockets that were barely operational. The British released hundreds of German Wehrmacht officers and "tradesmen" from POW camps to work as construction crews at the launch site. The project's director even admitted that "it was necessary to give them better treatment than the normal P.W." to make them cooperate. By September only three rockets had been launched, and the JCS angrily told the British that they wanted von Braun and other rocket experts sent to America at once.[15]

In addition to the delays, Operation Backfire succeeded in blocking an investigation of Rudolph's wartime activities at Mittelwerk. Canadian Field Service (FS Sec) officers uncovered information that Rudolph was Mittelwerk's production director and that foreign slave labor there "has been very badly mishandled according to Dir. Rudolph's own words." They also suspected that another Mittelwerk engineer, Hans Lindenberg, "may be wanted" in connection with Rudolph's activities. But the officers were not allowed to interrogate them, due to what they called the "delicate situation" at Cuxhaven.[16]

The question then arose of what to do with General Walter Dornberger, who had headed the V-2 operation at Peenemünde. He was separated from other Germans after trying to turn American and British officers against each other for his own benefit. During interrogation, he blithely mentioned that Russian, French, and Polish POWs had been used as forced laborers at Peenemünde. In fact, ten thousand foreign laborers had been imprisoned at a concentration camp in Karlshagen, located near the Peenemünde rocket base. The camp included political prisoners who had been taken from their countries by force to work as slave labor on V-2 rockets. Dornberger said that many of these prisoners had been killed when the Allies bombed the rocket base in 1943. Unfortunately, neither British nor American intelligence officers questioned Dornberger closely about the use of POWs and political prisoners as forced labor — and their possible mistreatment — in violation of international law.[17]

AAF General Knerr, of course, immediately pounced on the idea of bringing Dornberger to Wright Field, and once again his overenthusiasm for the Germans rankled other American officers. One general told Knerr not only that would he block AAF efforts to employ Dornberger, but that "in fact, we may trade him to the Russians for a dish of caviar." Dorn-

berger's other critics were lined up at FIAT, the agency formed
July 1 to oversee Overcast in the European theater. Everyone
at FIAT loathed Dornberger and felt he should be interned
as a menace. The British settled the matter by taking Dornberger to London, where they planned to hold war crimes
trials of German militarists. Although Dornberger was interned in British POW camps for two years, he immediately
went to work at Wright Field upon his release in 1947.[18]

On August 6 the first atomic bomb was dropped on Japan
followed by a second bomb three days later, quickly bringing
the war to an end. Overcast specialists began to arrive in the
United States from Germany a month later. They entered the
country without visas, outside normal immigration procedures, but all had employment contracts in their pockets. Although they were supposed to be under tight military custody,
Peenemünde's former guidance department chief, Ernst Steinhoff, wasn't even met at the boat. He ended up hitchhiking
to his job at Aberdeen Proving Ground, Maryland.[19]

Interrogation centers were set up at Fort Strong, Massachusetts, located on an island in Boston Harbor, where the
Germans were supposed to fill out forms and be interviewed.
Most escaped close scrutiny. Herbert Axster, Dornberger's
chief of staff at Peenemünde, recalled that the rocket group
knew they were protected from the beginning. "We knew
already that they wouldn't do anything to us, because they
wanted something from us," Axster said.[20]

Most officers conducting the interrogations did not even
inquire whether the new arrivals were ardent Nazis or wanted
for war crimes. One officer, obviously suspicious of Rudolph,
did comment on his form, "100% NAZI, dangerous type,
security threat. . . ! ! *Suggest internment.*" His remarks were
put in Rudolph's file, discussed occasionally during security
clearance investigations through the years, and generally ignored.[21]

It wasn't long before nearly 150 Overcast specialists were
working at various military bases across the country under this
lax policy. Rudolph, von Braun, and more than a hundred

other former Peenemünde and Mittelwerk employees worked for Colonel Toftoy at Fort Bliss, Texas. Other rocket technicians joined Steinhoff at Aberdeen Proving Ground. Colonel Putt brought thirty additional jet aircraft and rocket fuel specialists to Wright Field. Torpedo and submarine specialists joined Herbert Wagner and the Navy's group at an isolated mansion in Long Island, New York. Twenty other recruits helped reassemble the huge Kochel wind tunnel in White Oak, Maryland.

A false myth persists to this day that only scientists and technicians were brought to the United States under this project, while many men in neither category were included from the beginning, in violation of the policy. For example, Armin Stelzner, who had served as a major in the Wehrmacht in Poland, France, and Africa during the war, worked under Overcast as a translator of documents dealing with high frequency communication at Aberdeen Proving Ground.[22]

Colonel Putt favored high-ranking militarists, and by mid-December 1946, five Luftwaffe officers were employed at Wright Field to write a survey of the Luftwaffe's battles with the Soviets. The head of this group was General Herhudt von Rohden, commander of the Luftwaffe on the Russian front, who had worked for a U.S. military historian in Europe immediately following Nazi Germany's surrender.[23]

Herbert Axster was a patent attorney and a lieutenant colonel in the Wehrmacht in command of a unit fighting the Russians. In 1943 he met a director of Peenemünde while on furlough at his ranch near the rocket base. "All of a sudden I got a telegram from Dornberger telling me I'd been reassigned to be his chief of staff," Axster recalled. In 1945, von Braun and Colonel Toftoy told Axster he was going to America. "I said, 'Why? I'm not a technician.' And Toftoy said, 'The U.S. Army needs to know how Peenemünde was organized so we can organize our rocket program.' Of course, being chief of staff, I knew. And that's why I went to America."[24]

Project Overcast was badly organized and lacked funds to accomplish even the minimum standards set for the project.

Even the Germans complained about the situation. For example, Theodor Zobel and five other jet aircraft specialists arrived at Wright Field only to learn there was so little money allocated to the project that equipment damaged on the trip from Germany was not even replaced. Zobel angrily told Putt that he thought the entire project, "beginning with the extended enforced waiting period in Germany prior to arrival here, has been badly planned and carried out." The scientist was forced to rig lab apparatus in the corner of a warehouse, devising mounting platforms from empty cartons and crates.[25] The situation did not improve when additional scientists arrived. Jet fuel expert Ernst Eckert said he sat idle for months because of inadequate library facilities and the AAF officers' failure to provide him with even pencils and paper.[26]

Meanwhile, one of JIOA Director Gruhn's first actions as overall administrator of the project was to compile a hiring list of the best-qualified German and Austrian scientists that was used by both the United States and Great Britain as a recruitment tool for decades. Although this list has been mentioned in the past by journalists and historians, no one ever noted that it was partially compiled by Werner Osenberg, the notorious wartime commander of the Gestapo's scientific section. The decision to use Osenberg was made by U.S. Navy Captain Ransom Davis after consultation with the JCS.[27]

During the war, Osenberg was in charge of a special SS research council directly subordinate to Reichsmarshal Hermann Göring. Osenberg sent his Gestapo agents to investigate work in progress at scientific institutes and report back on each scientist's political reliability. From those reports and the Gestapo's files, Osenberg compiled a list of fifteen thousand names of scientists in the Third Reich. He wrote comments next to the scientists' names regarding their political affiliations, such as SS membership, and his opinion of their scientific abilities. Of course, those scientists who held fanatic Nazi views and SS membership were also those whom Osenberg considered to be the best qualified.[28]

Osenberg had been captured in 1945 by the Alsos team and

interned in a camp in Germany. Soon after the JIOA expressed interest in him, intelligence officers whisked him out of Germany to Versailles, France, where he set up business as usual, sifting through his files to suggest names of those he considered the best scientists in the Third Reich.[29]

Not surprisingly, when JIOA's hiring list began to circulate it caused an immediate uproar among American officers. One officer in Germany complained directly to the JCS that the list contained a "large number of former Nazis and mandatory unemployables." He was furious when he recognized the names of ardent Nazis he had just forced out of jobs in Germany, as JCS policy required.[30]

While Osenberg influenced the hiring of ardent Nazis, there is disturbing evidence suggesting that the project was penetrated by the Soviets from the beginning. Assistance in earmarking which German scientists to recruit also was offered by Donald Maclean, the first secretary of the British Embassy in Washington and liaison for atomic secrets. Maclean was a Soviet mole. Among the top secret documents in JIOA files is a letter advising that certain scientists were too unimportant to recruit. An attached list then contained derogatory comments about the qualifications of some of Germany's eminent nuclear physicists, including Otto Hahn and Carl von Weizsäcker. The most striking comment is about Hahn, winner of the Nobel Prize in chemistry, who was judged on the list as having "negligible value."[31]

Members of the Joint Research and Development Board, headed by Dr. Vannevar Bush, were shocked when they saw the derogatory comments. JIOA Director Gruhn had sent the comments to Bush and asked for an opinion of the scientists' eminence. As a result, Bush issued a scathing retort criticizing the military for not knowing even "elementary information on Germans whose names are as well known in scientific circles as Churchill, Roosevelt and Stalin are in political circles." He emphasized that Hahn and von Weizsäcker were "intellectual giants of Nobel Prize stature" and that their expertise would be of great value to America.[32]

Nevertheless, none of the physicists was placed on the list until the 1950s, although most worked as consultants under the project in Germany, and physicist Rudolph Fleishman was flown to the United States for interrogation prior to the dropping of atomic bombs on Japan. Major General Leslie Groves, as head of the Manhattan Project, had already told the director of intelligence that he was vehemently opposed to any of the German physicists working for the Manhattan Project, for security reasons. "If they are allowed to see or discuss the work of the [Manhattan] Project the security of our information could get out of control," Groves said. Of course, Groves had good reason to worry, since German-born Klaus Fuchs, another Soviet spy, had worked for the Manhattan Project during the war. Contrary to some published reports, Fuchs was not brought in under Paperclip. He fled Germany in 1934, worked in Great Britain, and then joined the bomb project in 1943, two years before Paperclip even existed.[33]

Another controversy ensued when French agents nearly exposed the well-kept U.S. secret that American officers were kidnapping scientists in the Soviet zone. The French asked the Joint Chiefs of Staff for permission to see JIOA's list, supposedly to check the scientists' movements in the divided zones of occupied Germany. The list identified scientists from the well-known Carl Zeiss optical works in Jena who were forcibly taken out of the Soviet zone by U.S. officers in 1945. The French request came at an embarrassing time, since U.S. and British government officials were publicly criticizing the Soviets for kidnapping scientists, in violation of international law. Now the JCS was afraid that if the public learned of the Jena incident, it would expose America's activities as equally illegal.[34]

The Jena group had been locked up in a detention camp for a year. In 1946 the group filed a damage claim seeking return of personal property and scientific equipment that had been confiscated and sent to Wright Field. Carl Zeiss himself complained bitterly to U.S. officers that two men in his group already had committed suicide and another had returned voluntarily to the Soviet zone as a result of their enforced idleness. JIOA officers inquired about employing the entire Zeiss staff under Overcast, but the plan was dropped. Colonel J. A. Johnson, who headed the board of officers processing the Zeiss group's claims, said the group wasn't worth the trouble. According to Johnson, most were automobile mechanics who "hopped on the band wagon and were attempting to make a good thing of the situation." A handful were brought in later to work for the Air Force.[35]

By spring 1946, policymakers in Washington still were trying to decide what to do about the project, whose codename had been changed to Paperclip. High-ranking policymakers in the State-War-Navy Coordinating Committee (SWNCC) worked on a policy to be submitted to President Truman.[36] And the Joint Chiefs of Staff were getting opinions on the subject from everyone, including the British, whose own project was coordinated in Washington through the Combined Chiefs of Staff. In fact, the two countries' projects were tightly linked; they coordinated policies, shared hiring lists, and U.S. and British intelligence agencies screened the Nazi backgrounds of the scientists. At the time, the British were exploiting several groups of Germans in their own country. In March 1946 British intelligence also began dumping German scientists on British Commonwealth countries, including Canada and Australia. In Operation Matchbox, twenty Germans secretly were sent to Canada to work. They included four wartime I. G. Farben chemists and a man described later by Canadian investigators as the "number one Nazi in the dental trade during the war." Some of those men would be brought to America in the late 1950s under Paperclip.[37]

Of course, the JIOA Governing Committee already had begun to set their own agenda. Officers attending their weekly meetings in the summer of 1946 included U.S. Navy Captain Francis Duborg, G-2 Exploitation Branch chief Hagood, and on various occasions other officers, including Putt and Toftoy.

The group was led by forty-two-year-old Navy Captain Bosquet Wev, who had been named chairman of JIOA's committee in early 1946. Wev was a career naval officer who had conducted antisubmarine operations against German subs along the entire coastline of America and the Caribbean during the war. He also had been a member of the occupying forces of Japan until November 1945, when he returned to America.[38]

Samuel Klaus was the State Department representative on the JIOA Governing Committee, but the forty-two-year-old lawyer was no bureaucrat. He was amused once in Europe when children followed him because they thought that he — with his bowler hat, cane, and mustache — was Charlie Chaplin. He once told his sister that he was like Javert, the detective in *Les Miserables*, in pursuit of justice, and his State Department career reflected that pursuit. During the war Klaus worked on the department's Safehaven project, tracing the intricate network of fronts and money-funneling operations used by German banks and corporations to smuggle their assets out of Nazi Germany before its collapse. He helped set up the State Department – run Berlin Document Center, which today still houses voluminous captured Nazi organization files. Klaus also conducted numerous investigations of human rights violations in Communist-bloc countries, riding through Armenia on horseback.[39]

Wev and Klaus clashed during the very first meeting and their relationship went downhill from there. Wev was, to put it bluntly, a loose cannon. He often tried to maneuver himself into a position where he could make decisions he did not have the authority to make, without the knowledge of either the State Department or the JIOA Governing Committee. In one meeting, he and Hagood accused Klaus of being uncooperative because he did not obtain Wev's permission to attend a meeting in the War Department. Klaus sarcastically informed them that the assistant secretary of state, who had arranged the meeting, was no doubt empowered to meet with the assistant secretary of war without clearing it first with a lowly Navy captain.[40]

Klaus and other State officials deliberately were kept out of the loop from the beginning. He complained that the JIOA and G-2 Exploitation Branch made decisions behind his back and refused to give him and Assistant Secretary of State General John Hilldring a list of the Germans employed under the project. "The situation therefore is one in which the State Department bears a public as well as governmental responsibility for a program over which it has in actual fact no control and not even any information," Klaus remarked. He also was shocked when he learned that the Navy had no money to employ scientists but wanted to bring them to America to work for private industry. Klaus thought it was unfair to expect the American taxpayer to foot the bill so that large corporations could hire new employees.[41]

In June Army Director of Intelligence Vandenberg's replacement came on board the project. Major General Stephen J. Chamberlin would be a significant figure in the early stages of Paperclip. This cold warrior knew how to play the game. His decisions, philosophy, and goals would set the project on its fateful course. The fifty-seven-year-old career officer had been General Douglas MacArthur's intelligence chief of planning and operations for the Pacific campaign. As director of intelligence Chamberlin served directly under Army Chief of Staff General Dwight Eisenhower until reassigned to another post in October 1948.[42]

While the SWNCC debated a new policy that still would include only scientists or technicians, the intelligence community had other ideas. Hagood's CPM Branch, AAF officers Putt and Knerr and Army Colonel Toftoy were among eleven officers holding meetings on their own — without Klaus — to work on changes they wanted made in the new project. Their agenda included expanding the category of people to include prisoners of war, militarists, SS officers, and anyone else who they thought would be of use to the military. One proposal would have included 558 German POWs held in the United States since the beginning of World War II. Some of these Germans already worked at Wright Field as cooks, waiters, and busboys; others cared for the animals used in mustard gas experiments at Edgewood Arsenal, Maryland. But the secretary of war opposed the idea and ordered the prisoners returned to Germany.[43]

One month after that proposal fell through, Hagood, Putt, and others in the Washington group, in conjunction with U.S. Army intelligence officers in Germany, secretly approved a scheme to include SS officers and former high ranking officials of the Third Reich who already were employed by Army intelligence in Germany. They would have to be smuggled into America, since their backgrounds clearly violated U.S. immigration laws. Although the identities of these dubious recruits are not known, the fact that Lieutenant Colonel Dale Garvey was among those involved in this plot in Germany gives some idea of the scurrilous group of individuals being discussed. Garvey was commander of Region IV of the 970th Army CIC in Germany and one of the officers who later approved the Army CIC's recruitment of Klaus Barbie.[44]

After the meeting, Hagood prepared a report for his superiors—Chamberlin and Eisenhower—but the group carefully expunged information they said was so "controversial" it would delay action if the generals knew the full story. Hagood then told Garvey and other intelligence agents in Germany to expedite procedures and begin shipping the Nazis as soon as the revised Paperclip policy was approved.[45]

It was not surprising that no one mentioned this plot to Klaus during the official JIOA meeting held later the same day. Yet Klaus certainly suspected that something was going on behind his back, judging from his comments in a memo. "I gathered in the course of the meeting that there had been meetings of the group to which I had not been invited," Klaus noted suspiciously.[46]

The intelligence officers quickly forged ahead with the schemes they had hatched in Klaus's absence. On July 30 Chamberlin asked Chief of Staff Eisenhower to approve a plan to smuggle in thirty ex-Nazi experts on the USSR among a thousand "scientists" in the new project. Chamberlin told Eisenhower that the Military Intelligence Division's experience in bringing similiar groups to America—Gehlen, Hilger, and others—"has proved that valuable intelligence on Russia and

Russian dominated countries can be developed more rapidly by this method than any other."[47]

Exactly one month later, Acting Secretary of State Dean Acheson sent a copy of Paperclip policy to the White House. The policy Truman was asked to approve expanded the project to include up to one thousand German and Austrian scientists or technicians whose scientific qualifications made their exploitation vital to the "interest of national security." The policy (SWNCC 257/22) also spelled out procedures the War Department was required to follow. The specialists would be under military custody, since they would enter the United States without visas. The War Department would screen their backgrounds and assure that "the best possible information" about their qualifications was submitted to the State and Justice Departments for visa consideration. Employment contracts would provide for their return to Germany if they were found not to be qualified or acceptable for permanent residence.

While war criminals were obviously excluded, one clause in the policy banned those active in nazism or militarism as well:

> No person found by the Commanding General, USFET, to have been a member of the Nazi party and more than a nominal participant in its activities, or an active supporter of Nazism or militarism shall be brought to the U.S. hereunder.

Acheson told the president that since the State, War, and Navy Departments had approved the policy, "I recommend your approval."[48]

At the same time, across the Potomac, Fort Hunt bustled with activity as Hagood's CPM Branch and other intelligence officers gathered in buildings isolated from the main area. Here, five aliens sifted through microfilm of captured records and were quizzed by interrogators. U.S. intelligence had used the German scientist project as a cover to bring the men to America. By no stretch of the imagination could they be called scientists. The new arrivals were Gehlen's spies, three Russian and two German intelligence experts on the Soviet Union.[49]

In the White House, Truman looked over Acheson's memo

about Paperclip. The acting secretary had assured the president that the Germans were merely scientists whose skills would benefit America's technology and that the War Department would exclude "persons with Nazi or militaristic records." On September 3 Truman gave Paperclip his official approval.[50]

3 Peenemünde on the Rio Grande

NIGHT had fallen by the time Army Ordnance was ready to launch the missile that stood like a bullet on the launch pad at White Sands Proving Ground (WSPG), New Mexico. The rocket was a modified V-2 made from captured German rocket parts shipped from Mittelwerk. It was the second in a series of rockets fired by General Electric and Army Ordnance in connection with their Hermes II missile project.[1]

The launch site was crowded as Army engineers and 118 Paperclip personnel made last-minute changes to assure a successful flight. As the countdown approached, Ernst Steinhoff moved to his post one mile south of the site. Another German, Theodor Vowe, was stationed west of the area. Both were assigned to observe the rocket's trajectory through high-powered telescopes and notify command officers in the blockhouse if the rocket veered off course. The command station could then cut off the fuel to the rocket's motors and stop its flight.[2]

The sound was deafening when the rocket lifted off the ground and soared into the evening sky. "It's a keeper," yelled Herbert Karsch from the bunkhouse. But the rocket began to go astray, reverse course and head straight south toward El Paso. Steinhoff knew the rocket was headed in the wrong direction but let it fly. It soared over El Paso, over the Mexican border, and finally crash-landed about three miles from a heavily populated Juarez business district. Mexican residents nearby fled in terror as the rocket exploded, leaving a huge crater 50 feet wide and 24 feet deep as it burrowed into the ground. The next day, red-faced officials in Washington had to explain to the Mexican government why the United States had launched a missile attack on their country.[3]

The controversy over the Juarez incident overshadowed a more serious problem at White Sands and Fort Bliss Army base in Texas. What happened there is a glaring example of the military's total lack of control over enemy aliens who were judged to be a threat to the internal security of the United States. Even though there were allegations of sabotage and evidence of gross violations of base security, as one intelligence agent bluntly put it, there was absolutely "no attempt to place them in anything resembling custody." Army officers in charge of the group maintained little or no surveillance over the Germans' activities either on or off the base.[4]

Security in the area itself was precarious. White Sands had been the site of rocket and missile testing for years. It was considered a perfect firing range for rockets, given the relative isolation of the million-acre base of New Mexico desert range land. During World War II a northern strip of the area was used as a bombing test range. On another portion, called Trinity Site, the first atomic bomb exploded on July 16, 1945.[5]

But White Sands was only forty miles from Mexico and Fort Bliss was near the Mexican border. Crossing that border, legally or illegally, was as easy then as it is today, and Mexico was a well-known haven for criminal and political refugees. FBI and Army CIC agents viewed northern Mexico as ripe for a potential unhampered operation of foreign agents or sympathizers. As one agent observed, "Former Nazi agents, interned during the late War in Mexico, are now given unlimited freedom within that country. The possibility of northern Mexico being used by Russian agents as an operating base against the guided missile project [is] felt to be obvious."[6]

The arrival of Paperclip personnel posed an additional problem. The War Department already had alerted all bases to step up security because "certain Paperclip personnel returned to Germany had technical documents in their possession upon arrival in the Theater." For example, Wright Field specialist Heinz Gartmann left America with turbojet rocket engine blueprints in his hand luggage. Gartmann claimed that a co-worker had packed the documents by mistake. But European investigators, who learned that Gartmann was negotiating with a Russian factory prior to his U.S. departure, reported, "It is believed here that the . . . documents were not taken accidentally."[7]

In addition, Army CIC counterespionage headquarters warned U.S. officials that Russian agents were making a concerted effort to obtain information about Paperclip. The mother of Helmut Groettrup, a German scientist who voluntarily went to Russia to work, was caught nosing around Landshut housing project in Germany, where families of Paperclip personnel lived. Thea Groettrup arrived at Landshut with Helmuth Thiele, an engineer known to the Army CIC as a Russian agent who recruited scientists for the Soviets. Frau Groettrup was trying to obtain information about the U.S. rocket project and the names of Paperclip scientists who were being returned to Germany from America.[8]

The Army also had been warned that the rocket group planned to withhold technical information from American personnel. The warning was contained in a report by Lieutenant Walter Jessel, an interrogator assigned to screen the rocket scientists for trustworthiness before they left Germany in 1945.

During the interrogations, Jessel uncovered evidence of a conspiracy among von Braun, Dornberger, and Dornberger's former chief of staff, Herbert Axster, to withhold information from U.S. officers. As a result Jessel concluded that to give security clearances to the group was "an obvious absurdity."[9]

In an interview Axster confirmed that they did indeed plot to withhold information to assure that the group would be sent to the United States. "I realized more and more that they wanted something from us," Axster said. "And of course that has to be paid for. We had to sell ourselves as expensively as possible." Once in America, the group's ultimate purpose was to find a more lucrative sponsor, such as General Electric, and then pull their group out from under the Army's control.[10]

Major James Hamill was directly in charge of the Paperclip group at Fort Bliss under Colonel Toftoy. The "tall, fair-headed" twenty-six-year-old major "looked good," according to Axster. Hamill was a graduate of Fordham University with a degree in physics. He had been a member of the regular Army when Colonel Toftoy assigned him to coordinate the entire V-2 mission in Germany. In that position Hamill played a key role in evacuating V-2 rockets from Mittelwerk tunnels to the United States.[11]

Some of Hamill's charges had been members of the SS and were considered to be potential security threats by European investigators. Wernher von Braun, for example, had joined the SS at the personal behest of SS chief Heinrich Himmler and had risen to the rank of major. And JIOA officers had even obtained a photograph of another Peenemünde engineer, Anton Beier, decked out in full SS uniform, complete with skull and crossbones on his SS cap. Beier had joined the SS the same year Hitler came into power, in 1933, and was also a member of the Nazi party and two other Nazi organizations.[12]

Kurt Debus, who later would be the first director of the Kennedy Space Center at Cape Canaveral, was another member of the SS, the SA, and two other Nazi groups. In 1942 he turned a colleague over to the Gestapo for making anti-Hitler statements during an argument over who had started World

War II. As a result the man was tried by a Nazi court and sentenced to two years' imprisonment. When questioned about the incident at Fort Bliss, Debus claimed that he had defended the colleague during the trial and that the man's prison sentence had been suspended "mainly due to my testimony." But the actual trial records tell a far different story. The man was convicted as a direct result of Debus's derogatory testimony. Furthermore, his prison sentence was suspended as a result of intervention by his employer, not Debus. Debus also claimed that he was only an "applicant" in the SS. But Berlin Document Center SS files show that he joined in 1939 and was assigned SS membership number 426559. Also, his wartime colleagues reported seeing him in a black SS uniform during the Nazi period.[13]

In addition to that evidence, over a dozen of Hamill's charges had worked in the Mittelwerk V-2 factory using concentration camp inmates as slave labor. Hamill had to know about the slave labor used there, since he visited the place in 1945. It would have been impossible for him not to see, or step over, the dead bodies of six thousand Dora prisoners covering the ground at Nordhausen.[14]

Wernher von Braun's younger brother Magnus was one of those who worked in that undergound hell. He was an engineer under Arthur Rudolph in Mittelwerk from 1943 until the Germans fled the area shortly before American troops arrived. Some German engineers at Fort Bliss felt he lacked experience and was included in the project only because he rode on the coattails of his older brother. And Army CIC agents at Fort Bliss believed he was a "dangerous German Nazi" because of his pro-Hitler views. "His type is a worse threat to security than a half a dozen discredited SS Generals," one agent remarked.[15]

All of this controversial information was being kept secret from the American public. However, Axster's wartime past eventually caught the attention of the press. Axster worked for Hamill in the Army Ordnance Research and Development Service, Suboffice (Rocket), where most of the Germans were engaged in planning, design, and drafting blueprints for rockets. "But my main task was as liaison with the commanding officer," Axster recalled. He was also in charge of a group that translated German measurements — kilograms, centimeters, and so on — into American measurements.[16]

JIOA Director Wev already had received numerous derogatory reports about Axster and his wife Ilse. The Axsters' wartime neighbors told a U.S. intelligence agent that they had mistreated a French prisoner of war and Poles and Ukrainians from the East who worked on their estates. In one instance Herbert Axster was accused of hitting a Frenchman caught laying rabbit traps. Villagers said the man was probably hungry, since the Axsters starved the workers and they frequently begged for food from the townspeople. Another time, when a Polish worker was seriously injured by a mowing machine, villagers said Axster did not do anything about it until a neighbor demanded that the man be taken to the hospital.[17]

"That's all lies," Axster exclaimed when confronted with the charges in 1989. He admitted that a Ukrainian couple had worked on his estate, but he said there were no Poles. Axster claimed that the Ukrainians had been offered a "vacation" in the Ukraine. "They said that they only would go if they were assured they would come back to the same place," he said. "So it seems to me they can't have been treated so badly." He denied mistreating the French POW and said the man did not work for him. Axster said he probably scared the man because Axster was carrying a shotgun while hunting when he saw the Frenchman with a rabbit. "So I shouted at him," Axster said. "That's all."[18]

The Axsters' neighbors were terrified of Ilse, whom they described as stalking through town wearing riding breeches and carrying a whip. This view of Ilse, now deceased, was confirmed in 1989 by relatives and acquaintances who remembered her as a "Nazi tyrant." In 1947, villagers said she frequently beat Polish workers with a horsewhip or called the police and asked them to beat the workers. Ilse was a leader of the *NS-Frauenschaft*, a women's Nazi party auxiliary in charge of teaching Nazi propaganda to youth groups. A fellow *NS-Frauenschaft* member told U.S. investigators that Ilse was the ideal person to represent "the godless principles in the Nazi education of children." As might be expected, Ilse hated Allied soldiers, and once, when she saw a British soldier parachuting to the ground, she told a Wehrmacht officer standing nearby that she would shoot the man if she only had a gun.[19]

The Axsters' neighbors angrily complained to U.S. officers in Germany that the couple escaped prosecution because of Paperclip. As a result, the story leaked to the press and Rabbi Stephen Wise at the American Jewish Congress began a vocal campaign to oust the couple from America. Wise stated his case in the first of many letters to Secretary of War Robert Patterson, charging that Axster held "responsible positions" with the Wehrmacht and Ilse was a "major offender" under denazification laws that were supposed to be enforced by the U.S. military government in Germany.[20] "These scientists and their families are supposed to have been 'screened,' " Wise told Patterson. "The Axsters prove that this 'screening' is a farce and the War Department 'screeners' are entirely incapable of performing this task."[21]

The rabbi was particularly disturbed that while Paperclip brought hundreds of Nazis to America, the State Department's obstructive immigration policies kept Jewish survivors of Nazi concentration camps out of the country. Wise reminded the secretary of war of this point in his scathing letter:

> Red tape, lack of shipping facilities, and every other possible handicap face these oppressed people while their oppressors are brought to this country with their families and are favorably housed and supported at our expense. As long as we reward former servants of Hitler while leaving his victims in D.P. camps, we cannot pretend that we are making any real effort to achieve the aims we fought for.[22]

Two weeks later Patterson sent Wise a terse, two-paragraph reply that investigators were looking into the "alleged Nazi affiliation" of Ilse Axster, and if the charges were proven, "you may be certain that appropriate remedial action will be taken." Wise's letter was forwarded to the "screeners" in the JIOA, who brushed it off as Jewish propaganda.[23]

Despite the charges against him, Axster was the one man whom Hamill chose to trust as the liaison between Hamill and the Germans. "I was always the one that was in contact with him," Axster said. "We were friends." Hamill's idea of insuring an efficient informant system in the rocket office was to use Axster as his key informant to surreptitiously gain information about possible security breaches by other Germans in the project. In a gross understatement, Hamill once remarked that Axster's "enthusiastic compliance with the directives of this office has at times brought him disfavor from his associates." Most German engineers strongly criticized von Braun for Axster's inclusion in the project and resented his high salary, since his experience was confined to military aspects of training troops.[24]

Not only were Axster and other Paperclip personnel allowed extensive access to classified information, but Hamill never even required the men to fill out federal governmental forms to apply for security clearances. In addition, Army Ordnance officers maintained such lax security over the group that there was no curfew, no checks of the Germans' mail, and little surveillance of their activities off the base. Three Germans had telephones in their quarters, but none were monitored, and no attempt was made to determine if any Paperclip personnel made long-distance telephone calls on local pay phones.[25]

This brazen laxity was allowed to flourish despite stiff security regulations issued by the secretary of war designed to curtail the Germans' activities and ensure that the country's internal security was protected. The regulations ordered Hamill and other officers in charge of Paperclip personnel to: (1) assure that each specialist would be exposed to "only such classified information as is necessary to the completion of his assignment"; (2) maintain limited surveillance over their activities, inspect their mail, make "sufficiently frequent" checks of their whereabouts, and file monthly reports on the results of that surveillance; and (3) report any attempt at "political proselytizing." Furthermore, neither the specialists nor their dependants were legal residents, thus security regulations emphasized that officers in charge should assure that no specialists leave the continental United States. And finally, each specialist was supposed to observe a "Code of Conduct" that required him to obtain permission to correspond with individuals overseas and forbade his transmitting classified information, including photographs of equipment.[26]

But just as soon as the regulations were circulated, Exploitation Branch chief Hagood sent Hamill a notice that Hamill interpreted as voiding the War Department's requirements. Hagood told him that, starting four months after the Germans signed contracts, there should be no further Army surveillance over their activities, even if they left the base on business or pleasure trips. In addition, Hagood said that more than 50-percent support of an individual constituted "dependent" status for contract purposes. The large number of so-called dependents — including mistresses and maids — brought to Fort Bliss as a result of Hagood's memo were subject to no off-the-post surveillance, even though it was assumed that they had access to at least some classified information because of their close contact with Paperclip personnel.[27]

Hamill's supervision was so arrogantly lax that it did not take long for trouble to surface. A Fort Bliss businessman reported engineer Hans Lindenmayr to the FBI for using his company's address as an illegal mail drop. As a result FBI agents intercepted a letter from Lindenmayr's wife in Germany, who was furious that Lindenmayr had brought his mistress to the United States posing as his wife, and she threatened to file a complaint with U.S. immigration officials unless the problem was solved.[28]

Army CIC Captain Paul R. Lutjens, head of branch intelligence at Fort Bliss, was assigned to investigate the case. In a meeting with Lutjens and Hamill, Lindenmayr admitted that the claims in the letter were true. He asserted that he had been arrested by SS troops in 1938 and charged with espionage. To avoid a one-year prison sentence and exile, Lindenmayr claimed, he married the prosecuting attorney's daughter and "lived with her several months before deserting her for the girl he is now living with. . . ." Despite evidence that Lindenmayr had helped the woman enter the U.S. illegally, Hamill recommended that he be retained in the project. Army Ordnance simply revised his contract and penalized him for his actions by cutting his salary by $2,000. They decided that Lindenmayr would file for a divorce, and when it cleared, his girlfriend would go to Germany, then turn around and come back as his wife and legal dependent.[29]

In addition to Lindenmayr, three other Germans had illegal mail drops in El Paso where they received money from foreign or unknown sources and coded messages from South America. One German received $1,000 in cash from Chile. Another specialist not only maintained an illegal postal box but deposited $953 in his bank account in one month, even though his monthly salary was only $290. Neither Army CIC nor FBI agents knew where that money came from, and by all appearances, no one cared to know how more than a third of the Paperclip group suddenly were able to buy expensive cars.[30]

Other incidents proved that security was a sham. Unsupervised German scientists with no visas illegally crossed the border into Mexico for a little cheap wine, women, and song. Other specialists made frequent trips from White Sands to the El Paso home of a German-born woman who was under FBI investigation and described by her neighbors as being so pro-Hitler during the war that local residents told her to "shut up or get out" of America.[31]

Compounding those problems, base security officers began to suspect that the rockets were being sabotaged, a suspicion that increased sharply after the Juarez incident. In one month, three out of four rockets fired at WSPG overshot the 90-mile-wide base and landed off course near heavily populated areas in New Mexico and Juarez. One landed four and a half miles south of Alamogordo, another crashed only two miles from

Las Cruces, and the third ended up in Juarez. In addition to unanswered questions about what caused the erratic flights, five cameras attached to one of the rockets were missing after the launch and parts from another missile that was launched never were found.[32]

Lutjens investigated the incidents, but when he began to talk with officers in charge of the rocket project he encountered turf fights between the Army and Navy, buck passing regarding the cause of problems, and criticism of the way the entire rocket program was run. None of the officers blamed the Germans for the problems. Hamill pointed his finger at the contractor for the Hermes II rocket, General Electric; Lieutenant Colonel Harold Turner, the Army's commanding officer at WSPG, said erratic flights were caused by "human error" and expressed little confidence in the officers under his own supervision. "I dare say, they are about the poorest qualified personnel of any government installation in the country," he told Lutjens. However, Lieutenant Commander R. B. McLaughlin, the Naval commander at White Sands, made no secret of the fact that he had no confidence in either Turner or his men. McLaughlin thought Turner's plan to construct seventy-five observation stations would not yield the desired result—namely, to enable the men controlling the rockets to know where they were headed in time to prevent a rocket from going out of control. "They can tell where the rocket is every second of its flight," McLaughlin scoffed, "but not until three months later."[33]

When Lutjens finished his investigation he was skeptical, since he felt that the officers could not be entirely certain that no sabotage had occurred. Most evidence pointed to incompetent Army personnel and bad V-2 parts. The parts were old, damaged, rusted, and totally worthless by the time they arrived from Germany. It was apparent that the boats carrying the rocket parts had leaked during the trip, because the parts were soaked with saltwater when they arrived in America.[34] The Juarez incident was caused by a rocket tilting program, preset to 7 degrees north, that never operated. The wind was from the south, and the rocket headed into the wind and began traveling in the wrong direction. Steinhoff did not tell the command station to stop the rocket because he figured it would land safely north of El Paso.[35]

Meanwhile, the lax security over Paperclip personnel became so obvious that even visitors to Fort Bliss complained. One War Department intelligence officer, Colonel Frank Reed, was shocked that Hamill and other ordnance officers had made no serious checks of the Germans' loyalty. Reed's concern about security was heightened because he had just returned from visiting Saint Louis, France, where a comparable group of German rocket engineers worked for the French government. While there, the French commandant told Reed he suspected the Germans under French control were receiving orders from Germany and working toward a reemergence of the Third Reich.[36]

All of a sudden, word came down that Wernher von Braun had been caught sending a map overseas to General Dornberger and concealing information from U.S. officials. It was an incident disturbingly similar to the plot that Walter Jessel had warned intelligence officers of in 1945. American officers in Europe were trying to locate V-2 rocket diagrams they believed were still hidden in Germany. When asked about the documents, von Braun told the Army he knew nothing about their location. Dornberger later told von Braun's brother that Army officers didn't trust von Braun and that officers had even told him that von Braun had lied to them. Von Braun then sent a map to his family in Europe showing the location of a burial place where sketches stuffed in a cigarette box were hidden. He told them to deliver the map to Dornberger's wife, since the general still was being held in a British POW camp. The way this scheme was supposed to work, the documents then would be located and given to German scientists, who would turn them over to von Braun when they arrived in the United States under Paperclip.[37]

U.S. officers reported that von Braun "apparently intended to use the location of certain hidden documents as a bargaining lever with U.S. officials."[38]

This plot was abruptly halted when Army officers confiscated the map from Dornberger's wife. Then the officers finagled Dornberger's release from the British and flew to Germany to look for the missing documents in a forest. Under Dornberger's direction, the officers wandered around the woods for days, digging up tree stumps that yielded nothing. The sketches eventually were found lying in the woods, practically worthless from rain and rot.[39]

Despite mounting security problems at Fort Bliss, investigator Lutjens's hands were tied. Even though the Intelligence Division in Washington was aware of the security breaches and had received copies of Lutjens's reports, the War Department had ruled the Paperclip group exempt from Army CIC control. All Lutjens was allowed to do was investigate suspicious incidents and turn over the information to his superiors. Army Ordnance had blocked CIC efforts to do anything about illegal activities that were uncovered.[40]

The FBI fared no better. When FBI agents reported a suspicious incident involving Magnus von Braun, the Army proceeded to squelch the investigation. FBI agents had learned that Magnus von Braun sold a bar of platinum to a local El Paso jeweler. It is still not known where he obtained the platinum bar, but when FBI agents reported the incident to Justice Department officials in Washington they were told to drop the case. The Army ordered that "action not be taken for security reasons and possible adverse publicity which might affect the long range objectives of the project on which the group of Germans was employed."[41]

Meanwhile, FBI Director J. Edgar Hoover had a pile of FBI reports sitting on his desk. One was by a General Electric manager whose employees at WSPG had fired rockets during various tests. The manager, A. K. Bushman, told an FBI agent that he thought the Army's lax security at White Sands bordered on "criminal neglect." Then Bushman ripped into Paperclip with a scathing critique of the Army's lax surveillance over the specialists. He was particularly upset that the Germans were allowed access to classified information about new discoveries, including a rocket fuel developed by GE's missile project in Malta, New York. Bushman told the FBI that the way the Army ran the project threatened the internal security of the United States, since around 350 of the Germans' former colleagues were working for the Russians and Bushman thought it reasonable to assume that friendships between members of those two groups continued.[42]

Hoover immediately sent a stinging two-page memo to Director of Intelligence Chamberlin. In minute detail, Hoover criticized the Army's loose security, summarized Bushman's report, and told Chamberlin that "if his information indicating a lack of restriction on the part of the movements of German scientists in the U.S. is, in fact, true, technical data made available to them concerning U.S. improvements of rockets and guided missiles . . . could very easily find its way back to Russian scientists."[43]

Once Chamberlin received Hoover's hand-delivered critique there was an instant flurry of activity in the Intelligence Division of the War Department. Chamberlin ordered the Exploitation Branch to investigate whether security had been breached at Fort Bliss.[44]

By then Lieutenant Colonel Montie Cone had replaced Hagood as chief of G-2's Exploitation Branch. Cone was a veteran Army intelligence officer who had been commanding officer at Fort Hunt in 1945 when Nazi spy chief Reinhard Gehlen was interrogated there. Cone would represent Chamberlin on the JIOA Governing Committee and help supervise Paperclip for over a decade.

Cone and Major Lyman White of the Special Investigations unit set out for Texas with a list of twenty-six items to investigate, everything from Wise's complaint against the Axsters to Jessel's conspiracy report. What they found was a group of Germans that Hamill allowed to run loose. White discovered that ordnance deliberately avoided surveillance over Paperclip personnel both on and off the base. The Germans were allowed to make unsupervised trips out of town and had to report to Army installations only when they arrived at their destinations.[45]

Their mail had only been spot-censored. Lists of their overseas correspondents showed none with addresses in Russia or its satellite nations, but no one had checked the names against G-2 files. A name check was crucial, since evidence showed that the Soviets used phony addresses to hide the location of Germans who worked in the USSR. For example, the CIA had sent President Truman information that the Soviets used an address in the U.S. zone of Germany as a cover for letters mailed by German scientists working in the USSR.[46]

During White's conversations with Hamill it became obvious that Hamill knew absolutely nothing about the Germans' off-base activities. Neither did Toftoy, who said that while he had no reason to believe that any of the scientists were engaged in illicit activities, his estimate was "based solely on their conduct at the installation." He did not have the slightest idea of what their activities were off the post. Furthermore, while Army CIC agents, the FBI, and G-2 considered some Germans at the base to be "under suspicion of being potential security risks," neither Hamill nor Toftoy was able to list accurately those individuals who should be watched or denied access to sensitive material. This was illustrated perfectly in the case of Axster, whom Hamill had chosen as his informant to insure ordnance's security.[47]

These were extremely important admissions. Hamill had filed *Sponsoring Agency Security Reports* with the JIOA on each German, attesting that there was no evidence that the individual had breached security at Fort Bliss. The reports were supposed to include the results of surveillance and interrogations of Germans on the base. In fact, there was little or no surveillance, and Hamill had no idea what the Germans' activities were out of the rocket office. The reports were important because JIOA officers submitted them and several other forms to the State and Justice Departments as evidence that the Germans were qualified for legal U.S. immigration. In addition, the JIOA used those reports repeatedly to discredit Paperclip detractors and excuse evidence of ardent nazism on the grounds that the Germans had done nothing to indicate that they were security threats since their arrival in America.[48]

Cone and White finished their investigation and returned to

Washington. Most of their suggestions to improve security were identical to the War Department's original regulations. In their final report they advised Major Hamill to curtail trips, censor mail, maintain lists of correspondents, forbid use of postal boxes, and monitor the Germans' telephone calls. They also suggested that restrictions on Lutjens's CIC unit should be lifted to allow the CIC more authority over Paperclip personnel and stop illegal activities uncovered by CIC investigations.[49]

Since Rabbi Wise's complaints about the Axsters had resulted in derogatory news stories, White was most concerned about controlling negative publicity, which he feared would shut Paperclip down. "While critical comment must be evaluated in the light of the natural Jewish bias against anything Nazi, it is, however a matter to be watched, and, if possible, counteracted lest it lead to official restrictive action against the project as a whole," White noted in his report. He felt that the press should be restrained before someone discovered the dubious backgrounds of other Germans at Fort Bliss. To solve the problem, an Army public relations officer was assigned to control the press and assure that it published "human interest" stories to take the focus away from controversial topics.[50]

In their report Cone and White suggested that officers in Europe "make a more thorough background investigation of all Paperclip personnel under Army jurisdiction." Cone noted, however, that Wernher von Braun was to be "fully justified" for legal immigration irrespective of his Nazi past.[51]

A Hell Called Dora

4

I N the fall of 1946 Air Materiel Command headquarters at Wright Field was bustling with activity. Dozens of reporters mingled with the large crowd that had gathered at the air base. The War Department's news blackout had been lifted. Wright Field and other bases were having an open house to introduce some of Nazi Germany's finest scientists. AAF officers put on frozen smiles as twenty Germans, in their best suits, went out to meet the press. The group was carefully selected from among eighty-six German jet engine, helicopter, and other aircraft specialists employed by the AAF at Wright Field or in cities where they worked under Army Air Forces contracts at aircraft factories or universities.

Alexander Lippisch showed the visitors a model of his new delta-wing supersonic jet. Lippisch was the inventor of the famous Messerschmitt ME-163 jet fighter plane, which set speed records. Theodor Knack, formerly of the Graf Zeppelin Institute, held up his ribbon-type parachute and told reporters it permitted safe jumps at high speeds. Eighty-year-old Hugo Eckener, former chairman of the Zeppelin Company, smiled brightly as AAF public relations officers said Goodyear was thrilled to have the dirigible designer working for them as a consultant under AAF contract. No one asked the former commander of the ill-fated Hindenberg blimp about the thirteen passengers and thirty-six crewmen who were killed when the infamous dirigible caught fire and burned in 1937.

The open house resulted in a flood of favorable newspaper and magazine stories which highly pleased the War Department. The Germans' Nazi past was forgotten. After all, reporters had been told that the Germans had been "exhaustively screened." *Life*, *Newsweek*, and other magazines gave prominent display to photographs of the Germans alongside their inventions. The local *Dayton Daily News* was less formal, showing a picture of six Germans sunning themselves after lunch. All of the news stories created the impression of a congenial, friendly relationship between the Germans and AAF officers at the base. Jet fuel expert Ernst Eckert, for example, was even photographed having a friendly talk with an American engineer about high-speed gas turbines. And American officers said they were thrilled to have the Germans working at the air base. "I wish we had more of them," one officer said, "they are wonderful workers."[1]

The problem was, the stories were beautifully orchestrated War Department propaganda. The congeniality between the Germans and AAF officers was staged. The press was required to clear their copy with military censors prior to publication. Most photographs had been provided by the U.S. military. Few stories deviated from a lengthy five-page War Department press release—a document full of half-truths and baldfaced lies. Unfortunately, this was only the beginning of one of the most successful military intelligence disinformation campaigns ever foisted on the American public. The Paperclip myth had just been hatched and was ready to fly.[2]

On the issue of the Germans' nazism, for example, Under

Secretary of War Patterson claimed that "no scientists who are alleged war criminals are brought to the United States." Additionally, military press officers were intent on creating an image of Germans working in a state of euphoric harmony with American officers. The War Department press release emphasized how closely the Germans worked with American personnel to impart their knowledge: "To date there has been no evidence of friction between these groups."[3]

Contrary to this propaganda, the Nazi past of the Paperclip group caused such violent disputes among officers at Wright Field that the air inspector once told Colonel Putt, "The mere mention of the German Scientist situation is enough to precipitate emotions in Air Corps personnel ranging from vehemence to frustration."[4]

Air Corps officers stationed in Germany began to arrive in Dayton and were outraged to find Germans working there whom they regarded as Nazi war criminals. Arguments and fights short of blows ensued. Two Germans and a U.S. Army officer filed reports on Theodor Zobel charging that he had "performed experiments on human beings while in charge of wind tunnels at Chalais Meudon, France." But before the allegations were even investigated, Putt sent AAF headquarters a recommendation that Zobel be approved for legal immigration.[5]

Other questions were raised about jet fuel expert Ernst Eckert's Nazi past, while working for the German Institute of Technology in Nazi-occupied Prague, Czechoslovakia. Berlin Document Center reports reveal that Eckert had been a member of the SA and had joined the Nazi party in 1938 and the SS a year later. Yet during an interview Eckert denied he had ever been a member of the SS—until confronted with his SS records. Then he talked about participating in SS meetings. "We did some sports, some exercises, talked about the state of the war, things like that," Eckert said. All of this information had been available to Putt and other AAF officers at Wright Field. "The Air Force knew," said Eckert, "they helped us fill out our forms."[6]

The controversies that arose over Zobel, Eckert, and others

were only the beginning. In October 1946 a letter written by a Paperclip scientist to his part-time employer set off a chain of events that instigated Georg Rickhey's trial for Nazi war crimes and a military coverup to assure that the Nazi past of the rocket group at Fort Bliss remained secret.[7]

Rickhey was an aggressive, cool, and calculating man, one who didn't mind attracting attention to himself or his high-ranking position during the war. He bragged on papers filed with both Wright Field and the JIOA that he was the wartime general manager of the Mittelwerk underground V-2 rocket factory. During the entire time Rickhey worked at Wright Field, from July 21, 1946, until his arrest nearly a year later, his name was prominently displayed on U.S. Army war crimes lists as being wanted for murder.[8]

His Paperclip job at the air base was analogous to putting a fox in a chicken coop. Rickhey was paid to translate forty-two boxes of Mittelwerk documents shipped from Nordhausen—the very same records a U.S. Army war crimes unit sought to use as evidence of his crimes. Rickhey had turned these records over to a Colonel Peter Beasley soon after the U.S. Army liberated Dora concentration camp. They were shipped first to London and then to Wright Field. Rickhey once described them as including Mittelwerk management papers, lists of managers, contracts, letters, and policy as well as information about V-2 rockets and underground tunnel construction.[9]

Judging from his description and the available documents, the boxes contained very important war crimes evidence. For example, management papers might have included sabotage reports signed by Rickhey, Rudolph, or other civilians that were filed with the SS. Sabotage reports resulted in hundreds of prisoners being hanged.[10]

Except for a meager handful, these Mittelwerk documents disappeared from view once they arrived at Wright Field. This is not surprising, since Putt had put Rickhey in charge of them at the air base. He certainly was given more than ample opportunity to destroy anything that could be used as evidence against him or other Germans at Fort Bliss whose names appeared in those files. Equally disturbing, however, is that Putt and other Wright Field officers allowed this to happen. Unfortunately, this is only one example of how Paperclip officials' callous attitude toward Nazi war crimes obstructed any possible justice.

Rickhey lived with 140 other Germans in a cluster of one-story barracks located on an isolated hilltop at Wright Field. Not satisfied with the money he earned under Paperclip, he used liquor and other goods given to him by relatives to set up a black market in his room, selling beer, candy, and cigarettes to other Germans at a profit. His room was frequently the site of noisy card games and drinking parties that extended long into the night.[11]

His card-playing partner, fifty-nine-year-old Albert Patin, had been a big-time industrialist who owned factories that manufactured automatic pilot devices for fighter planes. Patin had been a colonel in the SA storm troopers, a position he claimed was "honorary," and a director in the German Air Ministry. In a long, rambling affidavit turned over to Putt, Patin described how he had hobnobbed during the war with those in Hitler's inner circle. There were Mediterranean cruises with the nephew of Hermann Göring, the proclaimed successor to Hitler, and winter trips with Dieter Stahl, head of munitions production in Albert Speer's Armaments Ministry.[12]

Even more damaging, Patin brazenly admitted using Russian, French, and Dutch POWs, along with "500 pitifully dressed [Jewish] women with shorn hair," as slave laborers in his factory. "One of the first things I ordered [was] the issuance of scarves for the women to cover their heads as they suffered most because of their shorn hair," he said. Patin claimed he ignored "one of the basic rules when employing slave labor" by not putting electric fences around the "encampment" where his slaves were imprisoned.[13]

Patin's admission was totally ignored, even though both Putt and JIOA officers had to know that using slave labor was a crime warranting full investigation. The International Military Tribunal was front page news and had just sentenced Albert Speer to twenty years in prison for his involvement with slave labor. Yet Patin was the first German whom Putt recommended for legal immigration. And like Hamill's questionable use of Axster as a trusted informant, Putt used Patin to spy on the other Germans at Wright Field.[14]

One cold October night Rickhey, Patin, and another man were drinking booze, playing cards, and having a noisy good time. This was the second time in a month that Rickhey's loud parties had kept his neighbor, sixty-three-year-old Hermann Nehlson, awake past midnight. Rickhey soon would discover that Nehlson was the wrong man to cross. Unlike Rickhey's crowd, Nehlson had avoided even joining the Nazi party. During the war, Nehlson had been a consulting engineer for an aircraft company in Austria. He told friends that he had wanted to make a better life for his daughter in America, but was now surrounded by the same Nazis and anti-Semitic views that he had encountered in the Third Reich. In addition, Putt had promised Nehlson that he could work full time for Erwin Loewy, a close friend whose engineering company in New York City had contracts with the AAF. Instead he was allowed only short visits to New York and was otherwise confined to the air base.[15]

Angry that he couldn't sleep, Nehlson went to Rickhey's room and turned out the lights to stop the noise. The men around the card table lit a candle and continued with their game, as Rickhey yelled, "one could still play cards with a good 'kosher' candle." Nehlson attributed the anti-Semitic remark to the fact that Rickhey was drunk.[16]

When he returned to his room, Nehlson wrote a two-page letter to Loewy and told him of the unpleasant incident. He put more-damaging information about Rickhey on the second page of his letter, hoping it would slip by military censors. Nehlson accused Rickhey of being the "chief culprit" when twelve Dora prisoners were hanged in the V-2 factory. He thought Rickhey was guilty of the crime. But when he asked

Wright Field officers to do something about it, he was told that they would go to any extreme to protect the scientists at the air base. Nehlson guessed that included Rickhey as well as Patin, who had just been named camp spokesman. "That is how things are here," Nehlson sadly told his friend. Then he put the letter in the slot to be mailed.[17]

A few weeks later Nehlson left the air base without permission and spent four days with his brother-in-law in Ann Arbor, Michigan. As a result Putt accused him of security violations and transferred him to Mitchell Field, New York.[18]

However, Nehlson's letter eventually caught the attention of censors who screened the Paperclip group's mail. Colonel Millard Lewis, an officer in AAF Headquarters, asked Cone, G-2's Exploitation Branch chief, to investigate Nehlson's charges against Rickhey. Lewis also strongly suggested that "a more comprehensive investigation" of German scientists be made, "to avoid the possibility of undesirables being admitted to the U.S." Clearly, insufficient background investigations were not the problem. Nearly everyone at Wright Field, from the Germans to AAF officers in charge, openly discussed Rickhey's involvement in the hangings. As one employee put it, the whole story was "common knowledge."[19]

Seven months passed before AAF headquarters even assigned an investigator to the case. Meanwhile, Putt continued to consider Rickhey eligible for immigration. On May 2, the same day that Air Corps Major Eugene Smith was ordered to investigate Rickhey's case, AAF Headquarters signed Rickhey to a new five-year contract.[20]

Once Smith was on the case he quickly traveled to Wright Field. Little is known about Smith except his rank and serial number. He did note his personal opinions of Germans he interrogated in reports he filed with the air provost marshal. And his reports clearly show his frustration that headquarters had given him minimal information about Mittelwerk and Dora to begin his investigation.

Smith first discussed Rickhey's case with Captain Albert Abels, one of the officers in charge of Paperclip personnel at

Wright Field. Abels said he'd heard rumors about Rickhey but discounted them as "petty jealousy" among the Germans. Several other Americans at the air base also knew about the hangings but did nothing to investigate the stories. Smith wasn't so cavalier—at his insistence, Rickhey was arrested, searched, and given a physical exam. On May 19, 1947, he was returned to Germany under guard to face war crimes charges.[21]

Smith went to Mitchell Field to meet Nehlson and three other German scientists who also had heard about Rickhey's activities. All had met Rickhey for the first time in Germany when he boarded the ship for America with a trunk that had "Mittelwerk General Manager" boldly painted on its side. Once on board, a former Mittelwerk engineer, Werner Voss, openly discussed Rickhey's involvement with the hangings. Voss told the Germans that Rickhey had instigated several hangings of Dora prisoners in the factory. In one case, prisoners were hanged when some of them tried to revolt after British planes dropped leaflets on the area urging them to do so.[22]

The hangings were so gruesome that even today Dora survivors, such as Yves Beon, remember them vividly. In one case, twelve prisoners were simultaneously hanged on an overhead crane near Arthur Rudolph's office. With their hands tied behind their backs and wooden sticks in their mouths to stifle screams, the electric crane slowly lifted them above a crowd of engineers and prisoners gathered in the tunnel. "Instead of letting them drop and killing them on the spot immediately, they let them hang very slowly with pain that's absolutely horrible," said Beon. Their bodies were left hanging in the tunnel for hours as a warning to the other prisoners.[23]

Nehlson confided to Smith how odd it was that Rickhey was deliberately separated from Rudolph and other Mittelwerk engineers at Fort Bliss. "I think he is protected," Nehlson said in a guarded voice. "All those who had been at Nordhausen were already in this country. They were brought to this country to work."[24]

Two days later, when Smith arrived at Fort Bliss, he began to see that the Germans were protected there, too. Wernher von Braun and his brother Magnus, who had worked at Mittelwerk, were conveniently out of town on business when Smith arrived. Hans Lindenberg, whom the Canadians wanted to interrogate during Backfire, had died a few months earlier. And even though Major Hamill had visited Mittelwerk in 1945, he told Smith he knew nothing about the place.[25]

Information that surfaced years later certainly explains why Wernher von Braun would have wanted to avoid talking to Smith. A transcript of a meeting held in Rickhey's office in 1944 to discuss slave labor lists von Braun as one of those attending the meeting, along with high-ranking SS officers as well as Arthur Rudolph, General Dornberger, Ernst Steinhoff, Hans Lindenberg, and Hans Friedrich. The group discussed bringing more French civilians to work as slaves in the underground factory and the requirement that they wear striped concentration camp inmate uniforms. There was no indication that von Braun or anyone else at the meeting objected to this proposal.[26]

Of the Germans Smith did interrogate, three men gave him so little information that he did not bother to conduct formal interrogations under oath. That is unfortunate, since one of the men, Guenther Haukohl, is currently under active investigation by the Justice Department. Haukohl was assigned to Mittelwerk in 1943, helped design the assembly line, and supervised V-2 production. Yet he told Smith he had only heard rumors of hangings. Both Hans Palaoro and Rudolph Schlidt were tight-lipped about their activities. Palaoro said he never saw Rickhey at Mittelwerk and had no information other than what Smith already knew, which was very little. Schlidt said he had seen Rickhey only a couple of times and never witnessed any instances of prisoners being shot, hanged, or stabbed in the tunnels.[27]

Werner Voss, the source of the rumors about Rickhey, told Smith another story when he was interrogated. He said that twice he had seen up to twenty men at a time hanged in the tunnels, but he did not see Rickhey at the hangings. Voss denied telling Nehlson that Rickhey had instigated the hangings and said he had talked about the hangings with the men on board ship only because he had a personal grudge against Rickhey. Smith did not ask him what that was about.[28]

Eric Ball, an engineer on the Mittelwerk assembly line, told Smith that he had seen two hangings but that Rickhey was not present at either of them. He admitted seeing German engineers beating prisoners in his section. "These 8 or 10 times the beatings were done by Germans who were in charge of the section and it was very light," Ball said. He told Smith that while civilian engineers were not supposed to strike prisoners, if the beatings had been carried out by the SS instead, they would have been much worse.[29]

Smith did not know the extent to which the civilian engineers had physically abused prisoners or he might have questioned Ball more closely. According to Mittelwerk records, the beatings became so widespread that Dora's camp doctor complained that prisoners were hospitalized for being "beaten or even stabbed with sharp instruments by civilian employees for any petty offense." On June 22, 1944, Rickhey and the SS even warned the engineers in writing that punishing prisoners was the SS's exclusive domain.[30]

Smith also did not know about Mittelwerk's notorious Prisoner Labor Supply office or that it was directly subordinate to Rudolph. The office, run by a civilian named Brozsat, was responsible for the quantity of food the prisoners received, which was minimal. The office also was responsible for obtaining prisoners from Dora to work in the factory. This was done in coordination with an SS officer who ran a corresponding prisoner allocation office at Camp Dora. Decades later Rudolph would admit to Justice Department attorneys that it was he who requested prisoners from SS Sergeant Wilhelm Simon, who headed the camp's office. Civilian employees under Rudolph in Mittelwerk's supply office also were known to have beaten the prisoners frequently.[31]

What Smith did know was that he became suspicious of

Rudolph the minute he started interrogating him. Despite having little information, Smith was not stupid, and when Rudolph told him a conflicting story, Smith became suspicious. Rudolph admitted that he had visited the SS commandant at Camp Dora twice. But when Smith began to ask about prisoners who were hurt or killed, Rudolph first denied seeing prisoners abused, then later described incidents of abuse. In one breath, Rudolph first told Smith, "I did not see them punished, beaten, hung, or shot." Yet a few minutes later, when asked to describe the time twelve prisoners were hanged from the crossbeam of a crane, Rudolph said he did not know if they were dead when he arrived, but "I do know that one lifted his knees, after I got there."[32]

Smith was skeptical. From information he had obtained, a sketch had been made of Mittelwerk's tunnels showing that Rudolph's office had been located near the crane from which the prisoners were hanged. He figured that Rudolph must have seen the hangings and he repeatedly asked Rudolph about them, but was given even more conflicting answers. One exchange went like this:

"Did you ever see anybody die in the tunnel?" Smith asked Rudolph.
"No."
"Tell me about the day Rickhey ordered 12 men hung by a crane."
"The SS had control of things like that. There were 6 maybe 12."[33]

Rudolph's answers on the amount of food given to prisoners were equally evasive, since the food supply department was subordinate to him. At first Rudolph said German civilians either brought food from home or ate in a cafeteria, while prisoners only ate soup sent from Camp Dora. But later Rudolph claimed that the slave laborers' meals were "about the same" as his own meals. Smith did not believe him, but he did not have enough information to piece the real story together. He decided to talk with Rudolph again after he had met with everyone else.[34]

Hans Friedrich had been in charge of a consulting committee for V-2 electrical devices at Mittelwerk. But some of his activities may have resulted in prisoners being hanged. According to Dora records, German engineers turned prisoners over to the SS for minor offenses, such as leaning over to tie a shoelace, and the prisoners were hanged as a result. Friedrich admitted that he had once reported a prisoner to the Prisoner Labor Supply office for offering him a cigarette, and he believed the complaint was given to the SS. Unfortunately, Smith did not pursue this point with Friedrich.[35]

Friedrich said that once, while prisoners were hanging on a crane, he telephoned Rudolph to ask how long the crane would be out of operation. "He told me that the men would be hanging there the last 6 hours of one work shift and the first 6 hours of the next work shift, so that all Germans and Haeftlinge [prisoners] could see," Friedrich said. But when Smith questioned Rudolph a second time and asked about that incident, Rudolph said he did not remember the telephone conversation.[36]

Smith thought it was unusual that the men he interrogated knew so little about Mittelwerk's tunneling operations. Many of their answers were so alike that it was almost as though they had agreed on them beforehand. They claimed that the slave laborers' living, sanitary, and working conditions were the same as theirs, even though twenty thousand prisoners had died. All of them said they had seen only two hangings. And if prisoners were hurt, beaten for instance, the SS or prisoner capos were at fault. According to them, German engineers had nothing to do with punishing prisoners.[37]

Smith also was suspicious about Rudolph and he noted those suspicions in his final report:

> Mr. Rudolph impressed the undersigned as a very clever, shrewd individual. He did not wish to become involved in any investigations that might involve him in any way with illegal

actions in the underground factory and as a result, was cautious of his answers.[38]

On June 10, 1947, Smith sent the air provost marshal a detailed sixteen-page report and the sworn interrogations he had conducted at Fort Bliss and Mitchell Field. Smith included the sketch showing the location of Rudolph's office adjacent to the crane used to hang prisoners. All of this information was sent to Germany and introduced as evidence during Rickhey's trial.[39]

Rickhey was confined in an old barracks at the former Dachau concentration camp, awaiting trial as a Nazi war criminal. Armed American soldiers stood guard in watch towers from which the SS had once looked down on their victims. A large part of the Dachau complex had been turned into a prison for SS officers and other hardened criminals awaiting war crimes trials. One barracks was used as a courtroom for 489 war crimes cases conducted by U.S. Army military courts between 1945 and 1949. The Nordhausen cases were among those trials. They consisted of the main case, *U.S. v. Andrae et al.*, and the cases of five other individuals tried separately.

Rickhey posed a serious problem for the Army. On one hand, he was a sacrificial lamb. He was not a brilliant visionary like von Braun or a highly experienced engineer, but only a bureaucrat whose skills were expendable. On the other hand, the Army could not afford to make him too angry, since he knew too much.

Imprisonment did not dampen Rickhey's arrogant spirit. He thought he was still employed under the Paperclip contract he had signed at Wright Field shortly before his arrest. He sent reports of his exploits in Germany to Paperclip officers at Wright Field, reminding them of his valuable work. One report, directed to Putt, was pompously entitled "Report From Germany." In it Rickhey reminded Putt that he had generously turned over his Mittelwerk management records to the AAF. In a brazen lie, he told Putt he had been cleared of war crimes charges. "The suspicion manifested about me . . . was in error and was rectified by Col. Berman chief of the Nordhausen prosecution," he lied. His confinement at Dachau was a mere inconvenience, since he had to give "authentical information" in the war crimes case. But he soon would be free to visit Paperclip offices at Landshut to discuss technical information about underground tunnels with Germans he recommended be hired under Paperclip.[40]

Lieutenant Colonel William Berman was outraged when he heard about Rickhey's letter. He immediately contacted the commanding officer of the Army's war crimes unit, Lieutenant Colonel Clio Straight, and told him that no error had been committed. Rickhey was still imprisoned as a war crimes suspect and would be a defendant in the main Nordhausen case.[41]

Rickhey's chief defense attorney, Major Leon Poullada, demanded that von Braun and his group testify at Rickhey's trial. Poullada told War Department officials he wanted von Braun "as well as some engineers who worked in the different departments of the so-called Mittelwerk" as witnesses. Lieutenant Colonel Straight supported the request, emphasizing that Rickhey faced a death sentence and that the personal attendance of von Braun and other witnesses was essential: "Sworn statements would be inadequate due to necessity for detailed explanation of complicated managerial structure of Mittelwerk Company and overlapping chains of command in Nordhausen."[42]

Rickhey's trial posed a serious threat to the Germans working for the Army under Paperclip. Detailed explanations of Mittelwerk's management structure would expose Rudolph's authority over the Prisoner Labor Supply office and his connection to SS officer Simon, who was a defendant in the trial. Von Braun would be forced to explain his own dubious activities at Mittelwerk. Both might have to explain their attendance at the meeting in Rickhey's office in which the idea of sending more French civilians to Dora was discussed. And then there was the ultimate threat—Dora survivors, who were witnesses at the trial, might recognize them if they were present in the courtroom.

Army Ordnance officers solved the problem by flatly refusing to comply with Straight's request, saying that von Braun should not leave the United States for "security reasons." If this refusal stemmed from ostensible concern that von Braun might be kidnapped by Russians, it was a hollow excuse. Ordnance had allowed von Braun to travel to Europe exactly five months prior to Straight's request, on February 11, 1947. The sole purpose of his trip was to meet his girlfriend and bring her back to America. Ordnance officers first claimed that von Braun had made the trip to take care of his "personal affairs." But to get their superiors to approve of von Braun's trip, the officers quickly changed the story and claimed that the trip had been an "emergency." They pointed out that von Braun's Paperclip contract allowed his return to Germany when "a state of emergency exists."[43]

Ordnance officers won the battle: the group never appeared at the trial. The best Poullada got were sworn statements from von Braun, Rudolph, and others in which no questions were asked about their own involvement in Mittelwerk's sordid affairs.

Poullada's efforts to get Mittelwerk records from Wright Field also failed, even though General Clarence Huebner, commander in chief of the U.S. Army in Europe, told the War Department to turn over the documents as expeditiously as possible. Four months later Rickhey's family hired a lawyer in the United States and began to campaign for his release. They sent numerous irate letters to congressmen, including a gross accusation that the War Department had used "Gestapo" methods against Rickhey. Congressman John Anderson from California tried to get the Mittelwerk documents after Poullada's efforts failed. Anderson finally obtained a mere handful of records and sent them to Dachau with a request that Rickhey's cooperation under Paperclip be brought to the judges' attention at the trial.[44]

The *Andrae* trial began August 7, 1947. Except for Rickhey, the defendants were either SS officers or prisoner capos. The defendants were charged with the murders of at least twenty thousand prisoners who were starved, beaten, tortured, or hanged. Rickhey was specifically accused of instituting a system to increase V-2 rocket production that forced the slave laborers to work at such a fast pace that hundreds of them died from exhaustion. He also was charged with instigating hundreds of hangings in Mittelwerk's tunnels or at Camp Dora.[45]

SS officer Simon, Dora's labor allocation leader, also was sitting in the dock, charged with murder. This man was so brutal that Dora prisoners had nicknamed him "Simon Legree." An example of his brutality occurred one summer day in 1944, when a trainload of Hungarian Jews, including children, arrived from Auschwitz so weak from hunger they had to be carried into the camp. Simon immediately assigned the adults to a grueling work detail, forcing them to carry heavy wood planks to construct their own prison barracks. Soon many of them dropped dead from exhaustion. Then Simon went after the children, whom he considered useless because they were too young—no more than ten or twelve years old —to work in the tunnels. He ordered the SS to round them up in the camp yard and beat them to death with clubs.[46]

In his opening statement, Lieutenant Colonel Berman, the chief prosecutor, described Dora as unique among concentration camps in that it was created to serve the German war machine. The entire complex consisted of the main camp, Dora, and thirty-one subcamps clustererd around the town of Nordhausen, Germany, in the Harz mountains. The camps existed solely to provide forced labor in the top-secret V-weaponry factory. "Dora was a concentration camp with the avowed purpose of exterminating those who were sent to it," Berman said. "The method of extermination was not the gas chamber, but the method of working them to death, and this they proceeded to do."[47]

Of the 60,000 prisoners who had passed through the camp in less than two years, one-third died as a result of organized murder. Dora's hospital records graphically list the cause of death: 9,000 died from exhaustion and collapse, at least 350 were hanged, and the remainder were shot or died from disease or starvation. The bodies of those who died were shipped to Buchenwald until Dora's own crematory, designed to burn up to seventy-five bodies a day, was complete.[48]

During the trial Rickhey was described as a cold-blooded Nazi who ordered the SS to hang prisoners. Four months before American soldiers arrived, as Hitler was demanding that more rockets be produced, Rickhey took one of his daily walks through the tunnels dressed in full Nazi uniform and surrounded by heavily armed SS guards. He called the prisoners together in the tunnels and threatened to cut off their food entirely if they did not work faster. Witnesses said that was exactly what happened. Soup kettles dried up, potatoes rotted, and the death toll mounted. Both Rickhey and Rudolph knew the prisoners were dying. Simon's office sent them daily reports on the number of prisoners either working, sick, or dead.[49]

Rickhey's defense centered on his claim that he was an administrator in charge only of budgets, not of rocket production. He had had nothing to do with the prisoners' deaths and conveniently blamed everything on the technical director, Albin Sawatzki, who had never been located. Reports of his whereabouts were mixed. Dora survivors have claimed that American soldiers killed him at Nordhausen in 1945. One Army CIC agent reported that Sawatzki was buried in a hospital cemetery near Nordhausen. Two other reports, including an Army war crimes arrest warrant, noted that he might be in England. Another Army officer told his superior that Sawatzki was living in a large apartment near Mittelwerk, in what was by then Soviet-controlled East Germany.[50]

Rickhey begged the court to consider his work under Paperclip and his inability to obtain Mittelwerk documents or witnesses in his defense. "I have tried to get these records very hard and if I had gotten them I wouldn't be sitting here now," he said. Poullada submitted the affidavits filed by von Braun, Rudolph, and others at Fort Bliss who were not allowed to attend the trial. When von Braun's statement was introduced, noting that he had visited Mittelwerk fifteen to twenty times to discuss technical matters, the military judges asked Rickhey who he was. "Dr. von Braun was head of the development of the V-2 and always had close contact with all the data of Dr. Sawatzki constantly," said Rickhey.[51]

Chief Prosecutor Berman read portions of Smith's interrogation of Rudolph regarding Rickhey's position at Mittelwerk. Rudolph described the defendant as his chief and said that as Mittelwerk's general manager, Rickhey was responsible for everything that occurred in the factory. Rickhey had bragged about his powerful position when he was at Wright Field. During the trial, however, he tried to downplay his role. Berman and Rickhey argued a minute over Rudolph's description of his authority, and then this ironic exchange took place:

> "Mr. Rudolf [sic] is not only a scientist of repute, but personally a man of reputation as distinct, is he not?" the prosecutor asked Rickhey.
>
> "As far as I know, Mr. Rudolf's reputation is okay," Rickhey replied halfheartedly. The report that Major Smith filed with the court, noting his own skepticism about Rudolph, was ignored.[52]

Dora survivors told the court horrifying stories about how brutally they had been treated by vicious SS guards. There was also testimony about civilian engineers—such as Rudolph's subordinates in the Prisoner Labor Supply office—who ordered SS officers to hang prisoners or who beat prisoners on their own. At least 350 Dora prisoners were hanged, including 200 for sabotage. Prisoners who worked on assembly lines continually risked their lives by deliberately pulling out wires, urinating on wiring, and using other methods to assure that the rockets would not operate properly. They felt that their sabotage efforts helped save Allied soldiers' lives. In addition to those hanged for sabotage, others were hanged for such trivial offenses as leaning over to pick up a piece of wire from the ground or making a spoon during work.[53]

When civilian engineers saw a prisoner doing something suspicious they filed a sabotage report. These reports were turned over to the SS and then usually the prisoners were hanged. Rickhey was accused of having sent these reports to the SS, which had carried out the hangings. But Sawatzki's former secretary at Mittelwerk testified that it was Rudolph who had turned over the reports. Hannelore Bannasch said she saw the sabotage reports that crossed her desk at work. According to Bannasch the reports were handled by "the factory management," and Sawatzki heard of them only as "they were passed on by the factory management."

"Whom do you mean by that—what individual?" the prosecutor asked Bannasch.
"Director Rudolf," she replied.[54]

He then asked her who had signed the sabotage reports. Previous witnesses had testified to having seen a sabotage report signed by both Rickhey and a prisoner capo.

"That is impossible," said Bannasch, "a prisoner couldn't possibly sign a sabotage report and if anybody had signed it at the Werke, it would have been Mr. Rudolf, and never Rickhey, because he never had anything to do with that factory, itself."[55]

Civilian engineers even had taken more direct action by personally ordering the SS to hang prisoners. One Dora survivor named Josef Ackermann recalled that a group of Russian POWs were hanged because they were caught making a metal spoon. "The capo told a civilian engineer about it and the civilian engineer called the SS who was near him," said Ackermann. "The SS brought a piece of wire and hanged them over their machine." Another witness, Cecil Jay, was a British citizen living in Germany who had been arrested by the Gestapo for anti-Nazi activities and sent to Dora. Jay testified that he saw civilian personnel order SS guards to hang four prisoners in the tunnel. "The order was given from the civilians to the SS that the prisoners be punished for sabotage and it was carried out," Jay said.[56]

Rudolph's subordinates in the Prisoner Labor Supply office were notorious for beating prisoners. George Finkenzeller, a capo in Paperclip engineer Guenther Haukohl's detail from November 1943 until the summer of 1944, when he went to another area of the plant, was convicted in a separate Nordhausen trial. In his testimony Finkenzeller identified civilians by name from the Prisoner Labor Supply office and Rudolph's deputy, Karl Seidenstuecker, and said they ordered the SS to punish prisoners or beat prisoners themselves. "Practically all civilians who were working in the prisoner labor allocation and partly some of the civilians, especially during the first year, carried out beatings on their own," said Finkenzeller.[57]

Prisoners were brutally beaten by almost anyone in authority for any minor offense. "I was beaten by the SS, I was beaten by the civilian engineers, and I was even beaten by the capos," said former Dora prisoner Georges Kassimatis. He was beaten once with a large rubber hose because he was cold and had wrapped himself in a cement bag to keep warm. Another time he was beaten while carrying torpedo parts because he was not walking fast enough to suit his guards. He lagged behind the others in line because he was so weak from hunger his feet had gone numb.[58]

Toward the end of the trial Jean Michel was called to the witness stand. Michel had been a leader of the French Resistance in Paris when he was arrested by the Gestapo and sent to Dora. In late 1944 he organized a French underground movement in the camp to try to save prisoners' lives. "Everybody knew that the SS had decided to kill everybody at the end of the war," Michel said in an interview. "So, I decided to try to do something about it." He told the court that the Gestapo had caught him and thirty-seven other Frenchmen and threw them all in jail. Two men were beaten to death when they tried to escape. Then Michel and the others were taken one by one into another cell, where the SS beat them. "I would have been hanged if the end of the war didn't arrive as it happened," Michel said. After the war he was awarded the French Legion of Honor and the American Medal of Freedom.[59]

The trial lasted four months. When the verdicts were announced, fifteen defendants were found guilty and four were acquitted. Rickhey was found not guilty, and he immediately complained in a letter to Beasley that the trial had been a Communist plot. Rudolph had sent Simon's attorney a letter in Simon's defense claiming that the SS officer had tried to help the prisoners. The court, however, thought the evidence against Simon showed entirely the opposite and sentenced him to life imprisonment.[60]

In Washington, G-2 Exploitation Branch chief Montie Cone was busy in his office in the Intelligence Division when the telephone rang. State Department representative Henry Cox wanted to know if there had ever been a Paperclip specialist returned to Germany for a war crimes trial. "I thought a moment," said Cone, "and realizing that the Rickhey case was in the public domain . . . I did not dare deny the story." He told Cox that one Air Force case had been returned to Europe under suspicion and that he recollected that the man was cleared. In any event, Cone said, "we did not desire to take further chances on the case."[61]

Then, in an unprecedented move, the Army classified the entire trial record. The American public would not know that Rudolph, Magnus von Braun, and others at Fort Bliss had worked at Mittelwerk, not Peenemünde. The press would not be able to obtain Smith's report that noted his suspicions about Rudolph, or see trial testimony of witnesses who said it was Rudolph who had signed sabotage reports that were turned over to the SS. Wernher von Braun would be saved from having to answer awkward questions about his frequent visits to that underground hell. No one would know about twenty thousand men who died while working as slaves on Hitler's V-2. No one would even know that Camp Dora existed.

All of that evidence was now safely hidden from public scrutiny. And it stayed that way for decades.

5 Experiments in Death

T was mid-afternoon, March 16, 1946, when the guests arrived at the old Kaiser Wilhelm Institute in Heidelberg, Germany. Hundreds of Americans had been invited to the open house at the new AAF Aero Medical Center set up to exploit German aviation medicine. The center's commander, Air Corps Colonel Robert Benford, greeted guests at the door and sent them to the large library that had been transformed into a cheerful cocktail lounge decorated with brightly colored flowers. A bartender recruited from a local hotel kept the liquor flowing throughout the afternoon.[1]

The party provided an opportunity for the guests to meet more than a hundred German scientists working at the AAF Center under Paperclip. Benford and other AAF officers had recruited some of Germany's best-known specialists in aviation medicine. Many Americans at the party already knew Hubertus Strughold, who was in charge of the German staff. During the war, Strughold headed the Luftwaffe Institute for Aviation Medicine in Berlin under Oskar Schroeder, chief of the Luftwaffe's Medical Service. The German staff at the AAF Center included Strughold's former wartime subordinates at the institute, Konrad Schaefer, Otto Gauer, and Hans Clamann.[2]

As part of the festivities, guests toured the AAF Center to get firsthand information about the more interesting projects underway. Thousands of captured German documents and copies of the scientists' published and unpublished research were being translated into English for later publication in AAF monographs.[3]

Konrad Schaefer's study, "Thirst and Thirst Quenching in Emergency Situations at Sea," was part of this project. Schaefer had worked at Strughold's institute on problems of how to make seawater relatively safe to drink. The Luftwaffe—and now the AAF—considered this research an important step toward saving the lives of downed fliers with no water available to them except seawater.[4]

Other Paperclip scientists had conducted aeromedical experiments using the scientific equipment housed at the AAF Center. One was the well-known high-altitude specialist Siegfried Ruff—who works today as a consultant for Lufthansa German Airlines in West Germany. He was wartime head of aeromedicine at the German Experimental Institute for Aviation, the DVL (Deutsche Versuchsanstalt fuer Luftfahrt). Ruff and Strughold coauthored several articles and a book on aviation medicine.[5]

Ruff recalled his work under Paperclip at the AAF Center. "I worked on ejector seats," Ruff said in an interview. "We tested how much humans can stand." He and Gauer conducted experiments to test the body's ability to withstand sudden thrust accelerations simulating a flyer's experience when catapulted from an aircraft after an accident or ramming.[6]

Another Paperclip recruit, Hermann Becker-Freyseng, worked on high-altitude experiments with Ruff at the AAF Center. Becker-Freyseng was formerly head of the Department for Aviation Medicine under Schroeder and worked afternoons at Strughold's institute. Under Paperclip he and Ruff conducted seventy experiments with a German low-pressure chamber to study ways to prevent the bends. They put volunteer test subjects into a chamber and simulated an altitude of 39,260 feet to determine whether the bends were less painful when the body was in a prone position or sitting up.[7]

But a dark side of the Germans' work was kept secret from the guests at the party. Both Schaefer and Becker-Freyseng knew far more about seawater's effects on the human body than was stated in the published version of Schaefer's study. And men had been driven insane and died due to lack of oxygen when they ascended to simulated extreme high altitudes in the pressure chamber.

Karl Hoellenrainer was an innocent victim of gruesome seawater experiments at Dachau. The scars on his back where his liver had been punctured and his ruined health from being forced to drink putrid yellow seawater told the story of what was missing from Schaefer's study. SS chief Himmler had tried to eliminate gypsies from Nazi Germany. As a result Hoellenrainer was arrested by the Gestapo and sent to Auschwitz. He was only there a month, but that was long enough for the Nazis to kill his child, his sister, and both of her children, and throw their bodies into the smoldering furnaces at Birkenau. Then he was loaded onto a train bound for Buchenwald to be imprisoned until the SS decided his and other gypsies' fate.[8]

As Hoellenrainer sat waiting, Schaefer, Becker-Freyseng, and others held a conference at the German Air Ministry to discuss problems of fliers whose planes crashed at sea, forcing them to live on seawater. In 1944 the Luftwaffe's Medical Service had only two methods for making seawater potable. Schaefer's method was relatively safe but required substantial amounts of silver, which was in limited supply. The second method, called Berkatit, was a substance that changed the taste of seawater but did not remove the salt.[9]

During the conference, Becker-Freyseng reported that clinical experiments had not yet been conducted under sufficiently realistic conditions of sea distress. He and Schaefer were convinced that if a man took Berkatit his health would be damaged within six days and after twelve days it would kill him. Several meetings were held to plan the experiments, including one at Strughold's institute that Clamann also attended. The group agreed that a new set of experiments should be conducted using concentration camp prisoners, since experiments with Berkatit probably would result in deaths.[10]

Becker-Freyseng wrote a letter to SS chief Himmler, signed by Schroeder, asking for "40 healthy test subjects" and permission to conduct the experiments at Dachau. A particularly nauseating Nazi discussion ensued among SS officials over whether to use Jews or "asocial gypsy half-breeds." One SS man objected to gypsies because they were "of somewhat different racial composition" than Aryan Germans. Himmler finally arranged to transfer gypsies to Dachau for the experiments.[11]

Hoellenrainer got the word when the SS summoned him and forty other gypsies to the camp yard and said they were being transferred to a work detail at Dachau. When they arrived, however, they were sent to a hospital ward, stripped, and X-rayed. Wilhelm Beiglboeck, a Luftwaffe doctor in charge of the experiments, told them their fate. When one gypsy protested, Beiglboeck pulled out a gun and said, "If you are not quiet, and want to rebel, I will shoot you on the spot."[12]

The prisoners were fed cookies, rusks, and brown sugar during the first week of the experiments and then were starved. Over the next month they were forced to drink plain seawater or water that was treated in either the Schaefer or the Berkatit method. Those who refused to drink the putrid water, which made them violently ill, were tied up and force-fed with long tubes stuffed down their throats.[13]

"The people were crazy from thirst and hunger, we were so hungry—but the doctor had no pity on us," said Hoellenrainer. "Then one gypsy . . . ate a little piece of bread once, or drank some water. The doctor from the Luftwaffe got very angry and mad. He took the gypsy and tied him to a bed post and sealed his mouth."[14]

A number of victims suffered heart seizures and went into comas; others were seriously wounded when Beiglboeck took a long, sharp instrument and punctured their livers to drain the saltwater along with blood. When it was over, Hoellenrainer could barely walk, but he was still assigned to a work detail in another camp. The bodies of his dead companions were covered with sheets and carried across the camp yard to be burned in the crematories.[15]

The story behind the pressure chamber experiments involved Dachau prisoners who met an equally grim fate. Many victims died from being sent to high altitudes without oxygen, and others were driven mad from the horrifying experience. The idea for the experiments originated in 1941, when Sigmund Rascher attended a course in aviation medicine at the German air force headquarters in Munich. He told Himmler that he was disappointed to learn that no tests at extremely high altitudes had ever been made using human subjects, "as such experiments are very dangerous and nobody volunteers for them." Rascher asked the SS to make "two or three professional criminals" available to him for experiments that he boldly predicted would kill the participants. Himmler approved his using 200 Dachau inmates whose "crimes" were being Jews, Russian prisoners of war, or members of the Polish Resistance.[16]

Ruff and his subordinate at the DVL, Hans Romberg, agreed to help Rascher conduct the experiments. They held several planning meetings, including one at Dachau, where the SS commandant took them on a guided tour of the camp's experimental facilities. Ruff's low-pressure chamber was used for the experiments, but to hide DVL's collaboration the chamber was not delivered directly to the camp. DVL employees took the chamber to Munich, where they were met by SS drivers, who delivered it to the final destination.[17]

During the experiments victims were locked inside the windowed airtight chamber, with the pressure altered to simulate atmospheric conditions of altitudes up to 68,000 feet. According to one of Rascher's assistants, "Some experiments gave men such pressure in their heads that they would go mad and pull out their hair in an effort to relieve such pressure. They would tear their heads and faces with their fingernails. . . . They would beat the walls with their hands and head and scream in an effort to relieve pressure on their eardrums."[18]

Nearly eighty men died when they were kept at high altitudes without oxygen for up to thirty minutes. Others were dragged out of the chamber and held under water until they drowned. Rascher cut open their skulls, chest cavities, and abdomens underwater to determine the amount of air embolism in the vessels of their brains.[19]

Those who lived through the experiments were driven insane. One of the victims, a former Jewish delicatessen clerk, was used as a guinea pig in an experiment to simulate what would happen to a flier parachuting out of an airplane at high altitudes without an oxygen mask. The experiment was described in detail in a report signed by Ruff, Rascher, and Romberg. The victim was locked inside the chamber, given an oxygen mask, and raised to a simulated altitude of 47,000 feet. According to the report, when the mask was removed, Ruff reported that the victim "yells loudly" and "gives the impression of someone who is completely out of his mind." As the poor man huddled in the corner of the chamber, doubled over with convulsions and gasping for air, his tormentors cold-bloodedly filmed the experiment to make a faithful record of his agony.[20]

The U.S. military still viewed Ruff and Becker-Freyseng as valuable assets, despite their connection to these crimes. They were even employed under Paperclip to continue the same type of research that had resulted in the murder of Dachau prisoners! By June 1946 AAF headquarters in Washington was flooded with requests to bring Ruff and the others to America. Brigadier General Norris Harbold asked for Paperclip contracts for Ruff and Becker-Freyseng.[21]

At the same time, an Army war crimes unit also was interested in these men. Investigators sifted through SS chief

Himmler's files and found the records of the experiments. The scientists' names were placed on Army war crimes wanted lists. On September 16 Army CIC agents arrived at the AAF Center with a handful of arrest warrants. Colonel Benford recalled that when the CIC agents arrived, "some of my people were on their list," but he still believes that the charges against them were "nothing serious." Ruff, Schaefer, Becker-Frey-seng, Schroeder, and Theodor Benzinger were arrested and taken to a Nuremberg prison.[22]

Benzinger claims his arrest was a "set up" by Strughold to take the heat off Strughold's own questionable wartime activities. When he arrived at Nuremberg he was interrogated but not charged. His interrogators were interested in who had been present, besides Benzinger, at two meetings with high-ranking Nazis in which the experiments were openly discussed. Benzinger, former head of the Department of Aviation at the Luftwaffe institute in Rechlin, had attended one meeting in which film of high-altitude experiments was shown in the office of the secretary of the German Air Ministry. He also had attended a conference where Dachau cold experiments were discussed in detail, including information that concentration camp prisoners had died during the experiments. Benzinger's interrogators never mentioned Strughold or a dozen other Paperclip scientists who also had attended the conference, even though Strughold's subordinates, Schaefer and Clamann, had presented research papers at the conference.[23]

Benzinger said he and his colleagues had conducted explosive decompression experiments on themselves at his institute during the war. They were trying to find out what happens when the pressurized cabin in an aircraft fails. During one experiment Benzinger was sitting in a chamber across from a Junkers factory engineer. "I did not panic when the explosion came, [but] this man . . . fell right into my lap," Benzinger said. "After a few minutes he came to and he was all right." But one colleague died during the experiments. Benzinger said he was away from the institute at the time, flying a spy mission over England to photograph an aluminum factory near Oxford. Benzinger was released after spending a month in the Nuremberg prison. He was brought to the United States by the Navy and worked under Paperclip contract at the Naval Medical Research Institute in Bethesda, Maryland.[24]

Eight days after Becker-Freyseng's arrest, Nuremberg investigator Herbert Meyer questioned him at length about Strughold's role in the Dachau experiments. Strughold had been directly subordinate to Erich Hippke, chief of the Luftwaffe's Medical Service, and then to Schroeder when he replaced Hippke later in the war. Both men had signed orders that authorized experiments in the camps. Becker-Freyseng was intimately familiar with the three men's activities; he had been an assistant in Schroeder's office and also worked afternoons at Strughold's institute. He told the investigator that Strughold had advised Hippke and Schroeder on research matters, especially regarding high-altitude testing; that Strughold had known about the experiments; and that he had received copies of Becker-Freyseng's reports and those submitted by Ruff and Schaefer. Meyer then repeatedly asked Becker-Freyseng whether Strughold had had the authority to stop the experiments:[25]

"If Dr. Strughold did not agree with a specific experiment, could he interrupt it?" Meyer asked Becker-Freyseng.

"I would assume, yes," Becker-Freyseng replied.

"Did he have the power at his disposal?"

"Of course, he was the director of the Institute. He could do what he wanted there."

"If he had not agreed with the work of the doctors, could he have sent for them and said: 'You must stop that or go to another Institute.' "

"Yes. That is, he would have had to report to his superiors, because it was a military institution."

"As director of the Institute he could distribute and stop work?"

"Yes."[26]

Strughold was not arrested, interrogated, or even called as a witness at the trial, despite the derogatory information against him. It was a glaring example of how far the U.S. military went to protect him. His wartime superior, close associates, and a subordinate all were tried at Nuremberg, while Strughold blithely continued business as usual at the AAF Center.

The trial, known as the "Medical Case," was the first of twelve war crimes trials conducted by the U.S. government at Nuremberg. A tribunal of American judges presided over the trial. The case involved a long, grisly list of experiments and other medical crimes, such as experiments with bone transplant techniques, sterilization with X rays, and deliberate infection with malaria and typhoid.

On December 6, 1946, the chief of counsel for war crimes, Brigadier General Telford Taylor, stood before a podium in the makeshift courtroom crowded with spectators and delivered the prosecution's opening statement. He spoke of nameless victims who numbered in the millions and of those who still did not believe the crimes had occurred: "For them it is far more important that these incredible events be established by clear and public proof, so that no one can ever doubt that they were fact and not fable; and that this Court, as the agent of the United States and as the voice of humanity, stamp these acts, and the ideas which engendered them, as barbarous and criminal."[27]

To Taylor's right, twenty-three defendants sat in the dock accused of crimes committed under the guise of scientific research. Both Schroeder and Becker-Freyseng were charged with personal responsibility for high-altitude, freezing, sulfanilamide, seawater, epidemic jaundice, and typhus experiments. Schaefer was charged with participation in seawater experiments. Ruff and his associate, Romberg, were charged with being criminally implicated in the high-altitude experiments. Beiglboeck, also a defendant, was charged with conducting seawater experiments. All were accused of committing war crimes and crimes against humanity that included the murder of innocent civilians on political, racial, or religious grounds.[28]

Taylor pointed out that the defendants were not ignorant people. All but three were physicians. They had been department chiefs, members of German research institutes, or high officials of the Luftwaffe, Wehrmacht, or SS medical services. "Yet these defendants, all of whom were exceptionally qualified to form a moral and professional judgment in this respect, are responsible for wholesale murder and unspeakably cruel tortures," said Taylor.[29]

Nineteen German defense attorneys prepared for the battle. Four represented more than one defendant. They were paid by the U.S. government and received cheap meals, free cigarettes, and other benefits. Even former Nazis were allowed to act as defense counsel. Thirteen of these lawyers had been Nazi party members; one had been in the SS.[30]

There was no disposition for some of that group to worry about scruples when it came to their clients' defense. Beiglboeck's attorney submitted evidence in court that he knew had been altered by his client. Names of experimental subjects had been erased from clinical charts of the seawater experiments in an effort to stop prosecutors from locating survivors and using them as prosecution witnesses. Beiglboeck also admitted having erased information about how critically ill a prisoner had become as a result of the experiments. He and his attorney "were in agreement at all times" that the charts should be submitted in court only after derogatory information had been removed.[31]

Each of the defendants had an excuse for his behavior. They had merely carried out orders and their experiments were no different from those conducted by scientists in Allied countries. No one was a criminal. Becker-Freyseng said the experiments benefited society. Schaefer had only attended meetings. Ruff's victims were well-fed, model prisoners who had volunteered to be guinea pigs. Everyone blamed the dead. Rascher was the murderer; his experiments were the ones that had killed the prisoners. Ruff and his cohorts could not be blamed if their superiors had ordered them to work with that murderer.[32]

Defense attorneys also piled the blame on the victims. To them, all concentration camp inmates were criminals deserving of punishment. Their deaths were justified, since the experiments had been conducted in the national interest of the Third Reich. Hoellenrainer was caught in this crossfire when he was called as a witness and ruthlessly questioned by Beiglboeck's attorney. Did he beat his wife? Was he crazy? Mentally retarded? Mad? When he tried to answer, he was admonished not to be evasive, "as gypsies usually are."[33]

Hoellenrainer fought back in the court and paid for it. When prosecutors asked him to identify the Luftwaffe doctor who had punctured his liver at Dachau, he ran over to the dock and tried to assault Beiglboeck. The presiding judge had him restrained and told him he was in contempt of court.[34]

"This man is a murderer. He gave me salt water and he performed a liver puncture on me. I am still under medical treatment. Please do not send me to prison," he begged the judge.[35]

"That is no extenuation. The contempt before this court must be punished," said the judge, and he sentenced Hoellenrainer to ninety days in prison.[36]

The defendants who had worked under Paperclip played their American connections to the hilt. Strughold, Gauer, and Clamann submitted glowing references in their behalf. Strughold described Schaefer as "very humane and socially minded;" Ruff was "a scientist of extraordinary experimental talent and ingenuity." While prosecutors piled up evidence exposing Schroeder as a raving Nazi who personally had approved experiments tantamount to outright murder, Strughold portrayed him as "the typical honorable, conscientious and self sacrificing Medical Officer with a frank, natural and modest nature."[37]

Ruff's defense attorney told the court that he was most impressed with Gauer and emphasized that he was "working in America." Of course, it was no secret that Gauer, Strughold, and Clamann were all on the U.S. payroll. Gauer's comments were informative, but more for what they revealed about Gauer than about Ruff. He went into great detail about how he and Ruff had "frequently carried out experiments together" at the DVL and Strughold's institute. He made no apologies for Ruff's participation in Dachau experiments and surmised that Ruff had been "called" to Dachau "because he was *the* medical scientist who was best acquainted with the development of the stratosphere." Although Dachau victims had suffered "extraordinary" long periods of unconsciousness during the experiments, Gauer thought that was "no proof of a particularly reckless method of experimenting." Gauer cited a report that Ruff, Rascher, and the others had sent to Himmler that explicitly detailed the victims' plight and brazenly suggested that further experiments on humans should be conducted. "If we do not wish to stop half way, corresponding experiments are categorically demanded by the above-named results," he exclaimed. Using animals as subjects was "unsuitable" to him, since they differed from humans in size and metabolism.[38]

The trial lasted for nine months before the tribunal rendered a decision. Part of that decision included written guidelines covering the legal and ethical use of humans as experimental subjects. Throughout the trial, defendants had excused their crimes on the grounds that there was no consistency in international scientific circles regarding rules governing use of human subjects. The argument raised several pertinent questions: Should prisoners be used as experimental subjects? What rights should human volunteers have during experiments? Do the rules apply if a government contends that the experiments were conducted in the interest of national security? As a result of these and other questions, the tribunal listed ten basic principles that should be observed during any experiments using human subjects in order to satisfy moral, ethical, and legal concepts.

These important guidelines will surface later in the Paperclip story. First, in the 1950s Paperclip scientists at Edgewood Arsenal, Maryland, violated the guidelines—particularly the first rule, that the "voluntary consent of the human subject is absolutely essential"—when American soldiers were used in

LSD experiments in an atmosphere disturbingly similar to Dachau. Thirty years later, in 1986, the U.S. Supreme Court ignored the guidelines in the case of James Stanley, an American soldier who was an unwitting guinea pig in the LSD experiments.[39]

When the Nuremberg tribunal announced its verdict, Schroeder and Becker-Freyseng were found guilty and sentenced to life and twenty years' imprisonment, respectively. Beiglboeck was sentenced to fifteen years' imprisonment. Although Schaefer had attended meetings where the seawater experiments were planned, the tribunal acquitted him, stating, "Nowhere have we been able to find that Schaefer was a principal in, or accessory to, or was otherwise criminally involved in or connected with the experiments mentioned."[40]

The court's verdict concerning Ruff and his assistant, Romberg, was a closer call. Both admitted having been involved with high-altitude experiments. "At one time I went to Dachau while these experiments were carried on and I observed them," Ruff testified. But they maintained that two separate groups of experiments had been carried out at Dachau—one conducted by them with the use of "exhibition subjects" in which no one died; the other conducted by Rascher on a group of nonvolunteers in which seventy to eighty died. In the end Ruff was acquitted, but the court conceded that the question of his guilt or innocence was "close" and found "much in the record to create at least a grave suspicion" that Ruff was "implicated in criminal experiments at Dachau." Romberg was acquitted for the same reason.[41]

By the time the trial ended, Strughold, Gauer, Clamann, and others had already been brought to the United States under Paperclip. The AAF Aero Medical Center was shut down for violating U.S. law, which forbade certain types of military research from being conducted in the U.S. zone of Germany. Under a reorganization of the U.S. military in 1947, the AAF became a separate military service, the U.S. Air Force. Strughold headed a new Air Force School of Aviation Medicine at Randolph Field, Texas, and two years later was placed in charge of a newly created Department of Space Medicine.

Several Air Force officers complained angrily about Strug-hold's employment at Randolph. General Harry Armstrong, who was commandant of the school, admitted that he protected Strughold by appointing himself director of the new space medicine laboratory. "If it came down to a fight, I wanted to take the brunt of it," Armstrong said. "I thought if there was any adverse reaction it should fall on me and not on Dr. Strughold."[42]

Strughold also spent considerable time in Germany recruiting other German scientists to work for the Air Force under Paperclip. His colleague and friend Siegfried Ruff was once again recruited and the Air Force planned to bring him to America. The plan was squelched, however, after reporter Drew Pearson uncovered it and threatened to tell President Truman. Colonel Benford is still angry that the scheme to bring his "friend" Ruff to America failed. In his view, "the Air Force lost a great man."[43]

The Air Force did hire Schaefer, and when he arrived in San Antonio in 1950 he was touted as "the leading German authority on thirst and desalinization of seawater." No one, including JIOA Director Colonel Daniel Ellis, cared that he had been a Nuremberg defendant. Schaefer admitted on his entry papers that he had been arrested and tried at Nuremberg. Despite that admission, Ellis recommended his immigration and told the State Department that the JIOA had investigated Schaefer's background and found "nothing in his records indicating that he was a war criminal or an ardent Nazi, or is otherwise objectionable for admission into the United States as an immigrant."[44]

Nevertheless, it was not long before the Air Force repatriated Schaefer to Germany. After choosing to ignore his past, Air Force officers then raised questions about his competency. They said Schaefer had been assigned to three different departments at Randolph Field in a little over a year and had produced no finished work at any of them. Air Force Captain Seymour Schwartz told the director of intelligence that Schaefer had "displayed very little real scientific acumen" and recommended that he be returned to Germany. "The experience of this Headquarters indicates that this man is a most ineffective research worker and on the basis of his performance here his future worth to the U.S. Armed Forces is nil," said Schwartz. He also recommended that Schaefer not be placed on any future JIOA hiring lists, since "it is doubtful if he will be of interest to anyone."[45]

In 1949, Nuremberg prosecutor Telford Taylor submitted his *Final Report to the Secretary of the Army*, which outlined what had been accomplished by the Nuremberg trials. He felt that one significant accomplishment was that there was now a public record of the Nazis' crimes and of the United States' prosecution of the perpetrators. In the aftermath of Nazi Germany's defeat, the victors bore sole responsibility for stating the principles that should be followed regarding crimes "so calculated, so malignant, and so devastating that civilization cannot tolerate their being ignored because it cannot survive their being repeated." The Nuremberg trial records provided an unprecedented reminder of those principles. Taylor therefore strongly recommended that those records be published, so that future generations would know the terrible secrets of the men who sat in the dock at Nuremberg. But it would be years before all of the volumes of the twelve trials were printed.[46]

Around the same time, the Department of the Air Force expanded the Paperclip coverup when it proudly published translations of the Germans' wartime research in two volumes as *German Aviation Medicine: World War II*. In these books, the Air Force not only ignored the lessons of Nuremberg but embraced what the Nazis had done.[47]

The collection's introduction, alleged to be "a comprehensive and detailed picture" of the history of German aviation medicine, was written by Becker-Freyseng while imprisoned at Nuremberg for Nazi war crimes. It glorified the Nazis and boldly put forth their lies as fact. Hippke and convicted Nazi war criminal Schroeder were portrayed as heroic men who "showed great scientific understanding, interest, sincere helpfulness, and personal concern in aeromedical research." The

Luftwaffe's aeromedical institutes, which employed so many men, including Rascher and Ruff, who conducted experiments in the camps, suddenly became honorable institutions renowned for maintaining their "free and academic character" in Hitler's Third Reich. Regarding decompression chambers, other than accidents involving two physicians, "neither technical accidents nor permanent injuries . . . occurred in any of the chambers." Dachau prisoners murdered in the chamber were conveniently forgotten in the Air Force's revisionist history of Nazi science.[48]

The volumes contained heavily censored versions of the Nazi scientists' work. There was no mention that the authors of two chapters, Becker-Freyseng and Schroeder, were convicted Nazi war criminals whose research had involved cold-blooded murder. No reference was made to Ruff and Schaefer having been Nuremberg defendants. No information was revealed that would in any way raise suspicions about Strughold or others whom the Air Force now praised as great scientists.[49]

Their secret was safe.

6 Escape From Justice

N late 1947 numerous critics in Germany were charging that scientists had escaped denazification trials by fleeing to America under the auspices of Project Paperclip. Peenemünde Chief of Staff Herbert Axster and his wife Ilse were the focus of much of this criticism. Their former neighbors marched into the Public Safety Branch of the Office of Military Government U.S. (OMGUS), which enforced the denazification law in the U.S. zone of Germany. They were furious that the Axsters had escaped justice for mistreating foreign laborers during the war.[1]

JIOA Director Bosquet Wev had a serious problem with denazification, since the Axsters were not the only ones evading justice. Less than a handful of the 350 German specialists living in the United States had been through the process. New arrivals left Germany before their court cases were finalized. And

none of the early Overcast group had been denazified, including Wernher von Braun and Theodor Zobel, who had been
living in America for nearly two years.

At the same time, the director of intelligence of the European Command had a similar problem in Germany. U.S. Air
Force General Robert L. Walsh was employing another group
of Nazis who also had not been through the denazification
process. Fifty-three SS officers and Abwehr intelligence agents
were giving U.S. Army intelligence information about the
USSR under a project code-named "Greenhouse." Now their
work was over, but the men were unable to obtain regular jobs
in Germany because they had not been cleared by denazification courts.[2]

The solution to both groups' problems provides an example
of how Paperclip was used as a guide by other U.S. intelligence
agencies employing Nazis. As a result, both the JIOA and
EUCOM circumvented the law and helped accused criminals
escape justice.

Denazification was supposed to help democratize the German population. Under U.S. denazification law, every German
over the age of eighteen was required to disclose his or her
wartime Nazi affiliations on a *Fragebogen*, or questionnaire.
These forms were then submitted to a denazification court
(*Spruchkammer*) for review. The law categorized individuals
according to their Nazi activities. These categories ranged from
Class I "major offenders," which included war criminals, to
Class V, made up of persons who either actively resisted national socialism or showed a passive attitude toward Hitler's
policies. Penalties ranged from imprisonment to small fines.
Under the law, persons judged to be ardent Nazis were forbidden to work or hold public office in Germany. As noted
earlier, Paperclip policy barred war criminals and Class II
"offenders" from U.S. entry.[3]

Despite the law, denazification proved difficult, if not impossible, to execute. OMGUS status reports filed in 1947 noted
some of the problems encountered by Public Safety Branch
officers in Germany. OMGUS was understaffed, underfunded,

and overwhelmed with work, since they had to distribute questionnaires to over twelve million people. German denazification officials, who were supposed to be anti-Nazis, were accused of accepting bribes and threatening prosecution witnesses. One report noted that falsification of questionnaires was "flourishing." And despite American policies designed to eliminate nazism, the Germans blamed Jews for the Allies' policies and anti-Semitism was rampant, particularly in the schools. For example, a speaker at the Munich Institute of Technology was forced to cancel a lecture after students stomped their feet at the mere mention of Albert Einstein's name.[4]

General Lucius Clay was the man ultimately responsible for enforcing the denazification law. He was the military governor of the U.S. zone in Germany and served as commander in chief of EUCOM and head of OMGUS. His views on denazification were far different from those of the intelligence officers involved with Paperclip. He was a hard-liner when it came to America's attempt to "denazify" the entire German population and make them believers in democracy. "Our job, as I see it, is to see that only the right type of Germans are permitted to take leadership until democratic processes become a habit," Clay said.[5]

Clay strongly believed that all Germans, scientists included, needed denazifying. Once he fired a scientific adviser who insisted that German scientists were not Nazis, an attitude that caused extreme friction in OMGUS. Clay complained bitterly to Assistant Secretary of State John Hilldring that the scientific adviser "blamed Public Safety Branch severely for treating scientists as Nazis, even though the record is clear." That record included the Dachau experiments conducted by scientists who were tried for murder in the Nuremberg Medical Case.[6]

Clay was getting criticism from both sides over how OMGUS was handling the denazification of Paperclip recruits. On the one hand, *The New York Times* charged that Paperclip provided an escape route whereby ardent Nazis evaded the denazification process altogether. American officials in Europe generally absolved Clay of the blame. But critics told *The Times* that many of Clay's subordinates "do not know what makes a Nazi or do not care so long as the German has good table manners, speaks good English and is efficient in the job assigned to him."[7]

On the other hand, military officers who recruited scientists for Paperclip in Germany were angry that U.S. enforcement of denazification—stiffer than in the other three zones of Germany—hindered their recruiting efforts. Many Germans refused to sign Paperclip contracts because they were afraid that if they went to America prior to denazification, they risked being categorized as unemployable if they returned to Germany. Furthermore, competition was fierce, since the United States, Great Britain, France, and the USSR were all competing for the same men. The British offered the Germans a variety of places they could go, including Canada, Australia, and Pakistan. The French offered higher pay. And, as one American officer noted, the Soviets offered *everyone* contracts, even Germans whose names were on automatic arrest lists.[8]

In this atmosphere JIOA officers were trying to solve two types of problem cases under Paperclip. The first group consisted of specialists like Axster and Arthur Rudolph who had arrived in the United States before their denazification process even began. JIOA Governing Committee members suggested that General Clay handle these cases by trying the scientists in absentia. The scientists' *Fragebogen* would be submitted to a court in Germany, while the scientists stayed in America. JIOA Director Wev was afraid that pro-Communists might interrogate the scientists in court about their work in America if the group was returned to Germany.[9]

But Clay's decision on the matter went ever further than Wev's idea. He decided to forego trials of any sort for Paperclip recruits. Clay noted that trials in absentia were not permitted even in cases of Nazis located in Germany. Special treatment like that would only draw attention to the project and indicate to the German people that special procedures would be used if American interests were involved. "It would be much better to permit them to remain in the U.S. as Nazis without bringing them to trial than to establish special procedures not now within the purview of the German law," Clay concluded.[10]

Nevertheless, Clay's policy did in fact establish special procedures for the group. As one OMGUS official noted, "we are, for the first time, removing a group of Germans from normal denazificiation process." Paperclip policy already required U.S. agencies to conduct background investigations of the scientists' Nazi pasts. Clay thought those investigations would exclude ardent Nazis from the group. But as noted earlier, the JIOA "screeners" had turned those investigations into a farce.[11]

In the second type of cases, the JIOA officers brazenly flaunted the law. This group involved scientists whose denazification process had begun prior to their U.S. entry. First, JIOA Director Wev asked Clay's personal advisor, Dr. Walter Dorn, to expedite their trials. Dorn was against the scheme because it contravened normal procedures. But the Public Safety Branch did not think the request was unusual. "Assigning of priority of trials of individuals has been frequently carried out in the past so that it is almost routine," Public Safety Branch officer G. F. Corrigan said.[12]

Perhaps expediting trials in special cases had become routine, as Corrigan said. What was not routine, however, was that once courts judged some of the scientists as ardent Nazis, the Germans quickly left for America while U.S. intelligence officers in Europe intervened in the court decisions.

One case involved Hans Zeigler, chief scientist for the U.S. Army Signal Corps in Fort Monmouth, New Jersey. Zeigler had been a dues-paying member of the Nazi party and five other organizations and a candidate for membership in the SA. Denazification court officials accused him of falsifying information on his *Fragebogen*. But Zeigler left for the United States and never appeared at a scheduled hearing. When asked about his case, Zeigler stated in a sworn affidavit that Army CIC agents had obtained an "exemption" for him from the denazification law. One OMGUS officer, Captain Jack James, explained that dubious excuse in a report on Zeigler's denazification status: "The Subject never came to trial because of the interference of certain persons in Munich. The subsequent qualifications of Dr. Zeigler for Project Paperclip seemed to terminate all further actions in the denazification."[13]

Another case involved Rudolf Thauer, a medical specialist on the effect of heat on pilots during flight, who worked for the Navy Air Materiel Center in Philadelphia. During the war, Thauer had worked at the Institute for Animal Physiology in Frankfurt. A denazification court originally had judged him to be a Class II "offender" because of his membership in the Nazi party, the SS, the SA, and five other Nazi organizations. As a result Thauer should have been barred from employment under the project. Instead the court decision was changed and Thauer was reclassified as a mere Class IV "follower" after the court received twenty-one "trustworthy" statements from "well known personalities" in Thauer's behalf. Thereafter Thauer stopped mentioning his SS membership on Paperclip forms.[14]

But SS membership was not the only problem with Thauer's Nazi past. In October 1942 Thauer, along with more than a dozen other Paperclip specialists, had attended a scientific conference in Nuremberg at which Professor Holzlöhner openly discussed the freezing experiments he was conducting on Dachau prisoners. At the very least, JIOA officers or the Navy should have confronted Thauer and asked him what else he had learned about the Dachau experiments at the conference. The officers also should have confronted the other Paperclip scientists in attendance, including Hubertus Strughold and three of his associates, Hans Clamann, Konrad Schaefer, and Konrad Buettner, a speaker at the Nuremberg conference.[15]

Colonel Putt actively fought to get his specialists cleared of charges, and he was backed by Air Force Headquarters. The Germans' technical expertise was considered even more im-

SECRET AGENDA

portant after the birth of the U.S. Air Force in September
1947. Putt brought many new recruits to the air base in Dayton, Ohio, which was renamed Wright-Patterson Air Force
Base. When a *Spruchkammer* imposed a fine on Ernst Sielaff,
Putt asked the court to postpone the proceedings until Sielaff
returned to Germany—which, of course, he never did. Putt
got Winnibald Kamm's case postponed as well. Kamm had
been dismissed from his faculty position in Germany as a result
of denazification judgments that he was an ardent Nazi. Like
Sielaff, Kamm never returned to Germany.[16]

Putt even turned down one scientist's request for permission
to return to Germany voluntarily to clear his name. Radiation
specialist Heinz Fischer had signed a six-month contract and
wanted to return to Germany to settle his denazification. But
Putt was afraid that Fischer would not return, since the scientist had told him he was unhappy at Wright-Patterson because opportunities for new research assignments were limited.
The colonel denied Fischer's request and Air Force Headquarters backed him up.[17]

Even the most blatant Nazis in Putt's group slipped through
the net. Emil Salmon, a jet engineer, signed a Paperclip contract on June 2, 1947. One month later he was convicted by
a denazification court of helping the SS torch a synagogue and
participating in an SA assault unit assigned to squelch an anti-
Nazi revolt. The court sentenced him to six months of hard
labor. Police reports had noted that Salmon, a troop leader in
the SA, was a "good" Nazi who frequently wore his SA uniform and took his rifle to work. Witnesses said that Salmon
had bragged to co-workers about the torching incident the
next day. "There, we have done a proper job," Salmon re-
portedly had told them. He had said he did feel sorry for the
Jewish women who were forced to flee the synagogue as it
burst into flames.[18]

Two days after Salmon's conviction Paperclip officers
shipped him to America, where he went to work for Putt at
Wright-Patterson. Neither the Air Force nor JIOA officers
cared about Salmon's offenses or that he had escaped impris-

onment due to his Air Force contract. They were only worried that State or Justice Department officials might turn Salmon down for immigration to the United States, since Class II Nazis were barred from employment under Paperclip. Putt had Salmon sign a statement claiming that his SA activities had involved only "athletics and sports." The police reports detailing the synagogue torching, court records, and Salmon's *Fragebogen* were ignored.[19]

JIOA officers hid Salmon's dossier from State and Justice Department officials for three years because they were afraid that Salmon would be denied a visa as a result of his Class II status. JIOA officers finally settled the problem in 1950 when they told the Intelligence Division at EUCOM to change Salmon's court decision. A short time later Salmon was reclassified as a mere Class IV "follower." Air Force Headquarters admitted that the military was "cognizant of Mr. Salmon's Nazi activities and certain allegations made by some of his associates in Europe, but desires his immigration in spite of this."[20]

Meanwhile, EUCOM Director of Intelligence Robert Walsh had been observing the Paperclip process and decided to copy the JIOA's methods to help the Project Greenhouse group. Prior to this book, Walsh's significant involvement in Paperclip has not been exposed. The fifty-three-year-old general's wartime assignments had given him firsthand experience with Soviet operations. He had been commanding general of the U.S. Strategic Air Forces in the USSR and air member of the U.S. Military Mission to Moscow. Now, as director of intelligence at EUCOM, Walsh made decisions that directly involved Nazis employed by U.S. Army intelligence in Europe as well as the Paperclip group.[21]

Fifty-three individuals in Greenhouse worked at the EUCOM Intelligence Center in Oberusel. This was a high-level POW interrogation center, commonly known as Camp King, where Reinhard Gehlen's Nazi intelligence organization was reactivated by the CIA. Klaus Barbie was among the more notorious individuals who passed through the camp. The

Greenhouse group wrote reports and gave Army intelligence agents information about Soviet military tactics and the Soviet intelligence service.[22]

"At the time, we desperately needed intelligence information on the Russians," recalled former Army CIC agent Albert Losche, who ran operations using other types of Germans for intelligence purposes. "We thought there was going to be a Russian army invasion of the U.S. zone and the Germans were the only ones with good information on the Soviets."[23]

Most of the Greenhouse group had connections with Gehlen and all were knowledgeable about the USSR. For example, Herbert von Dirksen had been the German ambassador to Russia. Nazi historian Peter-Heinz Seraphim got his expertise on Eastern Europe by tracking the whereabouts of Jews in Poland and other areas in Eastern Europe. He had been brought to the United States for interrogation at Fort Hunt in 1945. Several other Greenhouse employees had served in the Waffen SS on the eastern front. Karl Herrnberger, for example, had been an officer in an SS battalion in Poland, Holland, Belgium, France, and Russia.[24]

Some men in the group had been Abwehr intelligence agents. Heinz Schmalschlaeger claimed he was the nephew of Abwehr chief Wilhelm Canaris, who was executed in connection with the July 20, 1944, plot on Hitler's life. Schmalschlaeger had been head of the Abwehr in Vienna and Poland. In 1941 he was named commander of Leitstelle III Ost, the center for tactical counterintelligence for the eastern front. Based in Warsaw, Schmalschlaeger had operated in Poland, Yugoslavia, Greece, and Hungary.[25]

Most of the Abwehr agents in Greenhouse were Russian-born citizens of Nazi Germany and had worked under Schmalschlaeger's command. Their fluency in Russian had made them valuable assets to Nazi Germany's intelligence service. Dietrich Abels, for example, had been in charge of a Leitstelle III Ost department that investigated the Soviet intelligence service. He had traveled along the entire eastern front and made a detailed psychological study of Soviet intelligence agents from information obtained from captured Russian POWs. Another Abwehr agent, Georg Striedter, had interrogated Russian POWs and translated captured Russian documents.[26]

In 1945 U.S. intelligence agents had even gotten Gestapo officers released from internment camps so they could work on the Greenhouse project. One Gestapo officer, Fritz Fischer, had been judged an "offender" under the denazification law and was imprisoned at Dachau. Another Gestapo officer, Franz Regnath, had been head of the criminal police in Munich until 1943, when he was transferred to Poland. At one point Regnath had run a unit that recruited spies to work for the Gestapo.[27]

Now they were about to be released from the project at Camp King, but they could not work in Germany because they had not been denazified. The men had not even turned in a *Fragebogen*, as required by American denazification law. On September 15, 1947, Walsh's executive officer, Major Thomas Grant, told the EUCOM Intelligence Division and the OMGUS Public Safety Branch that he wanted the Greenhouse group to be amnestied from the denazification proceedings. Walsh felt that the services they had rendered the United States were of such high value that a request for exemption under the law was justified.[28]

Intelligence officers were concerned about the denazification proceedings for the exact same reasons that the JIOA was concerned about Paperclip. Colonel W. L. Fagg, the executive officer in the Intelligence Division who also worked with Paperclip, agreed with Walsh's proposal and noted the division's concerns. If the Greenhouse group appeared before denazification courts, they might be forced to reveal the work they had done for U.S. intelligence. If any pro-Communists were on the courts, they might compromise U.S. intelligence activities or give the group harsher sentences because of their employment.[29]

But Public Safety Branch chief Theo Hall objected to the

amnesty proposal. He felt that an outright pardon would create a security hazard rather than protect information about U.S. intelligence activities. Germans on the courts certainly would speculate as to why they were being asked to pardon the group in the first place. Hall suggested they use Paperclip as the model for handling the cases. The denazification cases would proceed normally through the courts but would be "carefully watched." If any individuals were fined or given jail sentences, either the court decisions could be modified or the individuals could be amnestied.[30]

Hall sent his suggestions to Walsh and explained why he thought the procedure would work. "A procedure similiar to that outlined above has been applied with success in the cases of persons desired in connection with Operation Paperclip and other persons who had been employed on highly classified projects," he said. On November 20, 1947, Walsh approved the recommendation and told the Public Safety Branch to take action on the Greenhouse cases.[31]

The resulting legal action was a charade. Only a few individuals were even fined, and those cases were cleared upon appeal. Johannes Hoheisel originally was given three years' probation and fined DM 5,000 for his wartime Nazi activities. His case was immediately appealed with a change of venue to Frankfurt, where OMGUS officials watched over the proceedings. The Frankfurt court vacated the original decision and Hoheisel was cleared.[32]

SS officer Herrnberger was first jailed for falsifying papers he had submitted to the denazification court. During a hearing, he claimed he did not know about his SS membership. He had no idea how his signature got on the forms in his SS file from the Berlin Document Center. He merely had been a Wehrmacht soldier during the war. The court cleared him and issued no sanctions whatsoever. Herrnberger then obtained a position as chief of police in Garmisch.[33]

Other SS officers in Greenhouse received amnesty. Fritz Fischer's status suddenly plummeted from being an "offender" and jailed, to complete amnesty in 1948. Willi Fuellgraf's case was completely suspended. Fuellgraf had been an officer in the Waffen SS, a Hitler Youth leader, and a long-time member of the Nazi party. Former Gestapo officer Regnath also was exonerated.[34]

In addition, the favors extended to the Greenhouse group included more than merely taking care of their denazification. Former Abwehr agent Schmalschlaeger had been ordered evicted from his apartment to make room for homeless Jewish survivors of the Holocaust. German authorities cited an earlier Supreme Headquarters Allied Expeditionary Force (SHAEF) ruling that gave displaced persons priority in housing as the reason for the eviction. Intelligence officers quickly intervened, stopped the eviction order, and the Schmalschlaeger family remained in the apartment. According to Army intelligence files, in the 1950s Schmalschlaeger headed the Nuremberg branch of West Germany's intelligence service, which was run by Gehlen.[35]

Meanwhile in Washington, congressmen were listening to testimony that eight hundred Waffen SS officers and other incriminated individuals had entered the United States disguised as political refugees. "The American authorities have not, in fact, made any attempt even of a superficial nature, to check on the identity of these political refugees," one critic charged. "They have, as a matter of record, released collaborationist murderers who have been recognized as such by survivors."[36]

But the congressmen were more worried about Communists than they were about Nazis. By 1948 the whole U.S. denazification system crumbled, and war crimes trials soon met the same fate. Clay had been under constant pressure from right-wing congressmen to shut down the trials. The House Appropriations Committee was the most vocal congressional entity on this score, and it threatened to cut off Clay's funds. Clay was a realist in choosing between forces on the political Right or Left in Congress. "Between the two I have to choose the strong—the Right on whom our Congressional appropriations depend," he said.[37]

First Clay announced that the trials would cease by the end of 1948. Then both the United States and Great Britain decided they would no longer accept war crimes evidence or extradition orders against suspects after November 1, 1947.[38]

The cold war had begun.

1   The Dossiers

WHEN State Department representative Samuel Klaus entered the room, he immediately sensed that the military officers were about to gang up on him. For a long time Klaus had had the feeling that the men on the JIOA Governing Committee were laying plans in his absence. Now it seemed to him that one of those schemes was about to be hatched.[1]

He was the odd man out among those sitting around the table at the Pentagon. Nearly all members of the JIOA and G-2 Exploitation Branch were there: JIOA Governing Committee chairman Bosquet Wev; JIOA Director Colonel Thomas Ford; G-2's Exploitation Branch chief Montie Cone and his superior, Lieutenant Colonel H. B. St. Clair; JIOA member Francis Duborg; and a few men Klaus had not met before.

The purpose of this February 27, 1947, meeting was ostensibly to obtain Klaus's stamp of approval on a list of Germans the JIOA wanted to move through the pipeline. Over the past year Klaus had asked Ford repeatedly to give him names of all Paperclip scientists living in America, but Ford had refused. Klaus also had been unable to obtain a list of Germans on order. Even Assistant Secretary of State Hilldring had complained to the assistant secretary of war about the runaround they were giving Hilldring.[2]

Now a list was lying on the meeting-room table, but Ford was deliberately hiding it from Klaus's view. Ford then demanded that Klaus sign a waiver giving entry visas to the Germans on a list he was not even allowed to see. "I told him that of course I could do no such thing and that certification presupposed that the Department should have an opportunity to pass judgement of some kind before affixing its signature," Klaus later angrily noted in a memo.[3]

Ford told him that the list was classified and the State Department was not entitled to see it. Then Ford issued an ultimatum along with a McCarthyite threat. "Ford stated in various ways that if I did not accept the paper on behalf of the State Department he would give the information to several senators who would take care of the Department," Klaus wrote.[4]

The JIOA had a good reason for wanting to keep the lists secret, and it had nothing to do with classified information. At the time of the meeting, Wev and Cone were sitting on a powder keg. They had just received 146 investigative reports from Europe and nearly all of them were derogatory. They knew that the Germans' Nazi backgrounds violated the policy that Truman had signed. The *OMGUS Security Report* on the scientists disclosed allegations that Zobel and others had participated in experiments on humans, the Axsters had mistreated foreign laborers, Salmon had torched a synagogue, and SS member Debus had turned a colleague over to the Gestapo. Other men were accused of various crimes including theft and sexual perversion. Many had been early members of the Nazi party, the SS, or the SA.[5]

Wernher von Braun's report had been one of the first to arrive. The *OMGUS Security Report* noted that von Braun was considered an ardent Nazi and a security threat to the United States. His records indicated that he had been a major in the SS—having joined the SS at the personal behest of SS chief Himmler in 1940—a student at an SS riding school, and a Nazi party member since 1937. The JIOA had sent his report back to Germany and asked U.S. intelligence officers there to verify von Braun's political background and report any extenuating circumstances surrounding his SS membership.[6]

Klaus had not seen the reports, and since the JIOA withheld the complete list of names, he was unable to investigate the Germans on his own. The JIOA was supposed to give Klaus dossiers on the 334 Paperclip specialists living in the United States, who officially were considered enemy aliens under military custody. The *OMGUS Security Report* would be the key document in the dossiers, since it summarized the Army intelligence background investigations and judged whether or not an individual was an "ardent Nazi" and a security threat to the United States. Klaus already had received files on ten men who worked for Colonel Putt, but, unbeknownst to him, the files had been carefully censored. The file that Klaus received on Albert Patin, for example, did not include his admission to having used five hundred Jewish women and other innocent people as slave laborers.[7]

Nevertheless, Klaus was suspicious of the JIOA's methods, and his concerns heightened after the meeting. First he learned that the JIOA had expunged information about his confrontation with Ford from the meeting minutes that were submitted to JIOA's superiors in the Joint Intelligence Committee. Then he learned that Georg Rickhey had been returned to Germany for trial in the Dora case. Klaus thought the Rickhey incident represented a serious security problem. "That the Department's security fears were not baseless was recently demonstrated when a war criminal, wanted for war crimes of a bestial kind, was found here among these scientists, to be returned to Germany," he remarked.[8]

Animating the cabal of military officers who opposed Klaus

was a mind-set that would not hesitate to lie, violate President Truman's policy, or smear reputations to achieve its ends. The intelligence officers subscribed to the cold war philosophy. As they saw it, deceiving and undercutting one stubborn State Department official were certainly among the almost limitless means justified by the grand goal of containing communism.

Such convictions tend to endure. To this day Colonel Cone defends the project and the officers' actions. "Perhaps some mistakes were made that weren't rectified. I'm not aware of any, but I am convinced that we advanced our own interest greatly by this program," Cone said recently. "From a military point of view, we knew that these people were invaluable to us. Just think what we have from their research—all our satellites, jet aircraft, rockets, almost everything else."[9]

Wev was outspoken and impatient with anyone who opposed his views of what was good for America. The Navy captain frequently used Director of Intelligence Chamberlin as a sounding board for memos that attacked his enemies so fiercely that Cone had to tell him several times to tone down his fiery rhetoric. While Wev admitted that Truman's policy banned ardent Nazis from Paperclip, he felt that State's emphasis on "picayune details" such as SS records was absurd. Communism, not nazism, was the problem. To Wev, being forced to investigate the Germans' Nazi pasts was comparable to "beating a dead Nazi horse."[10]

By July 1947, the JIOA and State were deadlocked in an angry battle over immigration. Wev sent Chamberlin a scathing memo accusing Klaus of "sabotaging" the immigration process. He emphasized that it was imperative that "the most positive and drastic action possible be taken in order to break the impasse which currently exists." Wev expressed his concern that returning the Germans to Europe, where they could be used by potential enemies, "presents a far greater security threat to this country than any former Nazi affiliations which they may have had or even any Nazi sympathies which they may still have."[11]

Then JIOA and G-2 began to play hardball against Klaus.

Wev and Cone complained to right-wing congressmen that
Klaus was impeding the entire German scientist program.
Their complaints also were leaked to friendly reporters who
smeared Klaus's name in the press. At the same time they
were concealing allegations that some of the Paperclip specialists had been accused of complicity in murder and other
war crimes.[12]

In July, Klaus recommended to his superiors that the State
Department withdraw from the JIOA Governing Committee.
He thought continued participation in JIOA was unwise because "we were being estopped by some of their activities over
which we had no control." Klaus and the State Department
already were being unfairly blamed in the press for refusing
to give the scientists visas. "Apparently we were placed in
JIOA solely because someone assumes that by this device permanent immigration visas would be issued . . . over the
counter on demand," he said. "This is fundamentally unpleasant." Klaus recommended that State handle the project
internally in its Office of Controls, which was responsible for
the Visa Division, counterintelligence, and security.[13]

Hamilton Robinson, State's director of the Office of Controls, was put in charge of the Paperclip problem. Robinson
had been a law associate of John Foster Dulles when Dulles
was the Republican foreign policy adviser, and a legal adviser
to the State-War-Navy Coordinating Committee, which had
originated Paperclip policy. He was also a carbon copy of Klaus
in his suspicions of the military officers. Robinson immediately
sent five dossiers back to the JIOA and demanded that the
officers give him more information about the specialists' Nazi
pasts.[14]

The situation soon turned into a full-blown crisis for the
JIOA. The entire Visa Department was upset over the dossiers
they had seen thus far. Samuel Cummings was furious when
he discovered discrepancies between what the specialists said
about their Nazi pasts and actual Nazi records from the State
Department–run Berlin Document Center. Another visa official, Rebecca Wellington, thought the military was lying and

told the officers she took their statements about national security interests with "a grain of salt."[15]

State Department officials were not the only ones complaining about Paperclip. FBI Director Hoover constantly was reminding JIOA officers that he thought members of the Nazi party were security threats. And the FBI planned to conduct its own investigation of all Paperclip personnel.

The idea of a full-scale FBI investigation made the JIOA officers shudder. The FBI's own files already acknowledged that rocket technician Hans Giesecke had more to hide than just his SS membership. Members of Giesecke's family, who had lived in the U.S. during the war, had been under FBI investigation for Nazi espionage activities. The investigations were part of the FBI's massive wartime assault on the pro-Nazi German-American Bund, which resulted in the prosecution and deportation of German-born Nazi Bund leader Fritz Kuhn and others. FBI agents had staked out, photographed, and investigated Giesecke's parents, who were active Bund members in Portland, Oregon, and his brother Oscar, a Bund leader in Chicago. One undercover agent had attended weekly pro-Nazi rallies held in a back room at Earle's Cafe in downtown Portland. Speakers included radical leaders of the Silver Shirts, who patterned themselves after the SA. The agent learned that Giesecke regularly sent his parents anti-Semitic Nazi pamphlets from Germany which were distributed at the Bund meetings in Portland.[16]

It is important to remember that the American public was unaware of the scientists' sordid Nazi pasts. And Army public relations officials brazenly lied to them about it. For example, the Army's Intelligence Division had claimed that "no 'big' Nazis" were employed under Paperclip. Furthermore, the military told the American public that it had followed Truman's policy and barred ardent Nazis from the project. The Army defined "ardent Nazis" as those who had joined the Nazi party before Hitler came into power in 1933, Nazi party leaders, those convicted by denazification courts, and those accused or convicted of war crimes.[17]

Despite the Army's propaganda, vocal critics of Paperclip nearly blew the lid off the JIOA's cover story that the scientists had all been "carefully screened." Cone still views these critics with disdain. "There were elements in the country that were violently opposed to Paperclip, and they could stir up quite a lot of trouble," Cone recalled. "We had real problems with them." Rabbi Wise stepped up his campaign to oust the Axsters from America. Members of the American Federation of Scientists (AFS) complained directly to President Truman that the Germans were not the eminent scientists the military claimed they were.[18]

Reporter Drew Pearson repeatedly published stories raising disturbing questions about the military's false claim that it was following the rules. In one story that caused an uproar among high officials in Washington, Pearson reported that Carl Krauch, who had helped set up I. G. Farben's factory at Auschwitz, had been recruited into Paperclip. At the time Krauch was sitting in a Nuremberg prison awaiting trial as a Nazi war criminal. Dwight Eisenhower, then chief of staff, ordered Director of Intelligence Chamberlin to give him a full report after he heard about Pearson's story. Chamberlin and Colonel Hagood gave Eisenhower a brief history of the project and Hagood assured the general that all of the Germans had been carefully screened.[19]

The ideological battle lines were drawn between the intelligence officers and their critics. From then on, the fight was hard—and dirty. The officers gathered men of like mind to their side, held closed-door meetings with right-wing congressmen, and used the Army's enormous illegal domestic spy operation under Chamberlin's Military Intelligence Division (G-2) to spy on, investigate, and harass their critics.

G-2's operation was a powerful weapon that had been tooling up for Armageddon since the 1920s, when G-2 agents engaged in strikebreaking and ran private vigilante networks under Chamberlin's predecessor, World War I intelligence chief Colonel Ralph H. Van Deman. G-2 increased its domestic surveillance of American citizens during World War II, when its activities included bugging First Lady Eleanor Roosevelt's room in a Chicago hotel. This surveillance, which brazenly violated Americans' civil rights, continued nonstop for decades. G-2 agents engaged in countless unauthorized wiretaps, break-ins, and a spy operation that included a collection of eight million personal dossiers running the gamut from supporters of Senator Eugene McCarthy's presidential campaign to the Weathermen. The operation finally was exposed by a former intelligence agent in 1970 and shut down after a four-year congressional probe.[20]

In the late 1940s reporters who wrote stories critical of Paperclip were among G-2's prime targets—especially Drew Pearson. "He was a real troublemaker," remarked Cone. Pearson's telephone was bugged and he was spied on and investigated for years.[21]

Another reporter became a target when his article in the *New Republic* incensed G-2 officers in Cone's Exploitation Branch. Seymour Nagan's story "Top Secret: Nazis at Work" questioned the rationale of congressmen who worried about Communists infiltrating defense plants when four hundred Nazis with top-secret clearances worked on sensitive defense projects throughout the country. Nagan's story noted that some sources were afraid to talk because of "fear of reprisals." But it was Nagan who became the focus of attention when Cone initiated an investigation of him the same day his story hit the newsstands. Cone told an agent that Nagan's story "may cause trouble" and that he should read it and find out what he could about the reporter. "DON'T ask PID nor FBI nor US Branch," Cone warned the officer, "see if elsewhere you can dig up something on him for a blueslip." The officer eventually managed to "dig up" Nagan's personal telephone number and home address.[22]

The American Federation of Scientists was another target. First, intelligence agents tried—and failed—to prove that the group was a Communist front. Then, agents posing as AFS members attended meetings to collect information about the group's activities. In one instance Edward Wetter, chief of the

Intelligence Division's Chemical and Biological Warfare section, attended an AFS meeting in Philadelphia posing as a member. After the meeting, Wetter gave G-2 agents lists of names, notes of conversations, and other information about the group.[23]

The problem with the incriminating security reports, however, still had not been solved. JIOA officers knew they could not get the reports past State. JIOA Deputy Director Walter Rozamus sent Cone a copy of OMGUS's derogatory report on Adolf Thiel, summarized Thiel's Nazi past, and directed Cone's attention to the paragraph in Truman's policy "which indicates that active Nazis are not qualified under the Paperclip Program." Rozamus noted that Thiel's report described him as a security threat because of his long-time active membership in several Nazi groups. Thiel had joined the Hitler Youth at age seventeen, the SA at age eighteen, and the Nazi party when he was twenty-three.[24]

The solution was very simple. If State would not approve immigration due to derogatory OMGUS reports, the JIOA would change the reports to expunge derogatory information, in direct contravention of the president's policy. Furthermore, JIOA officers knew they could rely on their counterparts in Germany to help them do the job.

The Intelligence Division of the European Command ran Paperclip in Germany, under the directorship of Walsh, who was stationed in Berlin. The Paperclip office operated out of the Intelligence Division's headquarters in Heidelberg, under Deputy Director Colonel Robert Schow, who would become assistant director of the CIA in 1949 and assistant chief of staff for Intelligence in 1956. ACSI was the Army intelligence agency under which Cone's counterparts operated in the 1950s. Schow and his assistants, Colonel William Fagg and Colonel C. F. Fritzsche, signed many of the *OMGUS Security Report* forms. Some investigators were borrowed from OMGUS's Public Safety Branch, the denazification division. Military Governor Clay was commander in chief over both EUCOM and OMGUS.[25]

The plot to change the records was discussed during a JIOA Governing Committee meeting on November 14—a meeting that Klaus did not attend. Rozamus mentioned that many OMGUS reports listed individuals as security threats with what appeared to be insufficient data. Cone said the reports needed to be changed. "Someone should be sent from here to Europe to fully inform them there as to just what is wanted," Cone told the group. In the meantime, the officers withheld from the State and Justice Departments dossiers that contained derogatory information.[26]

Four days after the meeting, Rozamus sent Cone the dossiers of seven individuals who were wanted for denazification trials because of their Nazi activities, warning: "It is not considered advisable to submit any of the enclosed dossiers to the Departments of State and Justice at this time." Wernher von Braun's dossier was one of those enclosed. Rozamus said that von Braun's *OMGUS Security Report* "indicates that he is regarded as a potential security threat to the United States and he will be wanted for denazification trial in view of his party membership."[27]

Anton Beier's dossier also was withheld. Beier's SS records, which were over two inches thick, became such a hot item that G-2 classified the entire file "Top Secret." Beier had been in charge of assembling rocket testing stands at Peenemünde and now worked for the Army at Fort Bliss. His *OMGUS Security Report* noted that he "was an ardent Nazi and judging from the cap device on his SS uniform, was a member of the Death Head Division." He had been a platoon leader in the SS from 1933 until 1945. There was much consternation among the intelligence officers after they discovered that Beier's SS records from the Berlin Document Center included a photograph showing Beier decked out in full SS uniform.[28]

On November 28 Rozamus sent three more incriminating dossiers to Navy intelligence, quoted the paragraph in Truman's policy that barred ardent Nazis from the project, and said: "In view of this it is believed that there is little likelihood that the above scientists can be immigrated if the Theater Security Reports are forwarded to the State Department in their present form." Rozamus told the Navy that the JIOA intended to ask European Command to "reevaluate" the OMGUS reports to revise the ardent Nazi classification, "since such classification is a bar to immigration."[29]

The dossiers were those of Willi Heybey, Hermann Kurzweg, and Ernst Winkler, who worked on the Navy's wind tunnel project in White Oak, Maryland. Kurzweg, who had been chief of the wind tunnel project at Kochel, Germany, was judged by OMGUS to be an "ardent Nazi" because he had been a member of the SS Elite Guard from 1934 until the end of the war. Heybey had been a long-time member of the SA. Winkler had been a member of the SA from 1933 until 1939, the Nazi party, four other Nazi organizations, and the counterespionage branch of Abwehr intelligence.[30]

The same day that Rozamus returned those dossiers to the Navy, G-2's Cone told the JIOA that he recommended they ask the Intelligence Division in Europe to review and change the reports because they were having a negative effect on the scientists' immigration. Cone identified six individuals whom OMGUS classified as security threats and said that none were "politically active."[31]

The list included former Mittelwerk V-2 rocket technicians Guenther Haukohl and Hans Friedrich. Haukohl was judged by OMGUS to be an "ardent Nazi" because he had been a member of the SS from 1933 to 1939, the SA, the Nazi party, and two other Nazi organizations. Friedrich had joined the Nazi party in 1932—a year before Hitler came into power—and actively participated in SA election propaganda and party processions. In 1947 Friedrich was still touting Hitler's leadership as a positive force in Nazi Germany. "The entire living standards of the people rose, unemployment disappeared and most men seemed to be happier," Friedrich said in a sworn affidavit. No one asked Dora survivors if they had been happy working as slave laborers under Friedrich and Haukohl in the underground hell known as Mittelwerk.[32]

The coverup began in earnest on December 4, 1947, when JIOA Director Wev sent a lengthy memo to EUCOM Director of Intelligence Walsh and asked that the OMGUS reports of fourteen individuals, including Wernher von Braun, "be reviewed and that new security reports be submitted where such action is deemed appropriate." Wev made it clear that there was "very little possibility" that the State or Justice Departments would approve the immigration of any individual who was classified as a potential or actual security threat. "This may result in the return to Germany of specialists whose skill and knowledge should be denied other nations in the interest of national security," Wev told Walsh.[33]

In his memo Wev repeated Cone's assertion that the OMGUS reports were "unrealistic," since none of the specialists had been politically active. The list included Friedrich and Haukohl, former SS platoon leader Beier, and Major Hamill's chief spy at Fort Bliss, Herbert Axster, who was accused of starving foreign laborers by OMGUS investigators. Theodor Benzinger, who had been arrested as a Nuremberg war crimes suspect and was now working for the Navy, was also on the list. Wev even noted references submitted in behalf of Werner Gengelbach that described him as "devoted to his family" and "always reliable and humane." Wev considered the statements to be evidence of Gengelbach's nominal Nazi status and asked that the report be revised to reflect them.[34]

One OMGUS officer was outraged at Wev's request and refused to become involved in the coverup. "This headquarters should not revise merely to circumvent the rules set forth by the State and Justice Departments," Robert Bruce told his superiors. Bruce refused to change the reports on Gengelbach and Adolf Thiel because OMGUS denazification officers believed that their early membership in the Nazi party and numerous other Nazi affiliations were evidence of considerable political incrimination that made them security threats.[35]

He also refused to change Heinrich Kliewe's incriminating security report, thereby unwittingly squelching a secret intelligence plot to lure Kliewe out of the French zone of Germany and send him to the United States under Paperclip. Kliewe had been chief sanitary officer of the Wehrmacht, in charge of human experimentation for Hitler's biological warfare program. In 1946 he was judged merely a "follower" of nazism and fined DM 2,000 by a denazification court on the basis of favorable statements made by alleged anti-Fascists in his behalf. But later, OMGUS Public Safety officers discovered that some of the statements were entirely false and actually had been made by Kliewe's close friends, who were well-known ardent Nazis. A retrial was ordered and a warrant was issued for Kliewe's arrest. Nuremberg prosecutors also wanted him detained as a witness in the Nuremberg medical atrocities case. But Kliewe escaped arrest by slipping over the French zone border, where he joined other biowarfare experts on the run.[36]

Bruce was furious that the JIOA planned to include Kliewe's falsified statements, which were attached to his *OMGUS Security Report*, as well as statements claiming that Gengelbach was "reliable and humane," in dossiers sent to the State and Justice Departments. "Even [the] highly incriminated can produce good evidence with extreme ease," Bruce complained. OMGUS investigators had learned that in addition to statements made in behalf of Kliewe and Gengelbach, two hundred others that were submitted in defense of Paperclip specialists also were authored by close friends and contained false or misleading information.[37]

Nevertheless, the JIOA officers soon began to receive bundles of OMGUS security reports signed by Schow's executive officer in the Intelligence Division—all changed from "ardent Nazi" status to "not an ardent Nazi." Colonel Fagg and other intelligence officers had even signed most of the reports on the same day. The reports included numerous records of former SS members. Beier's twelve-year SS membership was excused by saying he was a mere "opportunist." Eckert, who had admitted attending SS meetings, was "not an ardent Nazi," according to the revised OMGUS report. Later, one officer involved in sanitizing the reports noticed glaring discrepancies between Friedrich Wazelt's report about his SS activities and the actual SS records, but he brushed it off and said, "I don't think it's worth checking on."[38]

Originally Wernher von Braun's September 18, 1947, report noted, "Subject is regarded as a potential security threat by the Military Governor." But five months later his new report said that since von Braun had been in the United States more than two years, if his conduct had been exemplary, "he may not constitute a security threat to the U.S." No information was placed in his dossier about his withholding information from the Army concerning the maps he mailed to Dornberger in London.[39]

Axster's first *OMGUS Security Report* stated:"He should— ideologically speaking—be considered a potential security threat to the United States." Six months later Axster's report was changed, despite additional incriminating information that had been obtained by investigators in Europe regarding Axster's treatment of laborers. Nevertheless, Axster's revised report concluded: "Subject was not a war criminal and was not an ardent Nazi. The record of Herbert Axster as an individual is reasonably clear and as such, it is believed that he constitutes no more of a security threat than do the other Germans who have come to the U.S. with clear records in entirety."[40]

Wilhelm Eitel, who had fled Berlin in 1945, worked for the Navy in a nuclear plant in Norris, Tennessee. His *OMGUS Security Report* originally had judged him to be an "ardent Nazi." Atomic Energy Commission security agents had expressed concern about Eitel's presence at the plant and his access to AEC workrooms. The Berlin police still had not closed the case of his wife's suicide. And Navy investigators had tracked down some of the Jewish scientists who had been fired from the Kaiser Wilhelm Institute in 1933 as a result of Eitel's compliance with Hitler's policies against Jews. One of those scientists had ended up in a concentration camp. Others told investigators that the famous chemist Fritz Haber had quit the KWI and fled to England rather than comply with the policies.[41]

Despite the incriminating evidence, Eitel's *OMGUS Secu-*

rity Report was changed to read that he was "not an ardent Nazi." During a meeting where Eitel's Nazi past was discussed, one Navy intelligence officer said, "it is admitted that while he was undoubtedly an adherent of Nazi ideology, even to the point of enthusiasm, it is felt that he is hardly the type of individual who would purposely and with malicious intent engage in activities to the extent attributed to him in statements" by the former KWI scientists. The officer concluded that the Navy considered Eitel to be a preeminent scientist and a valuable asset whose "previous political views appear to be of secondary importance at this time."[42]

The effect of the coverup involved far more than merely whitewashing the information in the dossiers. Serious allegations of crimes not only were expunged from the records, but were never even investigated. Regarding the specialists at Wright-Patterson, allegations against Theodor Zobel and Ernst Eckert, and Albert Patin's own admission that he had utilized slave labor, were never investigated. Statements from their friends or colleagues were simply put into their files as evidence that they were not ardent Nazis. Furthermore, none of the dossiers of the Mittelwerk group at Fort Bliss contained a shred of evidence that *Andrae*—the Dora trial—had ever taken place. At the very least, Major Eugene Smith's interrogations were relevant documents that should have been scrutinized by the State and Justice Departments when considering whether an individual such as Arthur Rudolph should be given a visa and, later, U.S. citizenship.[43]

The coverup was almost perfect. But for it to succeed, the intelligence officers had to get rid of their opponents in State. The whitewashed dossiers never would pass the scrutiny of either Klaus or Robinson. Less than two months after Wev first told European officers to change the reports, the officers' right-wing friend in Congress began to wage a full scale battle against the State officials. Congressman Fred Busby, from Illinois, was the perfect man for the job. Like Senator Joseph McCarthy, Busby was an extremist who used sympathetic members of the press and congressional committees as the public red-baiting platform for his effort to singlehandedly clean out the "subversive elements" in State.[44]

Much of the information that Busby used in his smear campaigns came from the Chicago Police Department's notorious intelligence unit known as the "red squad." The squad's activities included compiling dossiers and conducting illegal surveillance, break-ins, and terrorist-style raids that violated the civil rights of thousands of American citizens. The squad operated for decades in collaboration with G-2's illegal domestic spy operation and the Legion of Justice, a Chicago-based right-wing terrorist group.[45]

On March 10, 1948, Busby hauled Robinson before a House subcommittee, where the congressman wove a tale based on innuendo in an attempt to show that Robinson was "incompetent" in his job and had associated with a second cousin who Busby said was an alleged Communist. Eleven State Department officials already had been fired as a result of the McCarran rider to an appropriations act, which allowed the secretary of state to discharge any employee deemed to be a security risk. Busby wanted Robinson to be the twelfth, but subcommittee members shut down the hearings. "There was no substance," said Congressman John W. McCormack of the allegations against Robinson. "The only card-bearing organization of which he was a member was the Young Republicans Club of New York City. I think that is a mighty good American organization."[46]

Busby was forced to resign from the subcommittee because of his antics. But that did not stop him from attacking Robinson and Klaus in news broadcasts over NBC radio. "It's another chapter in a story of how a few minor officials in the State Department have succeeded in blocking a program of high military importance," reported NBC's Ned Brooks. He said the State Department had refused to give the German scientists visas even though Truman had approved Paperclip. Quoting Busby as his source, Brooks identified Klaus by name as being "the man most influential in sabotaging the program." A later broadcast blamed Robinson for the "ax work."[47]

On March 25, 1948, Busby lashed out again at the "sinister figures" in the State Department in a long speech in Congress. According to Busby, the State Department was infiltrated with Communists and Robinson had refused to go along with Busby's plan to fire employees accused of disloyalty. But Robinson's biggest crime, Busby said, was that he was in charge of a "clique" in the Visa Department, including Klaus and others, that had "sabotaged" the German scientist program. In Busby's view, all of these "fellow travelers" were at the root of the State Department's problems.[48]

Busby's campaign succeeded, and not just in the short term. With Robinson's resignation two days after Busby's speech, the last State Department watchdog was gone, leaving the JIOA conspirators free to proceed unimpeded with their scheme to circumvent Truman's policy.

Beyond these immediate effects, the smear campaign of which Busby was the mouthpiece left the historical record biased against the two State Department officials who strove to uphold the very policy they were accused of obstructing. Klaus, who died a few years after his losing battle with the JIOA officers, never was able to erase the undeserved stain on his record, a stain that endures to this day. More than twenty years after the events in question, Klaus still was being castigated for being, in historian Clarence Lasby's term, the "one man" in the State Department who was holding up progress. And to date, no history of those events has called to account those in the JIOA, in Congress, and in the press who plotted against this lonely, engaging figure with integrity and who dragged his name through the mud.[49]

On May 11, 1948, Director of Intelligence Chamberlin met with FBI Director Hoover and convinced him to change the FBI's long-standing policy that anyone with a record of Nazi party membership should be considered a security threat. Chamberlin told Hoover that immigration was the only way to successfully deny a "gold mine of brains" to the Russians. Regarding the specialists' Nazi pasts, although Chamberlin admitted that some were affiliated with nazism, he told Hoover that "none were active participants of the party or its political activities."[50]

After the meeting, Chamberlin told the JIOA officers the good news. FBI Director Hoover had volunteered to meet personally with the attorney general to eliminate bureaucratic red tape in order to expedite the visas. Hoover was on their team.[51]

As a result of whitewashed files, many Paperclip personnel would obtain visas, and later American citizenship, on the basis of false or misleading information in dossiers that the JIOA officers submitted to the State and Justice Departments. By 1949, JIOA officers bypassed the OMGUS security evaluations entirely in most cases. JIOA Director Daniel Ellis told a screening panel his reasoning behind that decision: "This action should be taken in view of the apparent inability of OMGUS to supply security evaluations *on a wholesale basis.*"[52]

8 CIA Dirty Tricks in the "National Interest"

THE cold war led to a major expansion of the German scientist operation. Heretofore, Paperclip was limited to German and Austrian scientists who worked for the U.S. military. But beginning in the summer of 1947, a new JIOA project lifted those constraints. Code-named "National Interest," the individuals brought to the United States under this program ran the gamut from Nazi scientists, including a convicted Nazi war criminal, to East Europeans involved in CIA covert operations overseas. The sole standard for these transfers was that they be deemed in the national interest.

National Interest operated on two levels. The more visible level included the cases of German or Austrian scientists employed by universities, defense contractors, or private industry. Their entry was considered to be in the national interest simply because it kept them from going to work for the Russians.

The second level was heavily cloaked in secrecy, and for good reason. The CIA and military intelligence used the project to bring intelligence sources or other assets to the United States, where they were given a safe haven in exchange for their services. In 1948 many of these individuals were of interest to the Office of Policy Coordination (OPC), the early covert action arm of the CIA, given the authority by Truman to conduct what is known in the intelligence trade as "dirty tricks." To put it bluntly, Project National Interest provided the escape mechanism to a haven in the United States that OSS chief William Donovan had wanted President Roosevelt to approve in 1944.[1]

National Interest policy assumed that all of these persons normally would have been barred from entry under U.S. immigration laws because of past Nazi or Communist party membership. Therefore, their entry was facilitated by the ninth proviso of the U.S. immigration law, which gave the attorney general the authority to admit cases with military implications or those affecting national security. The CIA cases were covered by a section in the CIA Act of 1949, which allowed U.S. entry of up to one hundred individuals a year "without regard to their inadmissibility under the immigration or any other laws. . . ." The JIOA Governing Committee approved the entry in the CIA cases and passed the names on to the attorney general for approval.[2]

The aliens in National Interest, like those in Paperclip, were sent to Canada and reentered the United States as resident aliens. Numerous historians and journalists have told the now-famous story of how Wernher von Braun and other Paperclip scientists were sent to Canada or Mexico and then reentered America. Yet not one has so much as mentioned the illegality of this or that Canadian officials were furious about it, since entry into Canada of these Nazis violated their own immigration laws.

In 1947, for example, the Royal Canadian Mounted Police

(RCMP) reported that they had been duped by U.S. officials into believing that the Nazis' backgrounds were such as to allow their entry under Canadian laws, when in fact the opposite was true. "Some of these people are admitted members of the Nazi party and others, I am informed, have criminal records," one RCMP officer reported after conducting his own investigation. In addition, the Canadians suspected that U.S. and British intelligence falsified background checks sent to the RCMP of Nazi scientists and "defectors" who were resettled in Canada in the 1950s. Following a 1981 investigation, Canadian officials uncovered evidence that some of these men were Nazi war criminals. As a result the Canadians thoroughly distrusted background checks conducted by the CIA and British intelligence. "No foreign agency should be considered a 'reliable source' in the sense that its reports can be accepted uncritically," a RCMP report noted.[3]

Prevailing myth has it that the first group in National Interest, the German scientists, were employed solely because of their scientific expertise. But there were other reasons as well. First, defense contractors and universities could hire German scientists for substantially less money than they could American employees. Salary statistics show that the Germans signed contracts for approximately $2,000 a year less than their American counterparts received in comparable positions. Of course, the Germans were unaware of the salary discrepancy, since they had earned even less money in West Germany. The JIOA, however, took advantage of the situation by promoting cheap salaries to convince corporations to participate in the project. Second, because of the Joint Chiefs of Staff connection with the National Interest project, German scientists could obtain necessary security clearances more easily than could American scientists. Defense contractors looking for new employees to work on classified projects found this aspect of National Interest to be particularly advantageous. By 1957, more than sixty companies were listed on JIOA's rosters, including Lockheed, W. R. Grace and Company, CBS Laboratories, and Martin Marietta.[4]

Originally the JIOA was concerned that National Interest would compete with Paperclip. This problem was solved by offering the military the first option to hire a German scientist on the JIOA's list. If the military was not interested in the individual, his name was added to the JIOA's National Interest roster and his services were offered to universities or corporations. The JIOA figured that it would be easy to keep private employers from hiring Paperclip scientists away from the military, since the JIOA could pull their federally funded research or defense contracts if they got out of line.[5]

The scientists who worked for universities or corporations were originally "sponsored" by either the Department of Commerce or the Department of Defense (Army, Air Force, or Navy). The Department of Commerce even sent its own recruiters to Germany. However, other than providing some help with the paperwork, this sponsorship was irrelevant: the individuals worked for and were paid by the universities or companies. The sponsorship did provide a way to meet JCS policy requirements of having some connection with the military or another governmental department. In the case of the second group, the sponsor provided a convenient cover to conceal the CIA-OPC connection.[6]

National Interest placed German scientists at major universities in research or teaching positions, regardless of their Nazi pasts. Even the U.S. Office of Education helped the JIOA send fliers to universities all over the country touting the advantages of hiring the Germans on federally financed research projects, since they could obtain security clearances more easily than Americans. The University of Texas, Washington University School of Medicine in St. Louis, Missouri, and Boston University were among the participants.[7]

The universities never even questioned whether Nazi professors might impart a skewed view of democracy or otherwise harm young students. And university officials certainly were aware that these men were Nazis, since their Nazi affiliations were noted on their résumés. In 1948, a representative of the University of North Carolina told the JIOA how pleased he was to have three Germans, including engineer Adolf von

Hoermann, working at the university and thanked the JIOA for its representations that the Germans had been screened. The JIOA's screening had revealed that von Hoermann was "a convinced adherent of the National Socialistic ideology" and had been a member of the Nazi party and four other Nazi organizations during the war.[8]

Still, there were angry disputes between American employees and Germans who still adhered to virulent Nazi views. One incident occurred at the Bechtel Corporation, where synthetic fuels expert Leonard Alberts worked under National Interest. Alberts had been a member of the SS, the Nazi party, the SA, and two other Nazi groups. He also had been a Gestapo informant in the Victor Works plant where he worked during the war. His job, as chief counterespionage agent for the Abwehr, was to uncover "spies and saboteurs" among the foreign forced laborers working at Victor and report them to the Gestapo. After he was brought to America under National Interest, Alberts changed jobs four times in two years as a result of American co-workers' complaints about his ardent nazism.[9]

The dispute at Bechtel occurred when the company learned that Alberts had failed to mention his SS and Abwehr connections on his forms. Alberts claimed that he did not recall his Nazi memberships, since "such matters were intrusted to my secretary." Bechtel officials also gave the FBI a pile of complaints from Alberts's co-workers and an Army security officer, Major Robert Humphries, who accused Alberts of being a security threat. Humphries told the FBI that Alberts "was and is a Nazi" and warned that he was "capable of dealing with Russia or any other group which would pay for his technical knowledge." Despite these complaints, the JIOA disregarded Humphries as being "opinionated" and transferred Alberts to Blaw-Knox in Pittsburgh. By then the FBI had collected even more unfavorable reports on Alberts's character and pro-Nazi stance. JIOA officers eventually helped Alberts obtain permanent residency, despite derogatory reports, because they were afraid he would work for the Russians if returned to Germany.[10]

National Interest was merely an entry mechanism to get the

person here first, ask questions later. Because of that, there was a potential for an even greater internal security risk with these cases than with Paperclip, which at least provided some semblance of military custody. In addition to hard-core Nazis, National Interest cases included former members of the Communist party and the Italian Fascist party.

One German was an accused Nazi spy who, though brought to the United States to work for a New York optical company, promptly disappeared once he arrived. This should have come as no surprise, considering Goerz Langfeld's track record. Langfeld had lived in America in the late 1930s and worked for Eastman Kodak in Rochester, New York. The FBI suspected that Langfeld and several top U.S. businessmen were meeting with a notorious Nazi spy, who later was convicted of espionage. Langfeld left America in 1941, and reports of his wartime activities are conflicting. Langfeld claimed on one form that he had gone to Tokyo as a "tourist." On another he said he had returned to Nazi Germany and joined the Luftwaffe. Yet another story was that he had worked for the German Naval headquarters in Berlin. One thing is certain: in late 1945 Army CIC agents thought he looked suspicious and threw him in jail. He was caught wearing a British uniform, brandishing a gun, and carrying falsified papers, including identity cards under several names. Langfeld escaped soon after his arrest and, under yet another alias, obtained a job at the Office of Military Government for Bavaria's film division. By the time he was brought to the United States in 1952 his records revealed that he had used at least five different aliases.[11]

Even convicted Nazi war criminals were accepted under the project. Otto Ambros's case is by far the most brazen example of how National Interest circumvented U.S. immigration laws. The fact that W. R. Grace and Company, headed by J. Peter Grace, employed Ambros as a consultant for decades is well known. But newly declassified JIOA and U.S. Army documents shed new light on this sordid affair.[12]

During the war, Ambros was a director of I. G. Farben, the chemical company that owned a firm that manufactured

Zyklon B, the gas used to kill millions of Jews in the camps. Ambros took part in the decision to use Zyklon B in the gas chambers and personally selected Auschwitz as the site of an I. G. Farben factory, which he later managed, because Auschwitz concentration camp prisoners could be used as slaves in the factory. Nuremberg trial witnesses recalled the deplorable conditions under which Auschwitz prisoners were forced to work at Ambros's I. G. Farben Auschwitz plant. "Thrashings, ill-treatment of the worst kind, even direct killings were the fashion," testified Rudolf Vitek, both a physician and an Auschwitz inmate. "The murderous work speed was responsible for the fact that while working many prisoners suddenly stretched out flat, turned blue, gasped for breath and died like beasts."[13]

I. G. Farben also manufactured nerve gas that was used in poison gas experiments on Auschwitz prisoners. These experiments, conducted in secret laboratories at I. G. Farben factories, were used to determine how fast nerve gas would kill Allied soldiers. The helpless victims of these experiments died instantly. According to British intelligence, Ambros and other I. G. Farben officials "justified the experiments not only on the grounds that the inmates of concentration camps would have been killed anyway by the Nazis, but also . . . that the experiments had a humanitarian aspect in that the lives of countless German workers were saved."[14]

Ambros was found guilty of slavery and mass murder at Nuremberg, but he was sentenced to a mere eight years' imprisonment. Chief prosecutor Josiah DuBois regarded the sentence as "light enough to please a chicken thief" and was so outraged that he wrote a scathing book about the men he called *The Devil's Chemists*. The JIOA had no such qualms and kept Ambros's name on JIOA hiring lists—even during his imprisonment. These lists were significant, since they contained the names of German scientists who had been cleared for employment under various JIOA and British projects. In addition, these Germans' families received benefits, including food supplements, not available to average German citizens.[15]

In 1951, General Clay's successor, the High Commissioner of Germany (HICOG), John McCloy, released from prison many convicted Nazi war criminals, including Ambros. The Nazi chemist immediately was hired as a consultant by Grace, Dow Chemical, and other American companies, as well as the U.S. Army Chemical Corps under a consultancy project that was run administratively in Germany by HICOG—conveniently the same agency whose chief had just set Ambros free. The full details of Ambros's consultancy with the U.S. military are unknown. The *effect* of that work, however, is abundantly clear. During the time that Ambros was a consultant, the chemical corps, using Auschwitz documents as a guide, conducted the same type of poison gas experiments that had been done in the secret I. G. Farben laboratories. This time, however, the experiments were conducted at Edgewood Arsenal, Maryland, and the unfortunate guinea pigs were more than seven thousand American soldiers.[16]

In the 1950s Grace repeatedly tried to get the State Department to issue Ambros a visa but was turned down because he was a convicted Nazi war criminal. Then National Interest entered the picture, as it provided a way to bring otherwise excludable individuals to the United States under the attorney general's waiver provision. According to State sources, the Justice Department approved Ambros's entry and he visited the United States at least three times.[17]

The CIA's tremendous influence on National Interest and Paperclip has been ignored prior to this book. The CIA was formed as a separate intelligence agency as a result of the National Security Act of 1947. A year later, the Office of Policy Coordination began operating as the CIA's covert action arm, headed by Frank Wisner, formerly chief of OSS operations in the Balkans during World War II. Wisner's OPC operated out of the State Department, which proved highly advantageous to the intelligence agents running Paperclip. His considerable influence in the State Department meant a more favorable climate, particularly since Samuel Klaus and other Paperclip detractors had been forced out of the picture. In addition,

Wisner handled the CIA investigations of individuals brought to America under all JIOA projects. Considering the well-publicized facts surrounding the CIA's own use of Nazi war criminals, it should not be surprising that the CIA name checks reported "no derogatory information."[18]

Wisner also helped the JIOA obtain visas for Paperclip scientists. For example, in February 1948 Director of Intelligence Stephen Chamberlin met with Wisner to discuss JIOA's problems with Klaus and the Visa Department. Chamberlin told Wisner that around 350 Germans were still living in the United States under military custody, but they could not become permanent residents without State Department approval. "This condition has resulted in an unfavorable reaction on specialists' morale," Chamberlin said. He asked Wisner to accelerate the visas and to support JIOA's efforts to change Paperclip policy to enable the Germans to get visas before their arrival in America.[19]

Less than a month later the State Department notified the JIOA that it would accelerate its processing of visas in the Paperclip cases. The new director of the Visa Department, Herve L'Heureux, also issued instructions to consuls in Germany that only major Nazi leaders would be barred from obtaining visas. By 1949 Paperclip scientists began to obtain visas prior to their arrival in the United States.[20]

The National Interest project provided a way to slip military or CIA intelligence assets into the country. The CIA group involved defectors or individuals who possessed information of significant intelligence value. JIOA officers passed on the names of the CIA group to the attorney general for final approval. "We just did the paperwork," recalled retired U.S. Army Colonel Bernard Geehan, who served on the JIOA from 1953 to 1957. But that approval process was crucial, because the law was designed to admit people who otherwise would be inadmissible. As one CIA attorney admitted in 1979, the provision allowing the CIA to bring a hundred persons to the United States waived all grounds of exclusion, so theoretically, drug traffickers or persons convicted of serious crimes could be admitted into the country under the law. The sole consideration for entry was that the aliens had performed significant services for the United States or had the potential for performing those services in the future. In some instances those services included working in CIA covert operations overseas.[21]

Some of these aliens had escaped to the West via an "underground railway" operated by a special unit of intelligence agents in Berlin. "We get some hot customers, hot with the breath of the Russian pursuers on their necks," one unidentified agent told *The New York Times* in 1947. The agents smuggled scientists, politicians, intelligence sources, and other individuals through Eastern Europe, using various modes of transportation and disguises to sneak them past Russian guards to the American or British zones of Germany.[22]

The aliens' backgrounds were varied. Some were Germans employed by U.S. intelligence at Camp King in Germany. Others were former Italian Fascists, including a wealthy businessman whom the JIOA was reluctant to approve for U.S. entry because his dubious business methods already had been an obstacle to negotiating a consultancy contract with the U.S. Air Force. Many were defectors, such as General Izydor Modelski, former military attaché with the Polish Embassy in Washington. Another defector, Peter Pirogov, was a Soviet Air Force officer who flew a jet plane out of the Ukraine to Austria, where he crash-landed and turned himself over to the Americans. According to JIOA records, the U.S. Air Force sponsored Pirogov's U.S. entry under National Interest. He then worked as a consultant for the Air Force and as a scriptwriter for the CIA-funded Radio Liberty.[23]

There was also a group of Finnish soldiers who wanted to form an underground guerrilla team to fight the Communists in their homeland. The Finns originally had sought asylum in Sweden and secured a transit visa to the United States en route to Venezuela. Upon arrival in America, they offered to join the armed forces. On October 21, 1947, JIOA Deputy Director Walter Rozamus notified the State Department that the Finns had been approved for admission under National Interest. The

Finns then went to Canada, reentered the country, and enlisted in the U.S. Army.[24]

One of the Finns, Alpo Marttinen, wrote to former OSS chief Donovan and asked that his group be transferred to the Intelligence Division in order to carry out a scheme that they had told Donovan about when they first arrived in the United States. The scheme included secretly recruiting a cadre of two thousand Finnish officers to be used to fight a guerrilla war against Soviet troops in Finland. "The first and foremost step in this campaign," Marttinen wrote, "would be to assist in the escape and to offer asylum to such persons whose services either in the underground activities or in war itself would be of most value." He explained that anti-Communist Finnish army officers living in exile in Venezuela and other countries were well qualified to fight this war, since they knew Scandinavian and Russian languages and terrains, were experts in winter warfare tactics, and were familiar with Soviet fighting methods.[25]

The idea was passed on to Major General Alfred Gruenther, chairman of the JCS, who asked several individuals for their comments. Most military officers thought the idea sounded too much like recruiting mercenaries. As one colonel put it, this cadre of guerrilla warriors might include "a large sprinkling of free-booters, criminals and petty racketeers." But the idea appealed to George Kennan, head of the State Department Policy Planning Staff, and architect of the political theory of Soviet containment. "We believe that Mr. Marttinen's project has merit and that a beginning should be made to carry it out," Kennan wrote to Gruenther. "It would seem advisable to start the project with these men and gradually to build it up as a top-secret undertaking." Soon, more Finnish soldiers began to arrive directly from Venezuela and other countries under Project National Interest. The influx continued well into the 1950s. Marttinen and other Finns trained with the U.S. Army winter warfare unit.[26]

National Interest also included Russian and Eastern European scientists who either had worked in Nazi Germany or had escaped to the West after the war. Alexander Papkow, for example, had been one of the first Russian physicists to work on nuclear fission. In 1943 Papkow moved to Germany and worked as a Russian translator for German intelligence and as a scientific assistant to Professor Walter Bothe at the Kaiser Wilhelm Institute in Heidelberg. Originally Papkow was going to be brought to the United States, but an investigation by Army CIC agents had raised suspicions about Papkow's wife and her Soviet connections. Army CIC agents normally kept the scientists on JIOA lists under surveillance. In Papkow's case Army CIC stakeouts gathered information about Papkow's émigré contacts that was used in an investigation of Soviet émigré espionage networks operating in the U.S. zone of Germany.[27]

The most interesting aspect of National Interest is the services some individuals actually performed for U.S. intelligence. The National Interest roster tells the story of nearly every early CIA-OPC covert operation that took place in the late 1940s. Under National Interest, U.S. immigration laws were juggled to allow some of them to travel in and out of the country with no questions asked. Two examples are enough to show the pattern.

One case was Teodor Manicatide, brought to the United States after being involved in a botched coup d'etat in Romania in late 1946. According to Robert Bishop, an American intelligence agent stationed in Bucharest at the time, the coup was planned by Lieutenant William Hamilton and Major Thomas Hall of the Strategic Services Unit (SSU). The full story of this operation still is unknown. And one key question that remains unanswered is whether anyone, especially the president, authorized the SSU officers' deliberate attempt to topple a foreign government. The SSU was an early War Department unit created basically as a caretaker agency for the disbanded OSS clandestine intelligence agencies until the CIA was formed in 1947.[28]

In Bishop's account of this debacle, Hamilton and Hall recruited factions of dissident political groups in Romania to form a resistance movement against the Communist-backed

Romanian government. The recruits included leaders of the National Peasant party, the strongest political opposition party in Romania, with a track record of having tried to overthrow the country's Nazi-puppet government in 1944. The American officers held meetings to plot a coup which they promised to finance with sixty thousand gold coins and support with arms and supplies. Manicatide served as Hamilton's translator at the meetings. The problem was, the meetings were held in the worst locations imaginable if the idea was to keep this plot secret from Russian intelligence agents. "A bar room, a garden restaurant, or a quiet place in the suburbs would have been foolproof by comparison," Bishop noted sarcastically. One meeting was held in an American officer's home located near the Russian Embassy. Another took place in a bombed-out palace that, as Bishop observed, was well known to Russian agents as being "a nest of reactionary activities." Hamilton and Hall were so incompetent as to have stenographic notes taken of the plots discussed at these meetings. Of course, the Russians soon obtained a copy of the notes, arrested the Romanians, and conducted show trials at which the stenographic notes were used as evidence.[29]

Manicatide, JIOA's National Interest subject, was given political asylum in the American Military Mission while being tried in absentia at the show trials. It is not known whether Manicatide unwittingly became ensnared in the activities of these renegade U.S. intelligence officers or if he took a more active role other than working as Hamilton's translator. Either way, it did not matter to the Romanian court, which considered his mere association with Hamilton enough evidence to convict him for participating in the plot. According to an account in *The New York Times* on November 20, 1946, of the sentencing of ninety-four persons on trial, Manicatide "was sentenced to life imprisonment on the grounds that he accompanied a Lieutenant Hamilton of the American Military Mission to a National Peasant congress." Manicatide was then smuggled out of Romania and provided with a haven in the United States under National Interest.[30]

The next case on the National Interest covert action roster

involved an Italian immigrant, Angelica Balabanoff, who helped the CIA secretly instigate a major upheaval in the Italian government that laid the groundwork for the successful election of CIA-backed candidates in 1948. Here the CIA, with the help of Wisner and other individuals, conducted full-scale clandestine political warfare. The CIA's dirty tricks were financed by $10 million in cash obtained from the U.S. Treasury's Exchange Stabilization Fund, which consisted of captured Nazi assets, including money and valuables that the Nazis had stolen from Jews. Ironically, Samuel Klaus originally had helped locate this loot while working on the Safehaven project, designed to stop Nazis from smuggling their assets out of Germany. The CIA funneled millions of dollars to Italian centrist political candidates. Circumstantial evidence indicates that CIA money backed Italy's Premier Alcide de Gasperi and a group of right-wing Socialists headed by Giuseppe Saraget. The CIA also financed media blitzes in the Italian press, supported armed goon squads used to intimidate voters, and published leaflets that smeared Communist candidates as being Fascists and sex perverts. The money was funneled through various fronts, including the Vatican, which is known to have helped smuggle numerous Nazi war criminals, including Klaus Barbie, to South America.[31]

In the 1970s U.S. congressmen investigating the CIA's secret involvement in Italy's affairs were led to believe that the CIA's operation had begun in 1948. In fact, the Balabanoff plot had begun a year earlier, in January 1947. Balabanoff was a former leader of the Italian Socialist and Labor movement who lived in New York as a resident alien. Because she was a former Communist, she risked being judged inadmissible to the United States if she traveled to Italy and then tried to reenter America. The National Interest project not only provided her reentry with no questions asked but allowed her to come and go between the United States and Italy at will in order to participate in this scheme.[32]

Raymond Murphy, the State Department's special assistant to the director in the Office of European Affairs, explained the reasoning behind the Balabanoff operation during a JIOA Governing Committee meeting on October 20, 1947. "This government is trying to evoke a response along democratic elements in Europe to organize resistance against the engulfment of their countries by an internal Communistic machine," Murphy said. Murphy told JIOA officers that Balabanoff, working in close cooperation "with certain officials of the American Embassy at Rome," had helped cause an upheaval and split in Italian politics that strengthened the CIA-backed Right Wing Socialists party headed by Giuseppe Saragat. Balabanoff made numerous speeches in Italy and held press conferences in the United States that publicized CIA-backed candidates. These trips were made possible by juggling U.S. immigration laws under National Interest.[33]

By 1948 the cold war had escalated National Interest and revitalized Paperclip. Washington already was full of rumors of war when General Lucius Clay sent his now-famous telegram from Berlin warning that war with the Soviets might be imminent. According to military historian Steven Rearden, "Evidence suggests that the idea of the telegram may have originated with Lt. Gen. Stephen J. Chamberlin." At the time, Director of Intelligence Chamberlin was desperately trying to salvage Paperclip. In February 1948, he told Wisner about his concern over the Army's "considerable burden of maintaining custody." The Army wanted to shut Paperclip down because there was no money to continue surveillance and other custodial duties over Paperclip scientists.[34]

The same month, Chamberlin went to Berlin and cautioned Clay as to the pitiful state of readiness of U.S. forces, the fact that military appropriation bills were pending before congressional committees, and the need to rally the public to support increased military expenditures. Chamberlin then asked Clay to sound an alarm to galvanize support. At first Clay insisted that his intelligence reports showed nothing to arouse suspicion about the Soviets, but later he decided to send a message to Washington. The primary purpose of Clay's telegram, according to the editor of Clay's papers, "was to assist the military chiefs in their Congressional testimony; it was not, in Clay's opinion, related to any change in Soviet strategy."[35]

On March 5 Clay sent Chamberlin the cable expressing his belief that war with the Russians might be imminent. "Within the last few weeks, I have felt a subtle change in Soviet attitudes which I cannot define but which now gives me a feeling that it may come with dramatic suddenness," Clay told Chamberlin. The fact that Clay's telegram went on to say that his opinion was not supported by data or hard evidence went unnoticed.[36]

Clay's "war warning," as it later was referred to in the Pentagon, hit Washington like an earthquake. Within hours Chamberlin and the assistant secretary of defense had briefed Secretary of Defense James Forrestal on the contents of Clay's message. By evening the word had reached the top echelons of the Navy and Air Force. Within a few weeks Forrestal had a full-blown war scare on his hands. "Papers this morning," Forrestal wrote in his diary, "[are] full of rumors and portents of war." *The New York Times* reported: "Top Military Men Urge U.S. To Arm to Show We Would Fight for Freedom," while Clay, trying to undo the damage, told reporters that he was "not the least bit apprehensive" and that "much too much is being made of this." Clay's comments went unheeded in Washington, where, during a Senate hearing, Secretary of the Navy John Sullivan announced that submarines "belonging to no nation west of the 'iron curtain' have been sighted off their shores." Ignoring the lack of evidence, the *Washington Times Herald* headlined the disclosure: "Russian Subs Prowl West Coast Waters."[37]

The significant effect of Clay's cable on JIOA projects previously has been ignored by historians and journalists who falsely assumed that the projects ended in the late 1940s. In fact, the resulting war scare escalated National Interest to such an extent that by 1950 U.S. intelligence was smuggling Eastern Europeans with false identities through immigration to Canada, where they were resettled. Later one Royal Canadian Mounted Police officer was shocked to discover that six files of incriminating information had been destroyed and replaced by a "false docket" on a Yugoslavian war crimes suspect who had been sent to Canada by U.S. intelligence. "I would be interested to know how the decision for destruction was reached for it is an action similar to the destruction of police files on Nazis in South America," the RCMP officer told his superior. British intelligence, which ran an identical project, also dumped their so-called "defectors" on Canada, as they had done with Nazi scientists. Canada's undersecretary of state recalled in November 1954 that Canada took in " 'British ex-agents' who were not in fact defectors as originally understood." A Canadian government investigation determined that many of these "ex-agents" were alleged war criminals or Nazi collaborators.[38]

The false war scare also invigorated Paperclip as the military received additional funds needed to keep the project going. Paperclip had been operating under a new policy that was supposed to eliminate the project's procurement phase. But JIOA Director Bosquet Wev aptly pointed out in a meeting that the JIOA never interpreted that to mean the end of Paperclip altogether. "In my mind there was no thought given to any ultimate termination date in this thing and [the policy] was a procedure to go on until such time as a peace treaty [with Germany] was signed or until the thing just petered out of its own accord," Wev said. As this book reveals, Paperclip finally "petered out" around 1973.[39]

An "escape clause" in the policy allowed the JIOA to procure scientists if certain conditions were met, such as a need for skilled workers for projects funded after the new policy went into effect. In the midst of the war scare, one Air Force officer remarked in a JIOA meeting that the "looming war psychology" in Washington had made the Department of Defense more receptive toward Paperclip. The Air Force believed that now it would be easier for the military to obtain money for new projects and bring more Paperclip scientists to America.[40]

Ultimately, the overall effect of the war scare on Paperclip was dramatic. The project's focus suddenly shifted toward one goal—to get German scientists out of Europe and away from the Russians by any means possible, even if that meant smuggling them to South American countries, such as the Argentine "Fourth Reich" of Juan and Eva Peron.

9 The Argentine Connection

ARGENTINA was a hotbed of fascism in exile. Nazi fugitives on the run arrived by the boatloads in Buenos Aires, carrying false papers provided by pro-Nazi Catholic priests who helped them travel Vatican escape routes to freedom in South America. Croatian Nazis, Italian Fascists, and a Norwegian Nazi doctor charged with conducting experiments on humans all arrived in Buenos Aires carrying their "irregular" documentation. One talkative Abwehr intelligence officer, Otto Wiedemann, even boasted when he arrived in 1949 that he had been allowed to escape from an American POW camp in Germany after bribing an Army Counter Intelligence Corps officer. "I would never have gotten out of American CIC hands, had there not been one second lieutenant who liked $300 more," Wiedemann said.[1]

By 1950 Argentina had become tightly linked to the German

scientist project. That connection represents yet another example of how the project expanded as a result of the cold war. The JIOA helped Argentina recruit German scientists and then used the Argentine connection to provide a safe haven for Nazi war criminals.

Had it not been for the cold war, Argentina never would have been considered habitable by anyone with democratic ideals. The country was swarming with Nazi war criminals. The chief butcher among them was Adolf Eichmann, the SS officer who was personally responsible for carrying out "the final solution of the Jewish problem." As America's outspoken Ambassador Spruille Braden bluntly stated, "there is no country in the world where the Nazis find themselves in such a strong position as . . . Argentina."[2]

The country was run by the smiling despot Juan Peron, characterized by Braden as "one of the few fascist dictators left in the world." In return, Peron looked upon his American adversary with disdain, bragging to supporters that he was going to "throw out the Yankee pig." For a brief moment in history, an explosive personal duel erupted between the two strong-willed men that personified the political expediency brought on by the cold war. Braden was determined to destroy Peron's political career and clean up Argentina's image as a "gangster-governed country."[3]

Instead of destroying Peron, the Argentinian was elected president and, with his blonde wife Eva by his side, became the most powerful man in the country. Braden was sent home—replaced by the pragmatic friend of U.S. business, John Bruce, who immediately began to repair the damage by praising Peron as the greatest leader in Latin America. The Nazis were forgotten and Peron's image was transformed by U.S. policy and the press from that of a regressive strongman to a key figure in the collective self defense of the Americas against Communist aggression.[4]

America's changing views included a policy to allow German scientists hired by "friendly nations"—including Argentina—to legally leave the U.S. zone of Germany and relocate in South

America. Having pressured Latin American nations after the war to deport Germans and reduce German influences in their country under the State Department's "Safehaven" program, State was now being asked to approve the Germans' legal migration to South America.[5]

General Robert Walsh played a key role in the Argentine connection, as he had in earlier Paperclip plots. It was Walsh who initiated the policy in 1948, when he was reassigned from his position as EUCOM director of intelligence to the U.S. Air Force representative on the Inter-American Defense Board in Washington. Walsh was already a familiar figure at the IADB. An IADB report describes him as "one of the oldest members in point of service in the history of the Inter-American Defense Board." He represented the Army Air Forces at the IADB's inaugural session in 1942, was AAF delegate on the IADB from 1945 to 1946, and was director of staff from 1948 to 1950. In addition, Walsh formulated the bases of the IADB's entire military plan when he was head of the U.S. delegation of the IADB from 1950 to 1952.[6]

The IADB still operates today in a shroud of secrecy, though its current activities certainly would interest Americans. Three of its member nations are headline news—Panama, Nicaragua, and El Salvador. And remember, this is the same IADB that received an award in 1986 from then Panamanian strongman Manuel Noriega when he attended an IADB conference in Washington. This dubious event occurred while Congress was investigating Noriega's involvement in assassinations and drug trafficking.[7]

The IADB is composed of military officers representing the highest echelons in the defense establishments of the member nations in the Organization of American States (OAS), including the United States. The U.S. delegation on the IADB is officially an agency of the Joint Chiefs of Staff, with military officers serving on the board as part of their regular military assignments. Although the IADB is a separate agency from the OAS, it receives its funding through that organization, which means that there is no public accounting of how that money is spent. There is also no public accounting of the IADB's secret activities, since Joint Chiefs of Staff records of the U.S. delegation are exempt from the Freedom of Information Act.[8]

In the late 1940s the U.S. delegation on the IADB was composed of military officers who were directly involved with the JIOA, Paperclip, or other U.S. intelligence operations using Nazis. In addition to Walsh, the IADB members included:

- former JIOA Director Francis Duborg, a Navy captain, who served on an IADB staff committee under an army general from Paraguay;
- Lieutenant General Alexander R. Bolling, who replaced Stephen Chamberlin as Army director of intelligence and godfather to the JIOA and Paperclip in late 1948, when Chamberlin became commander in chief of the Fifth Army in Illinois;
- General Edwin Sibert, who was chief of U.S. Army intelligence in Germany and supervised the operation to bring Hitler's spy chief Reinhard Gehlen to the United States in 1945;
- Army Chief of Staff Omar N. Bradley, who was Bolling's superior and later a guest speaker at an IADB meeting in 1952, when Bradley was chairman of the Joint Chiefs of Staff;
- Deputy Chief of Staff General Joseph Lawton Collins, who became Army chief of staff after Bradley in 1949; Collins also served on the Joint Intelligence Committee, which oversaw the JIOA's involvement with Paperclip.

All of these generals were criticized by Congress in 1948 when they were decorated by Peron himself and made honorary members of his armed forces while spending a week in expensive Buenos Aires villas as Peron's guests. Some congressmen thought it was inappropriate for U.S. military officers to accept honorary membership in the armed forces of a Fascist dictator who had collaborated openly with Hitler during World War II.[9]

Walsh and other U.S. delegates worked at the IADB with

Latin American nations, in addition to Argentina, whose dictators harbored Nazi war criminals and used Gestapo tactics to prop up their repressive military regimes. Bolivia, Chile, and Paraguay (and later, Anastasio Somoza of Nicaragua) were all members of the board. Like Noriega, notorious Latin American leaders were flown to Washington and touted as honored guests at special IADB assemblies held in their behalf. For example, the IADB's guest on June 19, 1953, was General Alfredo Stroessner of Paraguay, where Nazi doctor Josef Mengele, the "Angel of Death" in Auschwitz, was allowed to live in peace. Stroessner ruled Paraguay with an iron fist for over three decades until he was overthrown in a coup in 1989. He headed a government that repeatedly has been accused of genocide of ethnic Indians, child prostitution, gross human rights abuse, and heroin smuggling. In addition, in 1961 the IADB honored Brigadier General Alfredo Ovando Candia of Bolivia, where Klaus Barbie had taken refuge. Ovando, who was army chief of staff at the time, not only knew Barbie but served on the board of Barbie's shipping firm, Transmaritima.[10]

With this group of honorees connected to the IADB, it should not be surprising that the organization declared in one annual report that "the results of the work of this high inter-American body is anonymous and silent."[11]

Some of those "anonymous" activities began in 1948, when the IADB implemented a plan to reequip and retrain all Latin American armed forces as a major defense against Soviet aggression. As a result the United States sold Peron $4 million worth of surplus weapons and ammunition. This contrasted sharply with earlier U.S. policy that banned weapons sales to Argentina because Peron already had armed his military with a stockpile of weapons obtained from Nazis during the war and had used those weapons against his political opponents.[12]

Part of the IADB's strategy, in which Walsh played a large part, was to retrain the Latin American armies and air forces in tactics standardized to conform with those of the U.S. military. The Argentine air force included a number of ex-Luftwaffe pilots, including Hitler's flying ace, Hans Rudel. Rudel was a diehard Nazi who used his personal friendship with Peron to obtain jobs for around one hundred members of his wartime Luftwaffe staff in Argentina's air force. Rudel had paid a Croatian priest in the Vatican to smuggle his Nazi friends out of Germany.[13]

Peron's army was even more problematic. Many Gestapo criminals on the U.S. Army's war crimes wanted lists now served in Argentina's army. Wiedemann even talked about them when he first arrived in Buenos Aires. "There are now so many former Gestapo men in the intelligence service here that it is riskier to tell a joke about Argentine Government personages in German than in Spanish," Wiedemann quipped.[14]

Braden had charged that the Buenos Aires police force included Gestapo officers who were responsible for the sadistic torture methods used on political prisoners jailed for opposing Peron's regime. The prisoners had been stripped naked, savagely beaten, tortured with prolonged electrical shocks to their genitals, and burned with lighted matches and cigarettes. But when Braden complained about the torture methods, Police Chief Juan Filomeno Velazco, a known Nazi sympathizer, remarked that "the police assign no importance to the so-called Nazi and Fascist tendencies." The legacy of the Gestapo's torture methods would haunt Argentina decades later, when death squads used similar methods to torture and murder thousands of people in the country that is now called the land of the "disappeared."[15]

German scientists were in the forefront of the IADB's plan to revitalize Argentina's defense, and the board urged Latin American nations to pursue the "scientific research of the future." As a result Argentina, Chile, Bolivia, and other Latin American countries accelerated their recruiting of German scientists and other experts who could design new airplanes, tanks, and weapons to defend the Americas.[16]

One of Argentina's biggest enclaves of German scientists was headed by Kurt Tank, former director of the Focke-Wulf aircraft factory and well-known fighter plane designer. Peron

Two dying prisoners of Dora concentration camp lie among the hundred dead on barracks floors where U.S. Army soldiers found them on April 11, 1945. The prisoners had worked as slave laborers in an underground V-2 rocket factory. *(National Archives)*

A Dora concentration camp survivor shows a U.S. Army soldier one of the furnaces that was used to burn the bodies of dead prisoners at Dora. The furnaces were still smoldering when American troops arrived in Nordhausen on April 11, 1945. *(National Archives)*

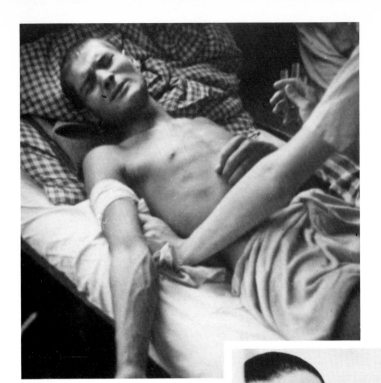

A Dachau inmate winces with pain during a seawater experiment. Over forty Gypsies were starved, forced to drink seawater, and had their livers punctured in the experiments at Dachau. *(National Archives)*

A Dachau prisoner gasps for air during a high-altitude experiment. Several prisoners died when they were locked inside an airtight chamber that was used to simulate extremely high altitudes during the experiments. *(National Archives)*

Major General Walter Dornberger (left), commander of the Peenemünde missile base, with Lieutenant Colonel Herbert Axster, Wernher von Braun (with sling), and Hans Lindenberg after they surrendered to U.S. Seventh Army troops May 3, 1945. Dornberger was contracted by the U.S. Air Force and Axster, von Braun, and Lindenberg by Army Ordnance under Paperclip. *(National Archives)*

Major General Walter Dornberger was wartime commander of the Peenemünde missile base. He later worked for the U.S. Air Force under Paperclip and was vice-president of Bell Aerosystems Company in Niagara Falls, New York. *(Smithsonian Institute)*

Defense counsel members Captain Paul Shrader, seated, and Major Leon Poullada are shown during the U.S. Army's trial of the atrocities at Dora concentration camp. The trial was held at Dachau, Germany, in 1947.
(National Archives)

Among the twenty-three defendants at the U.S. military tribunal at Nuremberg charged with conducting medical experiments on humans were four men who worked for the U.S. military: Kurt Blome (front bench, rightmost full figure), Siegfried Ruff (rear bench, leftmost), Hermann Becker-Freyseng (rear bench, fourth from left), and Conrad Schaefer (rear bench, sixth from left). Ruff and Schaefer were among the seven acquitted. *(National Archives)*

Herbert Wagner was the first German scientist to arrive in the United States, in May 1945, working for the U.S. Navy. Wagner had been the chief missile design engineer for the Henschel Aircraft Company and created the HS-293. *(National Archives)*

BASIC PERSONNEL RECORD
(Alien Enemy or Prisoner of War)

F. P. C.

(Internment serial number)		Height	5 ft. 7 in.	Reference
RICKHEY, Georg		Weight	165	INVENTORY
(Name of internee)				
Male		Eyes	grey	1.
(Sex)		Skin	light	2.
		Hair	brown	3.
		Age	47	4.

Distinguishing marks or characteristics:
scars on left cheek

5.
6.
7.
8.
9.

The above

(Date and place where processed (Army enclosure, naval station, or other place))

RIGHT HAND

1. Thumb	2. Index finger	3. Middle finger	4. Ring finger

LEFT HAND

6. Thumb	7. Index finger	8. Middle finger	9. Ring finger

W. D., P. M. G. Form No. 2
11 June 1943

Note Amputation in Proper Space

Paperclip recruit Georg Rickhey was returned to Germany to stand trial in the Dora war-crimes case, where he was acquitted. Rickhey had been general manager of the Mittelwerk V-2 rocket factory that used Dora prisoners as slave labor. *(National Archives)*

Samuel Klaus was the State Department representative on the Joint Intelligence Objectives Agency (JIOA) Governing Committee. He had numerous fights with JIOA officers over their investigations of the Paperclip scientists' Nazi pasts. *(U.S. State Department)*

U.S. Air Force Lieutenant General Donald Putt was in charge of the German jet aircraft specialists that worked under Paperclip at Wright-Patterson Air Force Base in Dayton, Ohio. *(Smithsonian Institute)*

U.S. Army soldier inspects a V-2 rocket that was found in the underground Mittelwerk rocket factory when American troops liberated Nordhausen in April 1945. Several V-2 rockets were sent to White Sands Proving Ground, New Mexico, for testing. *(National Archives)*

Members of the German rocket team who worked on rockets for Army Ordnance under Paperclip are shown at White Sands Proving Ground, New Mexico, in 1946. *(Smithsonian Institute)*

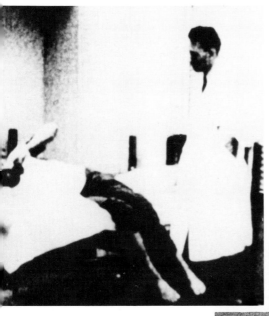

An unidentified U.S. Army doctor gives a soldier an injection of the hallucinogenic "BZ." These mind-control experiments were conducted in padded rooms at Edgewood Arsenal, Maryland. *(U.S. Army)*

An American soldier wears a gas mask and walks on a treadmill during a chemical-warfare experiment at Edgewood Arsenal, Maryland. Over seven thousand soldiers were used in chemical-warfare experiments at Edgewood from 1955 to 1975. *(National Archives)*

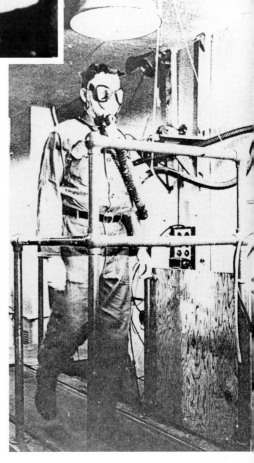

Hubertus Strughold, the "father of American space medicine," worked under Paperclip for the U.S. Air Force in San Antonio, Texas. *(U.S. Air Force)*

Hans Trurnit stands by a machine to measure thin films that he built while working for the Army Chemical Corps at Edgewood Arsenal, Maryland. Trurnit was one of eight Paperclip recruits who worked at the base on chemical-warfare agents or psychochemicals. *(National Archives)*

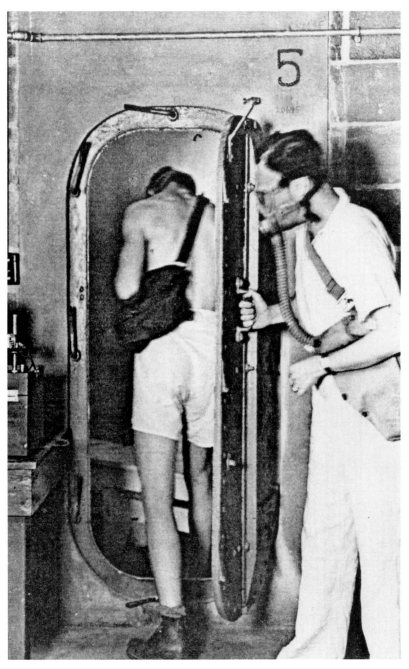

An American soldier enters the gas chamber at Edgewood Arsenal, Maryland. The chamber was used in experiments to expose humans to toxic chemical-warfare agents such as mustard or nerve gas. *(U.S. Army)*

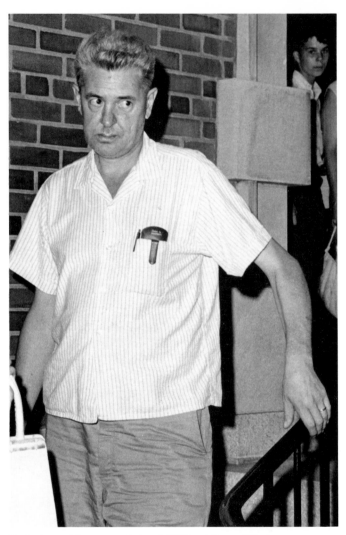

U.S. Army Lieutenant Colonel William Henry Whalen emerges from the U.S. District Courthouse in Alexandria, Virginia, on July 12, 1966, after his arrest on charges he sold atomic, missile, and bomber secrets to the Russians. Whalen was director of the JIOA and ran Paperclip during the time he was spying for the Russians. *(UPI/Bettmann)*

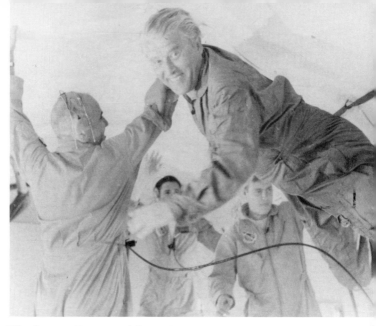

Wernher von Braun participates in tests that simulate the weightless conditions of space. Von Braun was director of NASA's Marshall Space Flight Center in Huntsville, Alabama. *(NASA)*

High-ranking NASA officials Kurt Debus (left) and Wernher von Braun had been members of the SS during World War II. Later Debus was director of the Kennedy Space Center in Cape Canaveral, Florida, and von Braun was director of the Marshall Space Flight Center in Huntsville, Alabama. *(NASA)*

Former U.S. congresswoman Elizabeth Holtzman initiated congressional investigations of Nazi war criminals living in the United States. She authored the "Holtzman Amendment" to the U.S. immigration law which provides a statutory basis to deport Nazi war criminals and to prevent their entry into the country. *(Lynda Fisher)*

Eli Rosenbaum initiated and directed the U.S. Justice Department investigation of Arthur Rudolph which resulted in Rudolph leaving the United States in 1984. Rosenbaum is Principal Deputy Director of the Justice Department's Office of Special Investigations. *(Linda Hunt)*

Members of the original German rocket team stand in front of a Saturn V rocket on April 26, 1985, at the Alabama Space and Rocket Museum in Huntsville, Alabama. Row 1, left to right: Eberhard Rees, Konrad Dannenberg. Row 2: Werner Sieber, Hannes Liebsten, Karl Heimburg, Otto Hirschler, Hannes Luehrsen, Walter Haeussermann, Helmut Horn. Row 3: Eric Neubert, Werner Voss, Bernard Tessmann, Guenther Haukohl, Ernst Lange, Dieter Grau, Wilhem Angele, Theodor Vowe. Row 4: Herbert Bergeler, Willie Kuberg, Walter Jacobi, Helmut Zoike, Robert Paetz. *(Linda Hunt)*

Convicted Nazi war criminal Otto Ambros admitted in 1986 that he was still working for U.S. companies. During the war Ambros ran the I.G. Farben synthetic rubber factory at Auschwitz. *(National Archives)*

Arthur Rudolph's supporters protest that the U.S. Justice Dapartment is conducting a "witchhunt" against the former NASA rocket scientist as Rudolph heads toward a Canadian immigration hearing on July 6, 1990, with his spokesman Hugh McInnish, left, and attorney Barbara Kulaszka, right. McInnish is an employee of the U.S. Army Strategic Defense Command who writes pro-Rudolph articles under the alias Thomas Franklin. *(Dave Dieter,* Huntsville Times)

put Tank back in the jet fighter business at the National Institute for Air Technology at Cordoba. Tank moved into a chalet near the institute so that he could travel the winding mountainous road to work in minutes.[17]

Argentina had been actively recruiting scientists in Germany since 1945, but that work was illegal and underground. The U.S. Military Governor of Germany Lucius Clay had to approve exit permits for any German who wanted to leave the U.S. zone in Germany legally. But that did not stop the scientists from quietly sneaking out of Germany through several illegal routes.

One route involved the INTR-Service, a Frankfurt travel bureau that was in reality a secret recruiting station for German scientists. One German engineer, Joachim Stauff, contacted INTR-Service in 1948 to find a job in Argentina. Stauff was told that he could obtain passage to Argentina more expeditiously if he would find a group of German scientists to go there with him. In the meantime Stauff signed a Paperclip contract and boarded a boat for America. During the trip, Stauff tried to convince Peenemünde's General Walter Dornberger and other Paperclip recruits who were on the ship to go to Argentina. Army intelligence agents investigated Stauff's recruiting tactics soon after he arrived in America. Later he was judged a security threat and sent back to Germany.[18]

Kurt Tank used another illegal route through Copenhagen, Denmark. He slipped out of Germany in disguise, with a phoney name and false papers provided by Peron himself. In Copenhagen a former aide to the German commander in chief in Denmark helped Tank slip through airport security along with more than one hundred other German scientists being smuggled to Argentina. Tank finally arrived in Buenos Aires via Denmark, London, and Lisbon, with microfilm of his fighter plane designs hidden safely in his trousers.[19]

Sixty of Tank's colleagues soon joined him by the same illegal route. Hans Schubert was among the first arrivals. Then came the former heads of the Focke-Wulf design offices, Wilheim Bansemir and Paul Klages. Ludwig Mittelhuber came, as did the theoretician Hebert Wolff and Dr. Otto Pabst, the specialist in the dynamics of gases. Heintzelmann arrived to deal with statics, and Wehrse and Plock, specializing in construction materials and questions of workshop techniques. Paul Rothkegal was there with a wide variety of specialists in design and mathematical calculation. They all left Germany illegally and brought their families to live on the mountain slopes near Cordoba and work for Tank at the aeronautical institute.[20]

Tank conducted business as usual in Argentina, designing a new high-speed fighter with swept wings based on the *Pulqui* for the Peron government. The original *Pulqui* was designed by a Frenchman, Emile Dewoitine, who had fled France to escape trial as a Nazi collaborator. By the time Tank's fighter, the *Pulqui II*, made its public debut in 1951, he and Peron were close friends. As the designer and test pilot flew the new plane over a cheering crowd, Peron expressed "the gratitude of the nation" to Tank for making a substantial contribution to Argentina's military aviation industry.[21]

In 1950 Walsh seized on the idea of not only legalizing exit routes but encouraging Germans to work in Latin America. To work out the plan, Walsh held several meetings with JIOA Director Daniel Ellis, who was a colonel in the U.S. Air Force. The sole purpose was to get the scientists away from the Russians. "From our viewpoint, which the British share, it is a big advantage to have these scientists in the safe areas of the Western Hemisphere, thereby denying them to the Russians," Ellis explained. The plan would provide jobs for a number of scientists whom neither America nor Britain wanted to employ. These included a group of Peenemünde rocket engineers who had fled to the West after working for the Soviets.[22]

But the U.S. political advisor in Germany, Robert Murphy, was vehemently against including Argentina in the plan. "Argentina has given asylum to many hundreds, if not thousands, of German specialists," Murphy told the secretary of state. "Quite apart from the problem raised by the infiltration of such elements into an area whose Government is not notably friendly towards the U.S., the question arises as to whether Argentina should be permitted to superimpose legal recruitment of German specialists on top of its large-scale illegal program."[23]

The plan was ultimately approved and became official U.S. policy, despite State's objections. Brazil was given first choice of the scientists on JIOA's list. At least that country had been an ally during World War II, unlike Argentina. The Germans recruited under the program were those whose skills were not desired by the United States or Great Britain. Ellis distributed 250 brochures describing Brazil's job opportunities to Germans on the JIOA list. He also arranged for Army intelligence agents to conduct limited background investigations in order to exclude Communist sympathizers from the employment lists. Ellis considered Nazi background checks irrelevant.[24]

Gerhard Schulze, a German engineer in Berlin, was one of the first scientists to leave Germany under the new policy. Schulze had worked in Brazil during the war and wanted to return. Eleven other scientists quickly signed up for the trip. All of them were working as consultants for the U.S. high commissioner in Germany. The group included chemical warfare expert Max Gruber.[25]

Other German and Austrian scientists eventually made Latin America their home. Franz Gerlach headed a biological warfare unit at the Bacteriological Institute in Santiago, Chile. In 1945 Gerlach had been fired from his position as director of the Veterinary Epidemiology Institute in Austria because of his wartime Nazi activities. Friedrich Fleischhacker worked in a forging plant in Brazil. And Ferdinand Porsche, the famous designer of Volkswagens and Panzer (Tiger) tanks, signed a contract with Argentina to produce automobiles on a large scale.[26]

Meanwhile, Walsh and the JIOA found an even more sinister use for their Argentine and IADB connections by arranging a safe haven for a scientist who was a notorious Nazi war criminal. General Walter Schreiber had been chief of the Sanitary Division of the Military Medical Academy—the division that had had jurisdiction over numerous experiments conducted in the camps. Schreiber also had been a member of the Reich Research Council, which had supported, funded, and commissioned these experiments.[27]

In one instance, he personally assigned doctors to work on epidemic jaundice experiments at the Sachsenhausen and Natzweiler camps, where prisoners died as a result of being deliberately infected with the disease. On another occasion Schreiber was the senior officer present at a meeting in which Dr. Ding-Schuler was ordered to inject Buchenwald camp prisoners with phenol to see how long it took them to die. Five prisoners were murdered in cold blood this way. "They sat down on a chair quickly, that is without emotion, near a light," Ding-Schuler later confessed. "During the injection they died in a momentary total cramp without any sign of other pain." He notified Schreiber's group in Berlin that the men had died in "about ½ second." After confessing to this and other crimes, Ding-Schuler later committed suicide in prison. SS Brigadier General Joachim Mrugowsky, who also attended the meeting, was convicted at Nuremberg and hanged.[28]

Schreiber, on the other hand, was captured by Russian troops in 1945 and held prisoner in various POW camps, including the infamous Lubjanka Prison in Moscow. He attended Antifa schools to undergo Communist indoctrination and was trained to take over as chief of sanitation for the East German police. In 1946 he was taken to Nuremberg to testify before the International Military Tribunal as a Soviet witness for the prosecution. Associate U.S. Prosecutor Alexander Hardy was shocked to see Schreiber, since his name was on a list of two hundred persons implicated in medical crimes who were supposed to be under arrest. Hardy and other American Nuremberg officials told the Soviets that Schreiber was wanted for interrogation and possible trial. But the Soviets quickly took him back to Russia. "I was unofficially informed that he was working on some 'hot' assignment for the Russians and that they required his services without interruption," Hardy reported.[29]

Two years later Schreiber reappeared in West Berlin and told reporters at a press conference that he had miraculously escaped from his captors. But his arrival in the West was amid rumors that he was a Soviet plant. A former Soviet POW told Army CIC agents that Schreiber had cooperated willingly with the Soviets during his capture and that his flight to freedom "was not a flight at all but a mission." Despite this warning, Army intelligence employed him for the next few years as a doctor at Camp King in Oberusal, Germany. He also was a CIA source of information on a project involving the use of drugs in interrogations.[30]

In September 1951 the JIOA brought Schreiber to the United States under Paperclip to work for the Air Force School of Aviation Medicine at Randolph Field, Texas, where General Harry Armstrong already was protecting Hubertus Strughold from being exposed to the public. Schreiber was employed in the Department of Global Preventative Medicine to work on military medical problems of survival, nutrition, and sanitation in remote areas of the world.[31]

But Schreiber's employment was short-lived as a result of complaints over his mere presence in America. Hardy and former Nuremberg medical investigator Leo Alexander complained to the White House and filed lengthy reports of Schreiber's crimes based on Nuremberg evidence that identified him by name.[32]

At the same time, a Ravensbrueck concentration camp survivor told U.S. immigration officials in Boston that she had seen Schreiber during a conference held at the camp to discuss experiments in which she was used as a guinea pig. Janina Iwanska was one of seventy-four female members of the Polish Resistance who were victims of gas gangrene and bone transplant experiments. The women underwent operations in which their legs were split open and deliberately infected with ground glass, wood shavings, and mustard gas. In some cases the bones were completely removed from their legs. Five women died from the experiments, six were shot, and the remainder were crippled for life.[33]

Schreiber was one of the biggest Nazi war criminals employed in the entire history of the project. Yet the attitude expressed by JIOA and Air Force officers when confronted with massive evidence of this man's crimes exemplified the anti-Semitism, the callous disregard for U.S. laws, and the total lack of any consideration of morality that plagued Paperclip for decades.

One glaring example of this attitude was expressed by General Armstrong, by now the surgeon general of the U.S. Air Force, when he told a group of physicians that "there is no evidence we know of that he is guilty of any crime other than serving his country during the war the same as I served mine." Remember that this is the same man who earlier admitted protecting Strughold and employed Nuremberg defendant Konrad Schaefer when Armstrong was in charge of the aeromedicine division in Texas.[34]

By February 1952 the Pentagon was besieged with complaints and bad publicity over Schreiber. Air Force Secretary Thomas Finletter finally told the American public that he had ordered the Air Force to drop Schreiber from its payroll and that the Air Force would "make no further use of him." Finletter also claimed that Schreiber was "under military custody" and expected to "leave the U.S. in a few weeks."[35]

The Air Force did not drop Schreiber, his Paperclip contract had expired. And when that contract ended, JIOA Director Benjamin Heckemeyer simply signed him up under a new short-term contract in another JIOA project, called "63." Furthermore, Schreiber was not under military custody, he was in hiding at his daughter's home in California. And despite Finletter's assertion that Schreiber would leave the country, no one quite knew what to do with him. The CIA had squelched plans to send him back to Germany out of fear that he would be kidnapped by the Russians. The commanding officer at Randolph Field, General Otis Benson, was even trying to get him a college teaching job. Benson told numerous universities that Schreiber was the victim of an organized movement of "medical men of Jewish ancestry" and asked them to hire Schreiber. "He is too hot for me to keep here on public funds, but I like and respect the man and hope I can help him in my role as a private citizen," Benson told one university representative.[36]

Schreiber settled the problem when he told the Air Force that he wanted to go to Buenos Aires, where his other daughter lived. That is when the IADB and General Walsh entered the picture. On February 12, 1952, JIOA Director Heckemeyer asked Walsh to help Schreiber find a job so that he could resettle in Argentina. Walsh began working on the problem the very same day, when he attended a special IADB function held in honor of Argentina's Brigadier Mayor Aristóbulo F. Reyes, whom he had known for a number of years. Reyes served as the Argentine delegate to the IADB from 1945 to 1949 and in 1955.[37]

Walsh's collaborator in this scheme was Lieutenant General Charles L. Bolté, who had replaced Walsh in 1948 as director of intelligence at EUCOM and now was chairman of the IADB. Walsh and Bolté held several meetings with Reyes to discuss Schreiber's case. They told him that Schreiber could make a valuable contribution to the Argentine government, considering his extensive experience in sanitary engineering and his research in the prevention of disease and epidemics. Of course, they did not mention that Schreiber had obtained his expertise as a result of experiments conducted on concentration camp inmates. Instead, in a memo Walsh portrayed Schreiber as an innocent victim of adverse publicity instigated by Jews in the United States. "Dr. Schreiber apparently had some association with the Nazi regime and I would believe in a completely military capacity," Walsh explained. He told Reyes that Finletter was aware of their negotiations, and as proof of their good faith, Walsh showed Reyes a copy of Finletter's public statement.[38]

Reyes returned to Argentina, and after he and a U.S. Air Force officer in Buenos Aires pulled a few strings, the Argentine government approved Schreiber's immigration. On May 22, 1952, Schreiber, his wife, his mother in-law, and his son left New Orleans to resettle in Buenos Aires.[39]

But that was not the end of the Argentina-Paperclip connection. By the late 1950s the JIOA was bringing German scientists who worked in Argentina to the United States under Paperclip and National Interest. Glenn Martin aircraft (now Martin Marietta) and Republic Aviation had recruited a large number of former Focke-Wulf aircraft engineers and designers who were part of Kurt Tank's group and brought them back to America.

One Focke-Wulf designer had been working for Martin since 1950. Hans Multhopp, a former Nazi party member, designed a jet fighter while working for Focke-Wulf in Bremen during the war that the Russians later developed into the MIG-15. After the war Multhopp and other German aviation experts worked at Farnborough, England, contributing to Britain's fighter plane development. Multhopp was brought to the United States in 1950 and became chief scientist at the Martin-Baltimore Division. In 1964 Martin proudly displayed another aircraft designed by Multhopp that could take off from the Pentagon courtyard with a 1,000-pound bomb and fly at a speed of 300 miles per hour.[40]

In 1957 the chief of personnel for the Army's rocket group in Huntsville, Alabama, which included Wernher von Braun, planned to go on a recruiting trip to Argentina. He asked JIOA officers for their opinions about hiring Tank's group. But the JIOA immediately squelched the idea. "The Germans remaining, with a couple of exceptions, are not outstanding," the JIOA officers replied. They went on to explain that the majority of Tank's group already was working in the United States.[41]

10 Spies, Spooks, and LSD

EDGEWOOD Arsenal, the most secret military base in the country, is located in a secluded area on the Chesapeake Bay twenty miles northeast of Baltimore, Maryland. A high fence stretches for miles around the facility to shield the Army's secret work on chemical warfare from the prying eyes of the American public. The arsenal has always been the Army's center for chemical warfare and the base's original mission has never changed. It is charged with finding out how and why poison gas works; discovering antidotes to its lethal effects; and inventing new, ever-deadlier clouds of poison that bring a swift, painful death.[1]

Edgewood was the first American installation to test lethal agents on humans. The experiments began in 1922, when the Chemical Warfare Service created a Medical Research Division charged with providing a defense against chemical agents.

157

Since that time, thousands of military and civilian "volunteers" have been used in experiments with mustard and nerve gas, riot-control agents, LSD, PCP, mescaline, and hundreds of other chemicals, including many that had been rejected by manufacturers for commercial use because they contained deadly poisons, such as dioxin.[2]

Some of those experiments were conducted at Edgewood's medical facilities, in isolation rooms with barred windows, padded walls, and furniture bolted to the floor. It was in such a room that Master Sergeant James Stanley was locked in February 1958. The young soldier was based at Fort Knox, Kentucky, and had volunteered to participate in experiments to test protective chemical warfare clothing. Instead Stanley became an unwitting victim of mind-control experiments with psychochemicals, including LSD.[3]

Stanley remembered sitting across a table from a white-coated doctor with two glasses of clear liquid between them. "Here, have a drink," said the doctor, as he handed Stanley one of them. "It's only water, nothing more than what I drink," the doctor promised, knowing full well that it contained LSD. An hour later Stanley thought he had gone insane. His head was filled with terrifying visions and his body seemed to tumble through time and space. Then his mind snapped and sent him into a frenzy of rage.[4]

"They told me the next day that I broke down the door and ran down the hall screaming," Stanley recalled. But his misery continued as he underwent three more experiments. In one he was given an even stronger dose of LSD, which made him violently ill. The other experiments were apparently an attempt to induce amnesia. Stanley was injected with an unknown substance and then asked if he knew where he was. The soldier felt as if his body was on fire, and he vaguely remembered telling the doctor that he was standing by a river. The last experiment was more successful at wiping away his memory. "I cannot account for that day at all," Stanley said.[5]

The story of Edgewood provides another glaring example of how information about Paperclip is still being covered up today—despite a massive congressional investigation in the 1970s into Edgewood's experiments, and despite legal action Stanley took that by 1986 had worked its way up to the U.S. Supreme Court. For all that, the secret Paperclip connections at the base remain unexposed.

The fact that Paperclip scientists worked at Edgewood at various times between 1947 and 1966 has been kept a closely guarded secret. Dr. Seymour Silver, who was scientific director of Edgewood during that time, is highly critical of the Paperclip project. "The whole judgment of who to pick, what they did, and who they selected was very faulty, very bad," Silver recalled, adding that none of the scientists were experts on chemical warfare.[6]

Kurt Rahr was one of the first Paperclip specialists to arrive at the base. Rahr was young, brash, and had a background in high-frequency electronics. When he arrived in September 1947, he was evading a prison sentence, having been convicted by German courts of bigamy, falsifying papers, using an alias, and lying about his Nazi past. JIOA officers had received numerous reports that Rahr was a compulsive liar and a security threat. His *OMGUS Security Report* noted: "Subject should be considered an absolute security threat to the United States."[7]

Despite the derogatory reports, JIOA approved Rahr's Paperclip contract and he was assigned to work at Edgewood. Army officers there did not know quite what to do with him. Lieutenant F. E. Van Sickle complained that Rahr made "conflicting statements" about his past, but he brushed them off as evidence of an "unusual imagination." The Army confined his work to unclassified areas, such as repairing equipment and translating Russian documents. In 1948 another German scientist, Hans Trurnit, accused Rahr of being a Communist, and Rahr was sent back to Germany.[8]

Trurnit himself arrived at Edgewood in 1947 and went to work in Silver's toxicology laboratory. During the war, Trurnit had joined the Nazi party and four other Nazi organizations. From 1934 until 1940 he was an assistant to the notorious

Professor Holzlöhner at the University of Kiel, though Trurnit left the university shortly before Holzlöhner became heavily involved in the cold experiments on Dachau prisoners discussed earlier. Trurnit then worked for a short time at the University of Heidelberg before joining the German military medical corps. "He was never in chemical warfare," Silver said. "He went to Stalingrad, got tuberculosis, and was medically discharged out of the Army for a couple of years until the war stopped." While Trurnit may not have been a Nazi ideologue, his wife was. "She was a Hitler lover who couldn't stand a democracy, so she went back to Germany," Silver said in an interview.[9]

Another Paperclip scientist, Theodor Wagner-Jauregg, arrived in 1948. He too had been a member of the Nazi party and four other Nazi organizations. Wagner-Jauregg had been chief of chemical research at the Institute for Chemotherapeutics in Frankfurt, where his research focused on the use of chemotherapy to cure leprosy, tuberculosis, and typhus. After the war Wagner-Jauregg worked on insecticides at the German Society for Pest Control. "His father was Sigmund Freud's antagonist," recalled Silver. The elder Wagner-Jauregg was the famous Austrian psychiatrist whom Freud publicly criticized for treating schizophrenia by injecting patients with malaria virus.[10]

Friedrich Hoffmann was the fourth Paperclip scientist to arrive at Edgewood in the late 1940s. He was not a Nazi party member, and although he applied for SA membership, he did not join that Nazi organization either. During the war Hoffmann was a chemist who synthesized poison gases and toxins for the University of Wuerzburg's Chemical Warfare Laboratories and the Luftwaffe's Technical Research Institute located near Berlin. In 1946 he worked as a consultant for the Chemical Section of OMGUS in Berlin.[11]

The German scientists' main job under Paperclip was to test the poison gases that had been invented by the Nazis during the war. Two nerve gases, Tabun and Sarin, were the most deadly agents the American military had ever encountered, and it was essential that new types of gas masks and protective clothing, as well as an antidote to their lethal effects, be developed. Wagner-Jauregg worked on an anti-inflammatory drug for poison gas infections. Hoffmann compiled bibliographies of literature on toxic chemicals, wrote reports, and conducted tests using some of the 10 tons of nerve and mustard gas that had been shipped from Germany to Edgewood and other American arsenals in 1946. Trurnit worked on physics problems and built a special machine in Silver's lab to measure thin films.[12]

To learn how Tabun affected humans, the scientists analyzed data in captured German documents dealing with Tabun nerve gas experiments on concentration camp inmates. One American scientist, Dr. J. H. Wills, used the camp experiment records to determine not only the amount needed to kill a human but the specific effects of Tabun, such as its ability to render a man unconscious within two minutes. Wills's final report noted an obvious conclusion: the "age of the subject seemed to make no difference in the lethality of the toxic vapor."[13]

Soldiers at the base were used as the guinea pigs in Tabun and mustard gas experiments conducted in Edgewood's own gassing chamber. In a scene horribly reminiscent of the Nazi death camps, Don Bowen remembered what it was like to sit in the large chamber and breathe the toxic fumes. After being led in, he was told to remove his gas mask at a given signal. As he waited he saw that there were dozens of animals, including dogs, cats, mice and rabbits, locked in cages covered with a clear plastic sheet along one side of the chamber. Then someone slammed the door shut and turned on the gas.[14]

"I waited five minutes and took off the mask," he said. The covers were ripped off the animals, and they went crazy. They ran around the cages, screaming, and then slumped onto the floor. "My immediate response was not to breathe. And when I finally did take a deep breath, the gas burned my nose, my lips and throat."[15]

Some of the soldiers were seriously injured in the mustard

tests. Two were hospitalized after being exposed to mustard gas up to fourteen separate times in the gassing chamber, and many others suffered serious skin injuries, including blistering that took several weeks to heal, after swatches of liquid mustard were taped to their arms. One Edgewood scientist noted in a report that in 1948 several soldiers who had been exposed to low concentrations of Tabun in Edgewood's chamber were "partially disabled for from one to three weeks with fatigue, lassitude, complete loss of initiative and interest, and apathy."[16]

In 1949 the direction of Edgewood's work abruptly changed. A consultant to the Chemical Division at EUCOM sent information about an amazing drug, LSD, that caused hallucinations and suicidal tendencies in humans. As a result, Edgewood's L. Wilson Greene seized the idea of conducting "psychochemical warfare." He listed sixty-one compounds, ranging from alcohol to mescaline, and speculated that if a small percentage of the enemy's troops or civilian population was exposed to those compounds they would suffer from symptoms of hysteria, panic, seizures, and hallucinations. "There can be no doubt that their will to resist would be weakened greatly, if not entirely destroyed, by the mass hysteria and panic which would ensue," Greene noted in his report. He then suggested that $50,000 be set aside in the 1950 budget to study psychochemicals.[17]

Ironically, Greene was trying to find a more humane way to wage war—one that would disable an enemy rather than kill him. But the CIA and military intelligence had a more sinister idea. They thought psychochemicals could be used as a cold war weapon to control the mind of an individual being interrogated. They suspected that the Soviets already were using brainwashing techniques, including hypnosis and drugs, on POWs and defendants in political trials. During the Hungarian government's trial of Cardinal József Mindszenty in 1949, for example, the cardinal confessed to crimes of treason he apparently did not commit, while sitting with a glazed look in his eyes.[18]

The intelligence agencies' key sources of information on anything related to chemical warfare were German or Austrian scientists who had worked for I. G. Farben—the company involved in manufacturing the Zyklon B gas used in concentration camps—many of whom were either in jail or under investigation by Nuremberg prosecutors. For example, Walter Reppe had been the chief chemist for I. G. Farben at Ludwigshaven and was jailed at Nuremberg shortly after the war. U.S. Army officers frequently got Reppe temporarily released from jail or transferred so that he could work on reports for the Army Chemical Corps. On September 14, 1948, Reppe and two of his former I. G. Farben associates were released into Army custody to work on an "opus" on acetylene derivatives. Colonel Patrick Fokers told a FIAT officer that Reppe's release from prison was justified because of the importance of acetylene chemistry to the U.S. Army. A year earlier U.S. Department of Commerce representative Robert Fry had told the State Department that even though Reppe was "very much a Nazi," he wanted to bring him to America under Paperclip. Fry's plans fell through when Reppe was taken to England to work for the British.[19]

One CIA source of information about "truth drugs" was Karl Tauboeck, I. G. Farben's leading wartime expert on sterilization drugs. Tauboeck had been the chief plant chemist at I. G. Farben's Ludwigshaven factory, where he specialized in the effects of drugs on animals and humans. After 1942 he devoted his time to research on the plant caladium seguenum, which the SS planned to use to sterilize mental patients and Jews. The SS wanted to keep this project secret, Tauboeck said, so that the "priests should not raise hell." Tauboeck testified at Nuremberg that he had recognized the criminal nature of the research and had not pursued it further. Others had, however. Hitler's personal physician, Karl Brandt, admitted that the plant was grown in a hothouse at Dachau and sterilization "experiments were conducted upon concentration camp prisoners."[20]

After the war, Tauboeck gave the CIA and the Office of

Naval Intelligence information about his secret wartime work on speech-inducing drugs. The Gestapo and Abwehr had been looking for a truth serum made from anabases aphylla plants to use on the German officers suspected of being involved in the plot to kill Hitler. They planned to slip the drug into the officers' drinks at a party, hoping they would confess. But Tauboeck said he could not locate enough plants to carry out the mission.[21]

Even with such information in hand, U.S. intelligence agents were tantalized by a number of unresolved questions: What chemical would force a man to reveal his secrets under interrogation? Could a drug cause total amnesia? Was there an antidote that would protect an American POW if the enemy used drugs on him? And the big question that preoccupied both Army intelligence and the CIA: could drugs or hypnosis, or a combination of both, serve as the ultimate mind-control weapon, sufficient to turn a man into a "Manchurian Candidate" (Richard Condon's fictional character who had been brainwashed and reprogrammed into an assassin)?

A combined CIA–military intelligence project code-named "Bluebird" and later renamed "Artichoke" was set up to find the answers to those questions. Significantly, the key military intelligence agency involved with this project—the Joint Intelligence Committee—had been involved in Paperclip from the beginning. The JIC members included U.S. Army Director of Intelligence Alexander Bolling and Brigadier General John Alexander Samford, the chief of Air Force intelligence who later headed the National Security Agency.

In addition to Bluebird, the CIA also began several mind-control projects of its own, including project MK-ULTRA, which involved LSD and other psychochemicals. The CIA's experiments eventually resulted in the death of Frank Olson, an Army scientist from Fort Detrick who jumped out of a hotel window after his CIA colleagues secretly slipped LSD into his drink.[22]

The link between Edgewood and the CIA was close. Many scientists who worked at Edgewood or under Edgewood contracts were on the CIA's payroll. Paperclip chemist Friedrich Hoffmann was a CIA consultant on psychochemicals. Dr. Ray Treichler was simultaneously assistant to the director of Edgewood's Medical Laboratories, the division in charge of human experimentation at the base, and a member of the CIA's Technical Services Staff (TSS), which was involved in the covert use of chemicals and germs against specific people. Psychiatrist Harold Abramson was a CIA consultant involved in the Olson case who also worked for Edgewood.[23]

At times the CIA used its covert methods on the Edgewood scientists themselves. "Do you know what a 'self-sustained, off-the-shelf operation' means?" Silver asked in an interview, referring to the Iran-contra scandal. "Well, the CIA was running one in my lab. They were testing psychochemicals and running experiments in my lab, using my people, and weren't telling me. They were spying on us. I said, 'You go spy on the enemy, not on us,' and I had the guard throw them out. It was a real off-the-shelf operation."[24]

By 1951, in the midst of the Korean War, the Paperclip scientists' primary job was to locate plants and poisons that could be turned into new hallucinogenic mind-control drugs. To find them Silver established an industrial liaison operation that was in contact with every major pharmaceutical company in the world. "We had worldwide reports of any observations that produced peculiar results or death," he said. "If you look for new chemicals, you have to look everywhere—into the Pacific Ocean, or follow a rumor about a Polynesian fisherman who goes into a trance."[25]

Paperclip scientist Hoffmann's skills as a chemist and his facility in several languages quickly were put to use. "He was our searcher," Silver said. "He was the guy who brought to our attention any discoveries that happened around the world and then said, 'Here's a new chemical, you'd better test it.'" Hoffmann's search led him all over the world. He traveled to foreign universities and visited marine labs and attended conferences in Switzerland, Czechoslovakia, Germany, England, Australia, Japan, and other countries. Toad venoms and poisonous fish from the South Pacific were among the samples that Hoffmann put into his black bag and brought back to Edgewood to be tested, synthesized, and turned into a new lethal agent or psychochemical. In Hawaii he found a conch shell that produced a highly active venom which it ejected through a hollow, needlelike tooth into its victim. The venom, according to Army intelligence records, caused "paralysis and visual blurring in man and has been responsible for several deaths."[26]

Hoffmann often used the University of Delaware as a cover at international symposiums to hide his connection to Edgewood and the CIA. In fact, Hoffmann had collaborated with William Mosher, the chairman of the university's chemistry department, and another scientist, on an article about marijuana for the *Journal of the American Chemical Society*. But Mosher's chemistry department itself may have been a CIA front. Mosher had been on the CIA's payroll for years, and another University of Delaware professor, James Moore, was heavily involved in the CIA's MK-ULTRA project as well as being funded openly by the Army Chemical Corps. "We were all being paid by the CIA," Moore said recently. Moore described his department chief as an "opportunist" who used the CIA's funds not only for research but to pay graduate students and generally to build up the university's chemistry program.[27]

Bluebird made full use of Hoffmann's discoveries with psychochemicals in experiments conducted at Edgewood or the Army intelligence base at Fort Holabird, Maryland. The participation of the CIA and JIC in the project was kept hidden by using a University of Maryland contract with Edgewood as a cover. At least a thousand soldiers, including James Stanley, were given up to twenty doses of LSD to test the drug as a possible interrogation weapon—even though Edgewood scientists already knew it could cause serious physical reactions in humans. In particular, Dr. Van Sim, the physician responsible for the human subjects used in Edgewood experiments, had worked at the British Chemical Defense Establishment at Porton Down, where similar psychochemical experiments were conducted on humans. Shortly after he returned to the United States, Sim warned that results of the British experiments had shown that "during acute LSD intoxication the subject is a potential danger to himself and to others; in some instances a delayed and exceptionally severe response may take place and be followed by serious after effects lasting several days."[28]

Nevertheless, test subjects at Edgewood or Fort Holabird were given LSD and other drugs, then subjected to hostile questioning by intelligence officers to deliberately create an extreme state of fear and anxiety. One soldier fought his way out of a locked box in stark terror during a Fort Holabird experiment. Several soldiers were seriously harmed by the tests. One man suffered a grand mal seisure; another went into an acute state of paranoia and had to be hospitalized for a week. Three others developed a history of epileptic seizures after the experiments. Like Stanley, none of the men knew what was happening to him.[29]

"I got shot in Korea and I can understand that," said Stanley. "That was part of my job because I was protecting my homeland. But when they give me LSD and use me as a guinea pig, then that is unforgivable."[30]

Another phase of the drug project involved interrogation teams, made up of three intelligence officers and a doctor, sent to Europe to assess how psychochemicals would work on suspected spies and defectors in a more "realistic" setting. The teams were under orders not to run their tests on Americans. But when a black American soldier, James Thornwell, emerged as a suspect in a document theft case in France, one team showed up to do a job on him. Thornwell later described in horrifying detail how he was locked in a room, pumped full of drugs, and grilled for days by interrogators who screamed obscenities at him. Thornwell later sued the government, claiming that the drugs had turned him into an epileptic. In 1984 Thornwell drowned in his own swimming pool. The coroner who examined him said the accident might have been caused by an epileptic seizure.[31]

With Bluebird off and running, Edgewood began preparing

for Armageddon amid the chill of the cold war not only by relying on Nazis here at home for their evil experiments but also by tapping the twisted minds of those still living in Germany. As mentioned earlier, U.S. laws governing the American zone of Germany forbade the Germans from doing research on chemical warfare. But that did not stop the Army Chemical Corps or the High Commissioner of Germany, the U.S. organization that replaced OMGUS, from hiring chemical warfare experts as "consultants" or funding German industries to produce chemical warfare materials for the United States.[32]

West Germany came under severe criticism when evidence surfaced in 1989 that German chemical companies had been helping Libya build a chemical warfare plant. In particular, a column written by influential *New York Times* columnist William Safire refering to "Auschwitz-in-the-Sand" ominously cited the reemergence of "the German problem." But neither Safire nor anyone else mentioned that it was the U.S. government who had put the German chemical warfare experts back to work soon after World War II, under the banner of the American flag.[33]

The U.S. agencies' employment of German scientists living in the American zone was an enormous operation. At one point HICOG's scientific director, Carl Nordstrom, had at least 150 Germans working for him as consultants. They offered advice or gave U.S. agencies information about their wartime research. At the same time, the Army Chemical Corps employed some thirty German chemical warfare experts to conduct secret nerve gas research for the Chemical Division of EUCOM. Many of these scientists met with Hoffmann when he traveled to Germany seeking information about psychochemicals or other new chemical discoveries. Others, like convicted Nazi war criminal Otto Ambros, were flown to the United States to work as consultants under National Interest for American corporations such as Ambros's employer, the W. R. Grace Company.[34]

Former SS Brigadier General Walter Schieber was among

the more notorious individuals on the U.S. payroll. One army officer called him "the prototype of an ardent and convinced Nazi who used the Party to further his own ambitions." Nevertheless, he worked for more than a decade for the Chemical Division at EUCOM, where he was given access to highly classified information about U.S. chemical warfare activities. At one point he even helped the division make nerve gas.[35]

Schieber, a chemist, had been in charge of the Nazi Armaments Supply office under Albert Speer during the war. He supervised the seizure of arms factories in France and other Nazi-occupied countries, and later in the war oversaw the Nazi's chemical warfare program. Thousands of civilians were forcibly brought to Nazi Germany to work as slave laborers in armaments factories under Schieber's control. In 1945 he was jailed as a war crimes suspect.[36]

Speer was convicted at Nuremberg and sentenced to twenty years in prison, but Schieber saved his skin by serving as a star witness at the Nuremberg trials and writing chemical warfare reports for the U.S. Army while he was still in jail. By 1947 U.S. intelligence agents had decided that Schieber's knowledge of chemical warfare was more important than his Nazi past. "Several obstacles were overcome by American authorities before Schieber's scientific knowledge could be exploited," one Army CIC agent noted. One of those obstacles was removed when U.S. intelligence officers got him released from prison. Within a short time Schieber was making DM 1,000 a month working for the Chemical Division at EUCOM.[37]

Air Force Colonel Donald Putt tried to bring Schieber to Wright-Patterson under Paperclip, but his scheme was squelched by an Army CIC investigation of Schieber's involvement with shady characters all over Europe. Schieber had French contacts who had offered him $50,000 for Nazi nerve gas formulas contained in documents he kept in his house. Some of his Swiss friends were arms smugglers who supplied weapons to SS officers on the run. And Schieber's frequent business dealings with Soviet officials in the eastern zone raised

Army CIC suspicions that he might be a spy. Schieber himself managed to kill the Army CIC's investigation by complaining to HICOG's Frank Perkerson that "convoys" of CIC agents constantly drove by his house and demanding that the CIC's investigation be stopped. Shortly afterward, one CIC agent wrote his superior in frustration, complaining that he "never received answers to leads forwarded, information requested or results of Central Registry checks." His investigation was squelched and Schieber continued working for the United States until 1956.[38]

The legacy of Paperclip back at home was set now that Edgewood had made its pact with the devil. The drug experimentation project quickly expanded to include psychiatric patients, who were drugged, shocked, and hypnotized in psychochemical experiments conducted under Army contracts with numerous universities and other institutions.

Some of the experiments duplicated those conducted by Nazi doctors in the concentration camps. American psychiatrist Paul Hoch's experiments on mental patients at the New York Psychiatric Institute, where he was working under Edgewood contracts and as a CIA consultant, killed one patient and seriously injured another. Harold Blauer died from an overdose of methyl di-amphetamine, or MDA, known on the street as the "love drug," the same day that another patient, a twenty-one-year-old girl, went into convulsions after being injected with the same drug. As a federal judge later stated, "no diagnostic or therapeutic purpose for Blauer, himself, was ever intended from the injections." Their sole purpose was to gather data for the Army's investigation of the use of mescaline derivatives for interrogations. Even after Blauer's death, the Army approved additional experiments on patients that included the use of hypnosis, drugs, and a polygraph exam to determine if "a particular personality type might 'break' more rapidly under a drug stress than another type" during military interrogations.[39]

In short, experiments on our own soldiers at Edgewood mirrored the horror stories that had unfolded in the dock at

Nuremberg. Thousands of American soldiers, seven thousand of them between 1955 and 1975 alone, were used as unwitting guinea pigs in the tests. They were gassed, maced, and drugged in the search for the ultimate mind-control weapon.[40]

Ironically, one part of the Nuremberg code was established to prevent a repeat of the Nazi atrocities. And the secretary of the Army ordered that the guidelines be followed at Edgewood. "The voluntary consent of the human subject is absolutely essential," the secretary directed in 1957. "This means that the person involved should have legal capacity to give consent; should be so situated as to be able to exercise free power of choice without the intervention of any element of force, fraud, deceit, duress, over-reaching, or other ulterior form of constraint or coercion." The secretary's directive further provided that "in all experiments involving volunteer test subjects, the individuals are thoroughly informed about all procedures, and what can be expected during each test."[41]

But a 1975 investigation by the Army's inspector general determined that "in spite of clear guidelines concerning the necessity for 'informed consent,' there was a willingness to dilute and in some cases negate the intent of the policy." The inspector general's report noted that soldiers who were duped into volunteering to test chemical warfare clothing and gas masks were then secretly given nerve gas, psychochemicals, incapacitating agents, and hundreds of other experimental and dangerous drugs. They were given no information about the chemicals used on them in the experiments, no warning that those chemicals might harm them, and no follow-up medical exam to determine whether they had been hurt by the tests.[42]

In one series of experiments the Army's search for a chemical that would produce total amnesia led them to Sernyl (SNA) —now commonly known as PCP or angel dust—an extremely dangerous drug. SNA originated as a general anesthetic but was taken off the market for human use because it caused delirium as patients emerged from the anesthesia. SNA is known to produce a delayed psychotic reaction similar to schizophrenia, and long-term effects can include permanent brain damage. Soldiers were given SNA orally or in aerosol form while walking on treadmills. The experiment apparently succeeded in producing total amnesia in at least one subject. Two other soldiers had intense "manic" reactions after being given doses of SNA with alcohol, and three more collapsed during the experiments.[43]

Other experiments involved at least 123 irritant chemicals, including one that had been contaminated with dioxin. These agents included Mace and CS, an even stronger riot-control agent that causes extreme irritation to mucous membranes. One group of men were subjected to five consecutive aerosol exposures of Mace. They stood inside a gas chamber and were told to take off their gas masks, then resist leaving until the pain became unbearable. Another 1,366 soldiers were exposed to CS, including some who had the agent dropped directly into their eyes.[44]

Steven Bonner was locked inside a padded room at Edgewood and given intravenous injections of CAR 302,688, an extremely potent incapacitating agent. The experiment itself was terrifying for him—Bonner imagined seeing enormous black spiders crawling all over the walls and ceiling of his room. Afterward, his life was cruelly endangered when he was shipped to a combat zone in Vietnam, where he had to fight off flashbacks while on guard duty.[45]

In late 1957 Edgewood doctors placed eight glasses of clear liquid in front of Kenneth Loeh and seven other men. Loeh remembered that things got "funny and giggly" before he and the others went outside to march. "It was about this time I began to realize something was wrong." A buzzing started over him, then he saw pulsating circles "like a Looney Tune cartoon. I remember falling out of ranks and walking to the side and telling this guy 'I want out of this!' I started feeling the tightness in my chest and the hands going numb." Loeh remembered falling down and hanging onto a soldier's pant leg.[46]

It was then that Loeh realized he was no longer a volunteer, but a victim. He tried to scream. "But when my mouth opened

I felt like I was swallowing myself. I thought I was going to die. Then I blacked out."[47]

Several soldiers suffered grand mal seizures as a result of experiments. One man went into a seizure three hours after having been injected with 2-PAM, a strong incapacitating agent. Another was hospitalized for anxiety, restlessness, and agitation after being given four different compounds, including an intravenous injection of the Soman nerve agent. Another soldier was sent to Walter Reed Army Hospital for psychiatric observation after being given a compound known to cause vomiting, nausea, and dehydration that gave him attacks of anxiety, acute agitation, and hysteria. Still another soldier reported having blood in his urine for at least a year after having been intravenously injected with a compound called EA3834.[48]

Many soldiers felt the residual effects of the experiments long after they left Edgewood. "I have experienced memory loss and my personality has changed dramatically," Bonner said. But that was only the beginning of Bonner's nightmare. His first child was born with multiple birth defects: an open spine, paralysis from the waist down, and water on the brain—all of which Bonner felt were caused by the drugs he was given at Edgewood.[49]

One soldier never got a chance to see what the long-term effects were; he committed suicide. Another attempted to commit suicide by slashing his wrists; still another tried to jump off a bridge.[50]

The Army's reaction to all of this was to close ranks and cover up information about the experiments. None of the soldiers could find out what had happened to them. Stanley could not understand why he was suffering memory loss and violent outbursts of temper. Thornwell did not know who was responsible for what had happened to him in that room in France. Loeh was hospitalized twenty-eight times for convulsions, and during the night he would constantly see flashbacks of the experiment, forcing him to live through the terror again and again. The Veterans Administration consistently denied him benefits. When Loeh cited the experiments, the Army denied that they had ever taken place.[51]

Twenty years would pass before Stanley finally learned the truth. And when he did, his observation about what had happened at Edgewood was chillingly close to the mark. "It was just like nazism to do me that way," he said.[52]

He didn't know how right he was.

Pipeline to the Alamac Hotel

11

T HE Alamac Hotel was located at Seventy-first Street and Broadway in New York City. Thousands of convention-eers, tourists, and other visitors had stayed in the nineteen-story hotel through the years. But the identities of some Alamac guests were kept a closely guarded secret from the American public. Army intelligence officers used a suite of rooms as a Paperclip office for decades, though they kept their Army connections secret by working in civilian clothes. They greeted scientists when their ships arrived, processed their immigration papers, and catered to their needs in the hotel. By the time Paperclip was shut down in the 1970s at least a thousand German and Austrian scientists had lived in the Alamac for months at a time while the military helped them find jobs.[1]

Paperclip, National Interest, and a new project, code-named

175

"63," operated nonstop during the 1950s despite numerous complaints that the projects were illegal and caused serious political tensions between the United States and the West German government. Up to 1950, 665 individuals were employed under Paperclip. Notwithstanding U.S. policies in force since 1948 that barred recruiting, and no matter who complained or what political problems were caused, the military stubbornly refused to stop the projects. The fact that 687 more Germans and Austrians were brought to the United States under Paperclip alone from 1950 through 1959 shows how little effect the complaints had on the projects.[2]

In November 1950, JIOA Director Daniel Ellis unleashed Project 63, which proved as controversial as Paperclip. This project's admitted sole purpose was to get the scientists out of Europe and away from the Russians. The scientists were paid $5,000 and given temporary visas to come to America for six months to look for jobs while being lodged in the Alamac Hotel. Most went to work for universities or defense contractors, not the U.S. government. Thus the American taxpayer footed the bill for a project to help former Nazis obtain jobs with Lockheed, Martin Marietta, North American Aviation, or other defense contractors during a time when many American engineers in the aircraft industry were being laid off.[3]

The European end of the operation was run by the Army's Special Projects Team from the Intelligence Division of U.S. Army headquarters. The team interviewed and contracted scientists for all JIOA projects in the field or from the team's offices in Frankfurt and Munich. For awhile, the Frankfurt office was located just inside the gate at Camp King, but later it was moved because of security reasons to two floors in a house across the street from the I. G. Farben building. Active recruitment was not necessary, since scientists all over West Germany already knew the location of the team's offices. Only the American public had been duped into believing that the project had ended in 1947.[4]

" 'Recruiting' was a nasty word," recalled retired U.S. Army Master Sergeant George Meidlein, who was with the project for over a decade at the Alamac and as a team contractor in Germany. "Everything was word of mouth. A scientist would get to the States and somebody would say, 'How'd you get here?' They'd say, 'Contact Mr. Meidlein in Frankfurt and he'll visit you.' And that's the way we got customers." Meidlein wore civilian clothes and traveled around West Germany in an Army car with German license plates so that the scientists' bosses would not know they were dealing with Americans. "We didn't want to jeopardize the scientist's job until we were prepared to offer him a contract," said Meidlein.[5]

Soon after Project 63 was in force, one of the team's recruiters, Ernest Richter, headed for Austria, where he found an untapped source of scientific talent. Geographer Karl Neumaier was making maps for the U.S. Forces in Austria, as he had done for German intelligence during the war in China, Romania, and the Balkans. Chemical warfare expert Rudolph Ulm headed a chemical lab in Tyrol. In 1945 Ulm had been interned by the British when A. K. Mills's technical intelligence team captured Ulm at the chemical warfare experimental station at Spandau. Another Austrian, Wilhelm Lohninger, ran a nitrogen works in Linz. During the war, Lohninger had been employed in the Speer Armaments Ministry supervising war munition factories confiscated by the Nazis in France and Belgium.[6]

Richter's efforts to hire the Austrians were hindered by their negative attitude toward the United States. "They consider the U.S., culturally speaking, a backward country," Richter observed. He suggested that recruiters could counter that attitude by mentioning television musical programs and the Metropolitan Opera as proof that America was not as lacking in culture as the Austrians believed.[7]

The team had more serious problems with the Russians. Like Germany, Austria had been divided into separate Allied zones, and some of the scientists were working in the Soviet zone or were members of the Communist party. For example, Karl Krejci-Graf, a well-known geological expert, was director of the Soviet's Geologic Institute in Vienna. In 1944 Krejci-

Graf had represented German oil interests when the Nazis occupied Hungary. He was arrested and interned in 1945 by U.S. authorities in Austria because of his high SS rank. Another Austrian, biological warfare expert Fritz Kress, was working for the Russians on a study of diseases that deliberately caused abortion in cattle.[8]

The Austrians' excuses as to why they had joined the Communist party were similar to those Germans made for having joined the Nazi party. For example, supersonics engineer Otto Golling told recruiters that he had been "forced to join" the Communist party to obtain employment after the war. He first had worked for the French Air Ministry in Paris and the British in London before returning to the Soviet zone in 1947. The team tried to reduce the Soviet influence over Golling by arranging for his relocation to the U.S. zone of Austria. Another Austrian, Ludwig Ettenreich, was director of the C. P. Goerz optical works in Vienna, which produced lenses exclusively for the Soviets. Ettenreich told the team that he had resigned from the Communist party and no longer held Communist views. But an investigation later determined that Ettenreich's name was still on the party's rolls.[9]

Other scientists had been ardent Nazis during the war. Alfred Kepka, the inventor of the Madrid rocket, had joined the Austrian Nazi party in 1927 and was such a Nazi activist that he had been awarded the Golden Party Badge. Others had been members of the SS. A well-known coal dust explosives expert, Mario Zippermayr, had joined the SS in 1933. And geologist Frederich Hecht had even been jailed by U.S. Forces in Austria officers and fired from the University of Graz because of his SS membership.[10]

Ellis and other JIOA officers were so unconcerned about the Nazi backgrounds of those they wanted to employ under Project 63 that they even considered contracting convicted Nazi war criminals who were still in prison. Take, for example, the case of Eduard Houdremont, who was still serving a prison sentence from his war crimes conviction at Nuremberg. Ellis and seven other officers discussed Houdremont and other dubious individuals during a meeting at which they decided which scientists on the JIOA's "K" list should be excluded from being hired under Project 63. Individuals in the "K" category were those whose skills should be denied to the Russians at any cost.[11]

Houdremont had been a top official of Krupp and was convicted at Nuremberg for his involvement in Krupp's massive slave labor program. Thousands of Eastern European Jews had been deported to Nazi Germany to work as slaves in Krupp factories, including a steel plant run by Houdremont. Yet the officers failed to mention this man's crimes or the fact that he had been convicted of complicity in the murder of hundreds of Jews who were beaten or starved to death. Instead the JIOA's brief discussion of whether to offer Houdremont a contract went like this:

> "The point to consider is whether the newspaper publicity would be adverse if he were brought over," JIOA member Max Brokaw said.
>
> "If the man is on the 'K' list and he should be brought over, we should do it regardless of the publicity," replied JIOA Deputy Director James H. Skinner.[12]

The JIOA officers did not even pretend to have screened other individuals on their list. Austrian Karl Kamptner was still on the JIOA's list even though the FBI was investigating him for having wrongfully obtained industrial information by posing as a member of the U.S. government. Although the officers did not indicate that they now planned to employ Kamptner again under Project 63, there was no explanation of why the list even included a man under FBI investigation.[13]

Brokaw told the group that although the Austrians' backgrounds had not been completely investigated, the plan was to put them under contract and bring them to the United States, "in which case some of them may have to be 'bought off' later if they are found inadmissible."[14]

Kurt Blome was one scientist whom the JIOA "bought off"

when the State Department refused to give him a visa because of his notorious Nazi past. Blome, who had held the rank of major general in the SA, had been a defendant in the Nuremberg Medical Case, in which he was charged with participating in euthanasia, extermination of tubercular Poles, biological warfare, and various deadly experiments. Blome had been the key biological warfare representative on the Reich Research Council, which had approved, funded, and commissioned experiments in the camps. Blome had told Alsos interrogators after the war that SS chief Himmler had ordered him in 1943 to conduct plague vaccine experiments on camp inmates. Blome had suggested to Himmler that Blome's new institute, then under construction in Poznan, would be better suited for the experiments than a camp because it was isolated. Himmler had then assigned an SS doctor to help with the work. The Alsos agent commented that during the interrogation Blome "had no hesitation in repeatedly referring to his intentions to use humans for his work on plague."[15]

Despite this admission, the Nuremberg tribunal acquitted Blome of all charges and concerning the biological warfare charge stated: "It may well be that defendant Blome was preparing to experiment on human beings in connection with bacteriological warfare, but the record fails to disclose that fact, or that he ever actually conducted the experiments." The Alsos interrogation was not submitted as evidence in the trial.[16]

Two months after Blome's acquittal, four representatives of Fort Detrick—the Maryland army base that was also headquarters of the CIA's biological warfare program—interviewed Blome about biological warfare. Dr. H. W. Batchelor set the tone for the meeting when he said, "We have friends in Germany, scientific friends, and this is an opportunity for us to enjoy meeting him [Blome] to discuss our various problems with him." During a lengthy interview Blome identified biological warfare experts and their locations and described different methods of conducting biological warfare.[17]

In 1951 JIOA's recruiters signed Blome under a Project 63 contract to work for the Army Chemical Corps. Not one background investigation reported Blome's Nuremberg trial or his 1945 arrest for high SA rank. On his personnel forms Blome conveniently omitted any reference to where he had been from 1945 to 1948. Despite Blome's cleaned-up files, the U.S. consul in Frankfurt ruled him inadmissible for immigration due to the incriminating Alsos report. JIOA officers were afraid that if they canceled Blome's contract, other German scientists might not sign contracts at all. In several meetings with Blome, an army officer told him that the reason he could not go to the United States was that the project had been canceled. After a long negotiation Blome finally agreed to work as a doctor at Camp King for the duration of his Project 63 contract.[18]

The way Ellis ran Project 63 was as controversial as the backgrounds of some of those the JIOA recruited. The State Department's scientific adviser, Dr. J. B. Koepfli, sent numerous complaints to the secretary of state and other officials in Washington about the questionable activities of some recruiters involved in the operation. One officer got into serious personal trouble during a recruiting trip in Germany. Another Special Projects Team member was a former diamond merchant from Los Angeles named Ehrman whose methods included handing out his personal business cards during meetings with German scientists. "You can imagine the reaction in German scientific circles of having a stranger and a diamond merchant calling on the most outstanding German scientists, including Nobel prize winners, offering a dubious contract in the name of the U.S. government," Koepfli reported.[19]

The team also sent fliers describing Project 63 to nearly every German scientist living in the U.S. zone. The sales pitch in these flyers would have been more suited to selling used cars than to convincing highly intelligent scientists to move to America. As a result, the Germans were either indignant over the crass approach or were convinced that the United States feared an immediate Soviet invasion of West Germany and was using this method to evacuate German scientists from the danger zone.[20]

A number of Germans complained angrily that the Special Projects Team had lied to them about the contracts. For example, Helmut Ruska was in charge of the Berlin Institute for Micromorphology and had signed on for Project 63 because he had wanted to find a position with an American university. After he arrived at the Alamac, however, the military pressured him to accept jobs at military bases and refused to pay for his transportation to attend job interviews at universities. Another Project 63 recruit was unhappy from the minute he arrived in the country. Former Luftwaffe parachute designer Wilhelm Buss worked under a short-term Project 63 contract at Edwards Air Force Base in California. Buss complained that the heat and altitude made him sick and that he had been charged for Alamac Hotel accommodations that he thought would be provided free.[21]

In 1952, American officials in West Germany dove for cover when they learned that a new twenty-man recruiting team for Project 63 was heading their way. This team included Air Force Colonel Gerold Crabbe, the JIOA deputy director; Air Force Colonel Arthur S. Randak; Colonel Edward Berry from G-2; four U.S. civilians, including ex–diamond merchant Ehrman; six Paperclip specialists; and an assortment of lesser military personnel. U.S. High Commissioner John McCloy warned the secretary of state that he had the "gravest fears" that this effort would result in a "violent reaction" from West German officials.[22]

Indeed, the situation reached such a crisis that even the CIA complained. Dr. Karl Weber ran a CIA operation collecting information about Soviet science by interrogating persons who had escaped from the east to West Germany. The JIOA's recruiters already had disrupted Weber's operation once, when they tried to recruit some of his people. He complained to the CIA's scientific advisor that the recruiters were "inept." But he was most concerned about the political repercussions. The West German government had threatened to intercede unless the recruiting was stopped, because it conflicted with NATO regulations and U.S. policies in West Germany.[23]

JIOA Deputy Director Crabbe was a week late for a scheduled meeting with Weber to discuss the problems. "In the meantime the JIOA group was well on its way to the repetition of previous blunders," Weber noted. When the meeting finally did take place, with Weber, HICOG's chief scientist Carl Nordstrom, Crabbe, and Berry, Weber complained that the JIOA's list of recruitment possibilities included people who were "too old, too rich, too busy and too thoroughly disgruntled with past experience with Americans" to justify trying to hire them. In return, Crabbe and Berry told Nordstrom that they regarded the CIA as "saboteurs and obstructionists."[24]

The JIOA's recruiting did not end, despite the complaints. In fact, they increased recruiting efforts for Paperclip as well. Even the reason for continuing that project was two-faced. On the one hand, Paperclip was defined in its policy as a project to exploit the skills of German scientists. But behind the scenes, the project was still viewed by those who ran it as a useful tool in the cold war game against the Russians. The military used the project to obtain military and political intelligence information about the USSR and the Soviet zone of Germany. As one Air Force history reported, "the loss of such intelligence and utilization to those powers not in sympathy with our way of life illustrated the program's 'denial value.' "[25]

Crabbe took over as JIOA director in 1953. "Crabbe was the typical pre–World War II aviator. If you couldn't shoot it or eat it, he didn't care about it," recalled retired Army Colonel Bernard Geehan, who served on the JIOA from 1953 to 1957. Geehan strongly believed that the United States received invaluable benefits from Paperclip and other JIOA projects. "It would have been an absolute sin to have wasted this opportunity," Geehan said.[26]

Geehan also claimed that there were no problems during his tenure with the JIOA. "There was nothing underhanded, we had nothing to conceal," he said. "There were no war criminals. We had to be careful." He described the State Department as uncooperative. "Their deadpan GS-12 bureaucrat asked no questions about morality, only about a misplaced comma in the paperwork."[27]

Geehan said the JIOA had several run-ins with the CIA

during the time he was in the agency. One incident occurred after the JIOA contracted with two German scientists from Darmstadt. "All of a sudden two guys in black suits showed up at my house," he recalled. "I thought, 'my God, it's the IRS.' But they were spooks from the CIA. They said they had a problem because our two German recruits were the CIA's undercover sources in R and D [Research and Development]."[28]

Paperclip also got entangled in a fierce turf fight between the CIA and the FBI in the United States. The CIA's 1947 charter forbids the agency from operating within the continental United States. Yet Geehan said the JIOA discovered that the CIA had spied on two Paperclip scientists who worked at Ohio State University. The scientists were terrified because they were being followed. "One man called the FBI and said it must be the Russians," Geehan recalled. "Now, I thought it might have been a football coach from a competitive university, but certainly not the Russians. We later found out it was the CIA."[29]

The practice of employing foreign rather than American workers led to strong complaints from the federal employees' union. Paperclip, it said, discriminated against American workers by granting Germans preferential treatment in the job market. But Air Force officers thought American workers were mediocre. In 1954, for example, the Air Force was trying to fill sixty-three vacancies at the Air Research and Development Command laboratories. Air Force recruiters interviewed engineers who had been laid off from North American Aviation in California, but reported that these workers were of "low caliber, essentially technicians, even though they termed themselves engineers." To fill the jobs, the Air Force sent its own six-man team to Germany, where they recruited thirty-five ex-Nazi colleagues of the German old-boy network working for Colonel Donald Putt at Wright-Paterson Air Force Base.[30]

The JIOA had problems clearing three of these recruits because they were agents in Germany's intelligence service. Herbert Alfke, for example, was a physicist and high-frequency specialist for the Plendl Institute in Austria. He also continued his connections with German intelligence that he had established during World War II. Alfke had been a lieutenant in the Wehrmacht from 1941 to 1944 and an Abwehr officer at the German Embassy in Spain, where he engaged in clandestine intelligence activities against the Allies. The Air Force contracted him under Paperclip despite FBI and CIA reports that Alfke was considered a "potential security threat" due to his foreign intelligence connections.[31]

Most new recruits were former colleagues of earlier Paperclip employee Albert Patin, who had obtained his U.S. citizenship despite having admitted using hundreds of Jewish women as slave laborers in his factory. In the early 1950s, Patin started his own company, Ampatco Laboratories in Chicago, to design and manufacture automatic pilot devices for jet fighter planes similar to those made by his factory in Nazi Germany.[32]

Patin had given Putt a list of Germans he wanted to hire and said that their backgrounds were clean. "None of the persons . . . had affiliations with any extreme political parties, neither Nazi nor Communist," Patin claimed. The list included Willy Hornauer, former chief engineer and assistant to Patin in his factory during the war; Gerhard Klein, chief of development at Siemens electric company; and several men who worked for the British government, including Johannes Gievers, chief engineer for Kreiselgeraete, a subsidiary of Askania that developed the gyro for the V-1 and V-2. But investigations uncovered derogatory information on Klein, despite Patin's claims to the contrary. Air Force Lieutenant Colonel Eugene Cook told the JIOA to drop Klein from the list "for security reasons."[33]

The Askania connections of some of the men also raised disturbing questions, since several top-level Askania officials, including a National Interest recruit, had been accused of collaborating with the Communists. In 1948, a German court charged Askania's technical director, Guido Wuensch, with "knowingly having delivered optical instruments to the Soviets" in an espionage case. Two years later, Wuensch was acquitted and brought to the United States to work for an Indiana company under a six-month contract. Wuensch then returned to Germany and resumed his position at Askania. He came under suspicion again in the mid-1950s when three Askania directors and several employees were convicted of selling half a million marks' worth of strategic military equipment to the Chinese Communists during the Korean War. Trial evidence revealed that some of Askania's directors, including Wuensch, were aware of the deal made with the Communists.[34]

In addition to the Air Force group, the Navy brought several biological warfare experts to the United States in the 1950s under Paperclip. For example, Anne Burger arrived in 1951 to work for a Navy biological warfare project at the Naval Medical Research Institute in Bethesda, Maryland. Burger had been a wartime assistant to Paperclip scientist Erich Traub, who arrived earlier. Their work for the Navy included conducting experiments on animals to determine the lethal doses of more than forty strains of highly infectious viruses.[35]

During the war Traub was in charge of biological warfare for the Reich Research Institute on the secluded island of Riems, where his biological warfare research specialty was viral and bacteriological diseases, including hoof and mouth disease and influenza. Traub's expertise fit right in with a scheme by SS chief Himmler to prepare a vaccine against the rinderpest virus and to conduct experiments to see whether the virus could be preserved for later use. Himmler had obtained a strain of rinderpest in Turkey and told Kurt Blome to send someone to collect it. Traub was chosen for the job, and after reporting to SS headquarters in Berlin he went to Turkey to get the rinderpest. Experiments were conducted at Riems on cows that were deliberately infected by smearing the virus on their lips. In 1945 the Riems institute was captured and reestablished by the Russians. Traub, Burger, and other biological warfare experts worked there for the Russians until 1948.[36]

Air Force Colonel Stone Christopher joined the JIOA in 1955. A veteran intelligence officer who had worked with British intelligence during World War II, Christopher was born in Stockholm, Sweden, and came to New York when he was eighteen. He joked about how his first name, Sten, was changed when he filled out his U.S. citizenship papers. "This guy looks at it says, 'well, that's Stone.' It's been Stone ever since."[37]

In October 1955, Christopher went to Frankfurt with Paperclip scientist Ernst Stuhlinger on a recruiting trip, traveling around West Germany to interview about five people a day who had been at Peenemünde during the war. Christopher said he felt that the men he interviewed were professionally unqualified to be included in the project. "I'm a stupid intelligence officer you know," he joked. "But everyone we investigated, we came up with the same conclusion that, well, 'he's a phony. . . .' " Christopher recalled that he also had met a group of former Peenemünde employees who now were working for the French government. The French would not allow the Germans to live in France, and consequently, they took them back over the border into West Germany each evening after work.[38]

Sixty-six-year-old Hermann Oberth, known as the "father of German rocketry," was hired in 1955 to work for the Army in Huntsville, Alabama, at Wernher von Braun's request. JIOA Deputy Director Geehan went to Oberth's castle in Bad Hamburg to make arrangements for the trip. "He always dressed in pre–World War II fashion, with a starched collar and a stick pin in his tie," recalled Geehan. The JIOA arranged to store Oberth's possessions in a warehouse near Washington, because there were truckloads of goods. "One day a guy from G-2 called and said, 'that Kraut's belongings have been here for six months. Either get it out or we're going to send you a bill.' " It was then that the JIOA discovered that Oberth's possessions included rare antique art and sculpture that had been taken out of West Germany in violation of that country's laws. "If the press would have gotten wind of that we would have had a real problem," Geehan said. The art was sent to a museum in Saint Louis for storage until Oberth returned to Germany a few years later.[39]

The German rocket group had moved from Fort Bliss to Huntsville in 1950 to work on guided missiles at Redstone Arsenal. Some of its members' backgrounds still were causing problems. One man left the country after the Army learned that he was a homosexual. In addition, the U.S. Justice Department refused to approve the legal immigration status of Herbert Axster and his wife because of their Nazi past. Axster said he finally told his boss, Major Hamill, that he was fed up. "I quit," he said. "I had a contract with the government and I told Hamill: 'End this contract any day you want.' They were happy to get rid of me." Axster opened a law firm with a friend in Milwaukee, Wisconsin, and later returned to West Germany.[40]

By the mid-1950s the Air Force had brought 153 new Paperclip specialists to various bases and research centers around the country. Ernst Czerlinsky, a former SS member, was sent to the Air Force Cambridge Research Center. Czerlinsky had been an aircraft engineer with the Experimental Institute for Aviation of the DVL in Berlin. In 1945, Army CIC agents arrested Czerlinsky to prevent him from interfering with U.S. expropriation of the DVL. OMGUS reports judged him to be an "ardent Nazi" because he had joined the SS and SA in the early 1930s.[41]

Some Paperclip recruits had worked for the Soviets for several years. Engineer Horst Gerlach had gone to East Germany shortly after the war ended because he objected to Allied restrictions in the western zones. In 1946, he was deported to the USSR, where he worked on radar installations at a research institute near Moscow until 1952. Another Paperclip recruit, physicist Fritz Klaiber, had worked for Siemens electric company in Berlin during the war. In 1945, he was kidnapped by the Russians and taken to a POW camp near Moscow, where he and other German POWs made electrical parts for guided missiles. When Klaiber was released in 1953, he provided U.S. and British intelligence with information about the Soviets' actvities.[42]

A group of chemical warfare experts went to Edgewood

Arsenal in the late 1950s. Eduard Wulkow had been a textile chemist for Lever Brothers in Berlin and at the Kaiser Wilhelm Institute during the war. He arrived at Edgewood in 1957 and developed fabrics for protective clothing that chemical warfare agents could not penetrate. Another specialist, Hermann Donnert, was a young Austrian nuclear physicist who graduated from the University of Innsbruck in 1951 and was working as a scientific assistant at the University of Cologne when he was hired under Paperclip. At Edgewood, he was assigned to the physics department to research and experiment with radioactive fallout.[43]

Edgewood scientists worked on several projects involving the airborne dissemination of chemical warfare agents, and another new Paperclip recruit, Albert Pfeiffer, was assigned to develop new ways to disseminate the toxic chemicals. During the war Pfeiffer was a chemical warfare specialist with the German navy's High Command, where he developed flame throwers, smoke bombs, and chemical warfare detectors. In 1944 Werner Osenberg, the SS representative on the Reich Research Council, personally assigned Pfeiffer as the council's representative to the Navy Chemical Testing Institute in Kiel.[44]

U.S. Army intelligence was still responsible for conducting background investigations on JIOA recruits. The system improved somewhat after 1955, when many applicants were given a polygraph exam before leaving Germany. "I instituted using a polygraph overseas because I couldn't see polygraphing people after they came in here," Christopher said. "Then we would have a 'disposal problem' you know. I went overseas myself and I picked my [polygraph] operator, because you don't use an operator that investigates crime to put a scientist on the box. You use a different technique." Some INSCOM dossiers on scientists considered for Paperclip after the mid-1950s contain copies of these polygraph tests. The scientists were asked questions to determine whether they had Communist affiliations or relatives living in Soviet territories.[45]

But no polygraph questions were asked regarding their Nazi

affiliations or activities during World War II. Neither Christopher nor any other officer connected to the project over the years believed that nazism posed a security threat. "What the heck would you think if you were in Germany under a dictator and you were a scientist and you wanted to work in your scientific field?" Christopher said. "They were Germans fighting for their country the same as we were fighting for ours."[46]

Apparently the Joint Chiefs of Staff felt the same way. The JCS had a secret plan to evacuate scientists from Europe in case of war with the USSR, and the JIOA maintained lists of those included in the plan. One list included individuals who normally would not be admitted to the United States, but whose work was considered so important that their skills should be denied to the Russians. In 1957 this list included convicted Nazi war criminal Houdremont, Nuremberg defendants Blome and Siegfried Ruff, who had returned to the DVL and later worked for Lufthansa German Airlines, and many biological or chemical warfare experts. Nerve gas discoverer Gerhard Schrader and biological warfare expert Wolfgang Wirth worked for I. G. Farben Bayer, of Bayer aspirin fame, located in the British zone of Germany.[47]

Willy Messerschmitt's name was also on JIOA's list. Messerschmitt's famous jet fighter planes, which ruled the skies over Nazi Germany during the war, had been built by Messerschmitt factories that used thousands of inmates from Mauthausen and Dachau as slave laborers. When Allied troops liberated Mauthausen they uncovered a mound of human bones surrounding the quarry that hid the Messerschmitt aircraft factory. Willy Messerschmitt went into exile in Spain, but he did not have to worry about being called to account for the deaths of the Jewish slaves. A German denazification court fined him a mere DM 2,000 for being a "fellow traveler" of the Nazis.[48]

By 1960, Messerschmitt's aircraft company, located in Augsburg, was back in business with assets of over DM 30 million. And Willy Messerschmitt was busy advising the Egyptian government on building rockets, which Egypt's President

Gamal Abdel Nasser declared would be used to destroy Israel. A large staff of Germans was in Cairo helping President Nasser develop his own aircraft, which the Israelis feared could carry high-explosive rocket warheads. *The New York Times* even reported that "a Munich physician wanted on charges of medical atrocities in concentration camps" was employed as a company doctor at the Messerschmitt factory near Cairo.[49]

The Syrians also were employing German scientists, and a few were brought to the United States in 1957 under Paperclip after they worked for Syria. One was Wilhelm Wessel, who was in charge of a rocket design team in Syria from 1951 to 1954. Wessel had been a design engineer for BMW during the war. Another employee in Syria, Otto Cerny, had been a rocket engineer at Peenemünde. From 1945 on, Cerny worked in Austria, primarily as a foreman at a steel works in Linz. He went to Syria in 1956 and then worked on rockets for the U.S. Army in Huntsville.[50]

By the late 1950s a great majority of those employed under JIOA projects were younger men with little, if any, post-university experience as scientists. In 1957 alone, ninety-four Germans or Austrians arrived under Paperclip. Unlike the earlier Paperclip group, these men had been soldiers, not scientists, during World War II.

Fifty-six specialists arrived during the first quarter of 1957 to work at Fort Monmouth, New Jersey, the nerve center of scientific research and development for the U.S. Army Signal Corps. Most had served in the Wehrmacht or Luftwaffe during the war and then obtained advanced degrees in science. One physicist, Josef Parth, had been a Luftwaffe pilot who flew fighter planes in France, Russia, and the Balkans. Another recruit, Hans Joachim Naake, was a radar engineer who had served in the Luftwaffe and had been interned in an American POW camp until the spring of 1946. Naake had been a member of the Nazi party and Hitler Youth during the war.[51]

These men joined the earlier Paperclip group, headed by chief scientist Hans Zeigler, who helped the Army hire scientists in Germany and kept a tight rein over them at Monmouth. One Austrian rebelled against the mail censorship regulations soon after he arrived. A code of conduct required the scientists to mail their letters at a base postal box so that censors could screen their correspondence. Henning Harmuth thought the practice violated the principles of democracy. "I told them right away that I don't intend to exchange Austrian censorship for an American one," he said. This led Zeigler to remark that Harmuth had a "fanatic conception about freedom in the U.S."[52]

But the controversy over mail was minor compared to the outrageous scandal that erupted when U.S. Army Chief Warrant Officer Ivan Simitch, head of the Foreign Scientists Section at Fort Monmouth, was caught in a motel room with Olaf Guzmann's wife. Simitch had rented a room in the Long Branch Motel and was living there secretly with Hilde Guzmann. The Paperclip scientist knocked on the door and, looking through a crack, was able to see his wife naked on the bed and Simitch rapidly crossing the room, clothed in a dressing gown.[53]

The Austrian engineer first met Simitch when he arrived at Fort Monmouth in late 1953. Guzmann, a wartime member of the SA, had been working for Philips telecommunications in Vienna. Almost immediately Simitch began spending all of his off-duty hours at Guzmann's apartment, and he even moved in for awhile. Soon Hilde told Guzmann she was leaving him for Simitch, who was a married man. "Toward the end of October Simitch's advice assumed a threatening manner," Guzmann said in a sworn affidavit. "Simitch told me if I did not sign [a property settlement] then my wife would take me to a divorce court, and since I have only a temporary visa, it would be hard for me to get a permanent visa thereafter. I considered this a veiled threat from Simitch. This frightened me because he was an officer of the U.S. Army and my supervisor."[54]

Unfortunately, Simitch was in a perfect position to prey on the Paperclip group. The scientists were vulnerable, since they were under military custody with no U.S. entry visas and depended on Simitch for their existence. "Mr. Simitch was my supervisor, he distributed pay checks, made arrangements for visas, censored all mail, provided for my aid or assistance under the terms of the contract," Guzmann stated in an affidavit. Most of the scientists did not speak English. And Simitch not only had access to their homes while they were at work, but he had used his security clearance to obtain information about their backgrounds.[55]

Army security officers interrogated Simitch and threatened to prosecute him for adultery, immoral behavior, and violating the federal Mann Act when Simitch took Hilde across state lines to spend a weekend in Washington, D.C. In a report, Colonel Frank Moses noted that "the conduct of CWO Simitch in an unofficial capacity after duty hours, seriously compromises his character and standing as a gentleman and makes him morally unworthy to remain a member of the honorable profession of arms." Hilde Guzmann was repatriated back to Austria. The JIOA and Army delayed Simitch's resignation from the Army until Hilde had left America, to stop Simitch from seeing her and avoid publicity.[56]

While the Army was keeping a lid on this scandal, other controversies arose in 1956 that threatened to expose the ongoing project to the American public. First, members of the Minnesota chapter of the American Chemical Society uncovered the Army's operation in the Alamac Hotel. They were furious when they learned that the large number of Germans living there were going to be employed by the military. The ACS was concerned that the Germans were taking jobs from Americans and it vowed to do everything possible to stop the recruitment of foreign nationals.[57]

Then the State Department found itself in the middle of a political controversy that jeopardized the friendly relations between the United States and West Germany. The West German government had complained for years about active recruitment of scientists by U.S. companies. Martin Marietta, Lockheed, and nearly every other major defense contractor sent their own teams to Germany to recruit scientists who then were brought

to the United States under National Interest. The German
government's complaints already had forced the secretary of
state to write those companies and tell them to stop recruiting.
Then the West Germans complained to Ambassador James
Conant about Paperclip and demanded that it be shut down.
Conant agreed and he urged Secretary of State John Foster
Dulles to quickly find a way to stop the project "before we
are faced with a formal complaint by the West German government against a continuing U.S. recruitment program which
has no parallel in any other Allied country."[58]

Nevertheless, West Germany's complaints did not stop the
projects. In November 1956, the U.S. Army Assistant Chief
of Staff for Intelligence (ACSI), Lieutenant General Robert
Schow, told the JIOA that the projects would continue but
recommended that they concentrate on processing current
cases and immediately discontinue active recruitment in Germany. Schow's comments reflected the views of the Joint
Chiefs of Staff, who felt that the recommendations would satisfy the German government while still allowing the project
to continue.[59]

In an effort to dupe the West German government into
believing that Paperclip had ended, JIOA Director Christopher changed the project's code name to the "Defense Scientists Immigration Program" (DEFSIP). "I changed the
name because the Germans objected to 'Paperclip,' " recalled
Christopher. The State Department was told that while applications would be accepted from interested German scientists, there was no longer a formal defense project to solicit
them.[60]

These changes made little difference. The Special Projects
Team stopped overtly recruiting German specialists, but if one
walked through the door, he would find a contract waiting for
him. And there were few, if any, scientists in West Germany
who did not know the team's address. The project's name
change fooled no one. Even the JIOA continued to refer to
the project as Paperclip.

A few months later the Russians' activities were used as an

excuse to escalate recruitment efforts again. On October 4, 1957, a Russian rocket launched *Sputnik I*, the first satellite to orbit the earth. Less than a month later, on November 3, a much larger satellite was launched that carried a dog, the first living creature to circle the earth.[61]

The space race had begun. At the time, former JIOA Director Benjamin Heckemeyer was working on Paperclip as chief of the Intelligence Collection Branch for ACSI in Europe. As a result of *Sputnik*, on November 1, 1957, Heckemeyer asked Schow for permission to recruit a large number of German scientists and "have them waiting at the Hotel Alamac when the go-ahead signal is given." He suggested accelerating the project by shortening the time spent on background investigations and eliminating the processing schedules altogether.[62]

Heckemeyer then told Schow, in a gross understatement, "we can ship a lot of talent when you give the word."

What Price Treason?

MOST mornings, JIOA Deputy Director William Henry Whalen arrived at his office in the Pentagon either drunk or suffering from a bad hangover. The forty-two-year-old Army lieutenant colonel was consuming at least a pint of liquor a day. His heavy drinking went hand-in-hand with the whirlwind social life that had become a habit by the time he was assigned to the JIOA in July 1957. For the previous two years, he had been assistant chief of the U.S. Army Foreign Liaison Office, where his job included attending as many as three foreign embassy–sponsored social events a night. Whalen and his wife were caught up in the glittering Washington social scene and continued to attend embassy parties after he joined the Joint Chiefs of Staff agency.[1]

Whalen had made several friends while making the rounds of diplomatic parties. One was Colonel Sergei Edemski, the acting Soviet military attaché and a known agent of the Soviet military intelligence agency, the GRU. Whalen had known Edemski since 1955 and the two men frequently socialized in each other's homes. The tall, forty-three-year-old, blond-haired Russian always appeared friendly and talkative. He was fluent in English, probably from having been stationed in London from 1944 to 1951, and his conversations were sprinkled with a lot of American slang.[2]

The smooth-talking Russian was a pro at using subtle coercion to snare someone into his spy net. As one Pentagon investigator noted years later, the tactic that Edemski used on Whalen was "a beautiful example of patient, calculated and well thought out, sophisticated recruitment of a source."[3] Edemski was like a spider who assessed his prey over a long period, found a weakness, and then spun a web tighter and tighter around his victim before moving in for the kill.

Edemski began to tighten the web soon after Whalen joined the JIOA. He asked the Army officer several times to give him some innocuous, unclassified U.S. Army manuals that Edemski easily could have obtained himself from the Government Printing Office. Whalen refused—for the moment—but the Soviet agent was a patient man. It would be only a matter of time before he put the pressure on Whalen's Achilles' heel. In addition to being an alcoholic, Whalen was deeply in debt to numerous credit bureaus and businesses throughout northern Virginia.[4]

It was worth the Russian's while to be patient with the Army officer who later would be called the highest-placed American military officer ever convicted of espionage. The Joint Chiefs of Staff is one of the nation's most super-secret agencies and forms the very heart of America's military defense system. And the world was in the midst of a chilling crisis that eventually would result in the construction of the Berlin Wall in 1961. Whalen's position on the JIOA gave him access to both America's and West Germany's defense secrets. With his top-secret security clearance, Whalen now could roam the JCS's heavily guarded Pentagon offices at will.[5]

The missile crisis between the United States and the USSR began to escalate almost from the moment that Sputnik was launched. By 1959 the missile gap had widened—the Russians were first to land an unmanned rocket on the moon. If Soviet rockets could reach the moon, they most certainly were capable of hitting targets in the United States. And Premier Nikita Khrushchev made that point abundantly clear in his public statements. "If we were attacked," he warned, "we could wipe off the face of the earth all our potential enemies." The tension heightened in 1959 when Khrushchev threatened to invade West Berlin, asserting that rockets with hydrogen bomb warheads were being manufactured in Soviet factories at the rate of 250 a year.[6]

Paperclip scientists were thrust into the middle of that crisis. Rocco Petrone, former director of NASA's Marshall Space Flight Center, was working for the Army at the time. Petrone recalls that Wernher von Braun's rocket team had been ready to launch a satellite on an Army rocket before Sputnik was launched in 1957. "There were six birds on the floor at Huntsville that could have gone into orbit at the time the Russians put up Sputnik, but they were given orders that they could not go all the way," Petrone said. Instead, politicians in Washington gave the Navy the go-ahead and its Vanguard rocket blew up on the launch pad. "Therefore, we denied ourselves the right to be first, and put the word *Sputnik* into our vocabulary."[7]

Whalen was already a familiar face to some of the men who ran Paperclip. Most of Whalen's military intelligence career since 1948 had been spent in various assignments with the Office of Assistant Chief of Staff for Intelligence. Colonel Montie Cone and other Army intelligence officers involved with the earlier Paperclip coverup of the scientists' Nazi pasts worked in a branch of the ACSI that had run Paperclip administratively from the beginning. In the late 1950s Cone was the executive officer of J-2, the Army intelligence directorate in the JCS. Christopher was JIOA director until he retired in the spring of 1958. Other officers on JIOA's staff included

Navy Captain Earle Gardner, Navy Commander William La-hodney, Army Lieutenant Colonel Don Davis, and Army Lieutenant Colonel Robinson Norris. As noted earlier, Heck-emeyer supervised the Special Projects Team recruiters as chief of the Intelligence Collection Division for ACSI in Europe.[8]

"Whalen was a big braggart," recalled Norris, who was on the JIOA in 1960–61. "One day he came in and announced to me and a couple of other people that 'I am going to be the assistant secretary of defense.' I said, 'Oh, how do you know that?' And he said, 'My mother delivered so many hundred thousand votes in New York state for John Kennedy and he's going to make me assistant secretary of defense.' " Norris laughed. "I thought that was rather presumptuous."[9]

State Department representative Walter Mueller described the vindictive way Whalen threatened to use that position. "Whalen griped about being discriminated against and said certain members in the Department of Defense would be sorry someday," Mueller told investigators. When Mueller asked what Whalen meant by that statement, Whalen indicated that when he became assistant secretary of defense he would see to it that certain persons were "given the works."[10]

Soon after Whalen joined the JIOA, Heckemeyer's earlier prediction that Paperclip would accelerate as a result of Sput-nik was proven correct. In early 1958 JIOA Director Christopher told Heckemeyer to keep the Special Projects Team "ready to go all out" on short notice. "Of course you must be careful that you are not accused of recruiting," Christopher warned. The military was going to bring more German and Austrian scientists to the United States even though they had yet to devise a plan to best utilize their skills.[11]

The project immediately underwent the same kind of ac-celeration that had taken place a decade earlier. A total of 361 Paperclip specialists were brought to the United States from 1957 through 1960, which was an increase over the previous few years. Ninety-four individuals arrived in 1957, compared with 64 the previous year. In 1958, the number increased again to a total of 109 specialists. In 1959 and 1960, while Whalen was spying for the Soviets, 158 specialists were brought to the United States under Paperclip. And in addition to the Paperclip group, a large number of scientists from Germany, Austria, and other countries were brought in under Project 63 and National Interest to work for universities and defense contractors, including Duke University, RCA (Princeton, New Jersey), Bell Laboratories, Douglas Aircraft, and Martin Marietta. Information about the number of defectors and other individuals brought in by the CIA and military intelligence agencies is unknown, since JIOA records concerning them were either shredded or pulled during the FBI's investigation in 1964.[12]

In 1958 the JIOA was still bringing in older scientists, primarily Austrians, who had obtained their scientific reputations during the time that Austria was willingly part of Hitler's Third Reich. One was Hans Nowotny, a professor at the University of Vienna who specialized in metallurgy and corrosion. Another Austrian, Alfred Popodi, was a former Nazi party member who had been a research engineer at Telefunken in Berlin during the war. Popodi then was senior engineer at the Laboratory Elektromedizin in Germany from 1948 until he came to America.[13]

Forty-five-year-old Heinz Gorges also was recruited in 1958. Gorges was a German rocket scientist who worked for the British after World War II and then immigrated to Australia. Paperclip scientists were supposed to be investigated and given polygraph exams before being brought to America. But that was not done in Gorges's case. In a memo to the State Department Visa Office, Whalen noted that Gorges's security investigation would not be completed before he began working with von Braun's group at the Army Ballistic Missile Agency in Huntsville. The results of that investigation are unknown. Among the few documents in Gorges's INSCOM file is a memo noting that the dossier would be destroyed March 6, 1959—the month that Whalen began spying for the Soviets.[14]

West Germans began complaining about Paperclip when it shifted back into high gear. For example, officials at Telefunken complained to the U.S. Embassy in Bonn that the Special Projects Team was actively recruiting its employees. Telefunken had a defense contract to make Hawk missiles and the company could not complete the contract if their best engineers left Germany to work in the United States under Paperclip.[15]

Around the same time, the *Bild-Zeitung* newspaper in West Germany published a scathing story about the plight of a blind, crippled space scientist who was losing his scientific helper because of Paperclip. Twenty-eight-year-old Hans Goslich was going to the United States to work for von Braun because the blind scientist could not afford to pay him. "Thus the sale on brains that started during those miserable years after 1945 goes on," the newspaper editorialized. A storm of publicity followed when a West German TV network held a fund-raising campaign on behalf of the blind scientist. The Special Projects Team's office was besieged with calls from German reporters wanting to know what was going on.[16]

Whalen coordinated a scheme with other officers to keep a lid on the story, which never was reported in the American press. German reporters were told that the "scientist exchange program" operated under State Department auspices and that the U.S. military did not recruit scientists. One reporter from a Cologne magazine was allowed into Camp King to talk with project officers, but they carefully kept him away from the team's offices, where a group of scientists was waiting to come to the United States.[17]

Paperclip recruiting continued to escalate in 1959 as tension between the United States and Russia grew stronger and the press reported rumors of war. Khrushchev announced a Soviet plan to turn West Berlin into a demilitarized "free city" and demanded that the Allied powers withdraw their troops by May 1959. Khrushchev's plan would leave the small island of democracy defenseless in the middle of Communist East Germany. The crisis escalated when Marshal Vasily Sokolovsky, chief of the Soviet armed forces, told a cheering crowd in Moscow that even if it meant starting a war, the Soviets would retaliate with force if the Western powers used force to remain in Berlin. "And the United States will not succeed in sitting it out on either side of the ocean with impunity," Sokolovsky warned. "The Soviet Union has intercontinental rockets, and no oceans will save the United States from retaliation."[18]

Then, in March 1959, President Eisenhower announced that he had not ruled out using atomic bombs if the Berlin crisis escalated into a war. Eisenhower said he thought fighting a ground war against Soviet troops in Europe was hopeless. "What good would it do to send a few more thousands or indeed, a few divisions of troops to Europe?" he asked. To attempt to fight the vastly greater number of Soviet forces on the ground would be "a miscalculation" and an "error," Eisenhower said, but he emphasized that he had not discounted nuclear war. "I think we might as well understand this—might as well all of us understand this: I didn't say that nuclear war is a complete impossibility."[19]

That same month, Whalen made the fateful decision to betray his country. He met Edemski at a shopping center in Alexandria, Virginia, and agreed to turn over America's defense secrets. From that day in March 1959 Whalen was a paid Soviet agent until he stopped spying in early 1963. He eventually gave the Soviets at least thirty to thirty-five U.S. Army manuals and oral information, for which he was paid approximately $14,000 in cash.[20]

Edemski and another Soviet agent gave Whalen specific instructions about the kinds of information they wanted. They asked him to obtain documents relating to U.S. defense plans for West Berlin, including U.S. troop movements and plans to reinforce the U.S. forces in Germany. The Berlin crisis had resulted in a number of military exercises involving the airlift of combat troops from the United States to Europe and vice versa while Whalen was in the JIOA. The Soviets directed Whalen to get information concerning the timetables of the airlifts and the specific destinations of the U.S. troops involved. The Soviets also wanted information concerning the realignment and streamlining of U.S. Army combat units, including details of combat strategy utilizing atomic bombs.[21]

The full extent of Whalen's espionage activities and of the information he gave the Soviets is unknown. This account is based primarily on federal court records and Whalen's massive eight-volume dossier from the U.S. Army Intelligence and Security Command. The FBI refused the author's FOIA request for Whalen's file. But Whalen had told FBI interrogators that he could not remember everything he had given the Soviet agents. For instance, he claimed that he could positively identify only seventeen of the thirty to thirty-five manuals he had given them. In addition, INSCOM reports note that he had shredded "thousands of documents" while working in the JIOA.[22]

Nevertheless, as one Department of Defense investigator reported, "it must be assumed that he probably gave them any information to which he had access." Army intelligence documents show that that definitely included information about the German scientist projects.[23]

Four months after Whalen began actively spying, he was promoted to director of the JIOA, on July 2, 1959. In that position Whalen sent lists of German or Austrian scientists to the State Department's visa director, Thomas G. Spence, asking State to issue visas so that they could enter the United States. Whalen's memos certified that "these aliens are not now, nor likely to become security threats to the United States," even though investigations on several scientists had not been completed. Whalen also sent the scientists' personal history forms to the FBI, noting that a complete security investigation had been conducted "with favorable results."[24]

Ninety-four individuals were brought to the United States under Paperclip in 1959. Most were employed by the Army in Huntsville or at Fort Monmouth. Others worked for the Navy at China Lake, California, or White Oak, Maryland, where the earlier wind tunnel group was based. The Air Force's group primarily went to Wright-Patterson in Dayton. In addition to Paperclip recruits, an unknown number of others worked under Project 63 or National Interest for Martin Marietta, General Electric, and other defense contractors or for universities, including Yale.[25]

Friedwardt Winterberg was one German scientist who was named as a candidate for JIOA's denial Project 63 in 1959. As the reader will learn later, in 1985 Winterberg positioned himself as media spokesman for Arthur Rudolph when Rudolph left the country rather than face war crimes charges. In January 1959 the thirty-year-old physicist was demanding a salary of over $1,000 a month. ACSI Director of Plans Brigadier General Richard Collins told the Special Projects Team that Winterberg might be considered for JIOA's project if he discontinued that demand. "Age and lack of experience would cause prospective employers to be reluctant to offer such a salary," Collins wrote. It was suggested that Winterberg be sent to the Alamac Hotel for job interviews. Winterberg accepted a position at Ohio's Case University in 1959 and currently is with the Desert Research Institute in Reno, Nevada.[26]

The 1959 group also included older scientists who had established their careers under Hitler. One was forty-seven-year-old Hans Dolezalek, a German meteorologist who had worked for the Wehrmacht Weather Service during World War II and had been an early member of the SA, the brown-shirted stormtroopers. The JIOA was not supposed to actively recruit scientists after 1948. Yet the team's recruiter, Knut Lossbom, had approached Dolezalek as early as 1953, sending him forms to apply for work in America. Dolezalek visited America in 1958 to attend a conference of meteorological experts. He accepted a position under Paperclip at AVCO in Wilmington, Massachusetts, for $13,000 a year, twice the salary offered by Fort Monmouth.[27]

Another 1959 recruit was working as a dishwasher in Canada when he asked Wernher von Braun for a job. Sixty-one-year-old Friedrich Wigand was first touted as a top German rocket scientist, but after he arrived in Huntsville he admitted that he had never even seen a rocket. He had been a lieutenant in the Wehrmacht stationed for a time at Kummersdorf, where some of Germany's rocket work was being done. After the war, Wigand immigrated to Canada and worked on a farm picking sugar beets. In 1956, he got a job washing dishes at a hospital in Calgary. "Every night after my work in the kitchen, I studied my chemistry and my physics," said the self-taught chemist. He arrived in Huntsville in May 1959 and obtained a position as a lab technician at Brown Engineering Company.[28]

One physicist was returned to Germany when he could not find permanent employment in America. Fritz Rossmann, a former SS member, had worked for the Army Ballistic Missile Agency in Huntsville and the Patrick Air Force Base in Florida. Despite a more lenient immigration law, Rossmann had problems obtaining permanent residency because of his SS and Nazi party memberships and the fact that he had been arrested twice by Army CIC agents and convicted by a denazification court. During the war he had been chief of the atmospheric electricity section of the German Glider Research Institute in Braunschwieg. Rossmann returned to Germany in 1959 and joined the faculty at the University of Munich.[29]

Whalen's position as JIOA director in charge of the German scientist program gives rise to disturbing questions about further services he might have provided his Soviet handlers.

- Did he bring in a spy or saboteur? Whalen could have inserted a specialist hand-picked by the Soviets into a crucial area of American defense-related research, where the scientist-agent could then either sabotage our efforts or report on them to his spy masters.
- Did he use blackmail to recruit a spy or saboteur from among the approximately sixteen hundred Paperclip specialists and hundreds of other JIOA recruits brought to this country since 1945? It certainly is clear from the evidence that many of them had a lot to hide.
- Did he give the Soviets information on research being done by JIOA specialists all across the country? These specialists worked on guided missiles for the Army, the Navy, and the Air Force. They worked in the NASA space program, in aeromedical research, in atomic, biological, and chemical warfare research, and on the latest designs in jet aircraft and

submarines. They worked at nearly every military installation and for most key defense contractors across the country, and in all of those locations they had access to classified information.

Whalen did pass on information gleaned from the JIOA's watch list of scientists working on defense projects in West Germany. The scientists' research was closely monitored by Army CIC agents and other individuals. This information obviously would have provided the Soviets with up-to-date knowledge of West Germany's defense research.

The issue of how much use Whalen made of the intelligence information obtained from scientists also is important. It should be clear by now that JIOA officers viewed Paperclip as an intelligence project, not an exploitation project. This view was discussed during a March 1960 meeting to decide whether the three projects should be continued. In that meeting, Whalen concluded that the projects had produced a "vast amount" of intelligence information and should be continued for that reason. Project 63, the denial project, was even defined as "definitely an intelligence program." Army intelligence officers interrogated scientists in America who corresponded with foreign scientists and attended international scientific conferences to learn what other countries were doing.[30]

Whatever use the Soviets made of Whalen's connection with the JIOA projects, the material he provided them from other sources was damaging enough. Because of his position in the JCS, Whalen was able to requisition documents to meet the demands of his Soviet handlers. He sold the Soviets army manuals, which were classified as secret, that gave details of U.S. Army nuclear artillery and missile capabilities and included information on Hawk and Nike missiles. One manual was entitled "Field Artillery Missile Group." Another was a Department of the Army technical bulletin that described the Nike-Ajax and Nike-Hercules antiaircraft guided missile systems and included detailed information on electronic countermeasures. Whalen, as one of the destruction officers for the

JCS, was able to destroy the documents after they were returned by the Soviets.[31]

In addition to selling classified documents, Whalen made oral and handwritten reports based on his conversations with colleagues in the JIOA, the Foreign Liaison Office, the ACSI, and the Joint Chiefs of Staff office. One 1970 investigation noted that none of the officers from whom Whalen obtained information was involved in espionage. The report stated:

> There is absolutely no evidence of connivance by others. In effect, Whalen used friendship as a vehicle to move conversations to a topic in which he had immediate interest in satisfying his handlers. These innocent parties were guilty of nothing more than a certain laxity in security in that they allowed themselves to be duped into discussing sensitive material to which subject had no established need-to-know.[32]

Whalen took advantage of casual conversations with associates in the Pentagon to obtain information for the Soviets concerning the movement of troops and the reorganization of U.S. Army combat units. Some of that information included data regarding mobile combat units equipped with Honest John rockets.[33]

Whalen met Edemski once a month in shopping center parking lots in Alexandria, Virginia, where they held operational planning meetings. On three or four occasions Whalen gave Edemski classified information about plans to evacuate U.S. civilians in West Germany in the event of a surprise attack by the Soviets. Several other times Edemski took notes on a three-by-five-inch pad of paper while Whalen made oral reports about the U.S. buildup or reduction of troops in Europe and defense plans for West Germany and France.[34]

Other oral reports to Edemski contained information from Washington Liaison Group projects in which Whalen had participated. He was the Department of Defense representative on the Liaison Group, whose purpose was to devise worldwide plans to evacuate and save the lives of U.S. citizens abroad in

saying he drank, he borrowed money," recalled Colonel Christopher, who rejoined the project in 1962. "I said, 'Why the hell didn't you tell somebody? That's an indication.' "[38]

Yet JIOA officer Gardner did consider a college student as being suspect simply because he was researching Paperclip. Clarence Lasby was a student at the University of California at Los Angeles and had decided to write his doctoral dissertation on Project Paperclip. As part of his research Lasby sent questionnaires to a number of Paperclip scientists, including Hans Ziegler at Fort Monmouth, where the Guzmann sex scandal took place. And remember, earlier Ziegler had been given a little help by Army CIC agents with his denazification court decision.[39]

On August 5, 1960, Ziegler telephoned Gardner, expressing "grave concern" that Lasby had asked several German scientists at Monmouth to fill out a questionnaire regarding their Paperclip experiences. Ziegler then turned Lasby's questionnaires over to E. M. McDermott, the security control officer at Monmouth, who advised the recipients of the questionnaires to "stand fast" and refrain from responding.[40]

Gardner alerted other officers that he intended "to check the possible Communist affiliations of Laspy [sic] through appropriate agencies." And so he did. Gardner notified the FBI, the ACSI, and the Office of Naval Intelligence and asked them to check out Lasby. In addition Gardner contacted a Captain Howell, described as the "JCS watchdog in the field of adverse or undesirable publicity." Gardner's investigation did not uncover any derogatory evidence against Lasby. But while Gardner was busy checking out an innocent college student, Whalen was wandering freely around the Pentagon gathering information to sell to the Soviets.[41]

In 1960 the JIOA brought fifty-five more Paperclip recruits to the United States. "We weren't overwhelmed with applications," recalled Norris. "They were mostly younger people with a bright future who didn't think they could get the opportunity to utilize their talents in Germany." Several went to work for the Army Signal Corps at Fort Monmouth: Karl

Moeller had just obtained a doctorate in physics from the University of Heidelberg and Rupert Brand had been an engineer with Siemens. In addition, the U.S. Bureau of Standards in Boulder, Colorado, hired physicist Adalbert Goertz and Watervliet Arsenal in New York employed engineer Friedhelm Bachmann.[42]

A number of others came in 1960 to work for universities, defense contractors, or private firms, including General Electric, Union Carbide, and the Case Institute of Technology. Thirty-year-old physicist Kurt Breitschwerdt obtained a position with Remington Rand. Thirty-five-year-old Reinhard Buchner parlayed his doctorate in experimental physics to become senior research engineer at AC Spark Plug in Boston. The Austrian Herwig Kogelnik, who had a doctorate in electronics from the Institute of Technology in Vienna, arrived in 1960 to work under a short-term government contract until his employment term began with Bell Telephone Laboratories in 1961.[43]

Meanwhile, Whalen's contact in Soviet intelligence was changed in February 1960 when Edemski was transferred to London and immediately promoted to the rank of general. During his farewell party at the Soviet Embassy in Washington, Edemski introduced Whalen to "Mike" and told Whalen to help the new man in the same way that he'd been helping Edemski. Mikhail "Mike" Shumaev was a known GRU agent and first secretary of the Soviet Embassy.[44]

Following Edemski's departure, Whalen met with Shumaev approximately eleven times in Alexandria shopping center parking lots. He received $3,000 in cash between March and July 1960 alone for turning over America's defense secrets to the Soviets. Some of that information was included in oral reports and approximately ten to fifteen U.S. Army manuals and documents that were classified either confidential or secret. Whalen later told the FBI that he could not remember the content of the information he gave Shumaev. In June 1960, for example, Whalen gave Shumaev a written report pertaining to three or four subjects, none of which Whalen could recall later, although he did remember that the information was classified confidential or secret and that he had obtained the information from conversations with other officers at the JCS.[45]

By July Whalen's health had deteriorated dramatically due to his heavy drinking. His once-towering six feet three frame was now painfully stooped over from arthritis and recurring bouts of multiple sclerosis. He could not stay seated in one position for long and as a result was constantly pacing the floor. On July 4 he had his first heart attack and was hospitalized at DeWitt Army Hospital in Fort Belvoir, Virginia, where doctors told him to take it easy. He had another heart attack the day before Thanksgiving.[46]

Whalen did not return to active duty after his first heart attack and he officially retired from the military in February 1961. But anyone who might think Whalen let serious health problems or retirement get in the way of his espionage activities would be dead wrong. One confidential source familiar with this and other espionage cases said that he had never seen as persistent and tenacious a spy as Whalen.[47]

Whalen continued to roam the halls of the Pentagon *until early 1963* to get information for the Soviets through conversations with officers he knew. This shocking example of Whalen's tenacity also raises serious questions about security—or lack of it—at the Pentagon. One officer reported that he saw Whalen sitting at a desk "reading papers" in a highly secret Joint Chiefs of Staff office a few months after Whalen had been hospitalized for his first heart attack. Another officer said that he had seen Whalen in a secret Army intelligence office where visitors were barred and that he had passed Whalen in the Pentagon corridors on one or two other occasions.[48]

Just one month after Whalen retired from the military, he received $1,000 in cash for turning over more secret information during a meeting with Shumaev. After Whalen's retirement Shumaev instructed him to develop a contact within the Pentagon who could furnish Whalen with information and documents for the Soviets; to obtain civilian employment in the Pentagon that would provide him access to information of interest to the Soviets; and to visit the Pentagon in order to develop information through conversations with former military colleagues. Whalen indicated that he would try to comply with these instructions.[49]

Whalen apparently was unsuccessful at finding an accomplice in his espionage activities. During the Cuban missile crisis, at the direction of Soviet intelligence, he did seek employment at the Defense Intelligence Agency and the ACSI. One ACSI officer said Whalen walked freely into his office, which was located in a highly sensitive Pentagon area that is off limits to visitors, to ask about a civilian job. Fortunately Whalen failed to obtain employment. Nevertheless, for two months following his retirement Whalen made frequent visits to the Pentagon to talk with acquaintances in the JIOA. In April 1961, based on conversations with those persons and discussions he had overheard, Whalen prepared an oral report for Shumaev dealing with U.S. armed forces, defenses, and plans pertaining to the European theater. Thereafter, Whalen visited the ACSI section at the Pentagon in quest of information for the Soviets.[50]

From February 1961 until the last operational meeting that Whalen had with Shumaev in early 1963, the Soviet agent frequently upbraided him for lack of production. During their last meeting Whalen indicated that he would be unable to obtain further information and suggested that their relationship be ended. The Soviet tried to persuade Whalen to keep trying, but to no avail. After the meeting Shumaev persisted by telephoning Whalen several times—again to no avail.[51]

Meanwhile, the FBI had begun to sift through the evidence from an espionage case involving one Colonel Stig Wennerström, a Swedish Defense Ministry official who was convicted of espionage in 1964 and sentenced to life imprisonment for compromising the entire Swedish air defense system. Wennerström had been air attaché in the Swedish Embassy in Washington from 1952 to 1957 and had frequently attended embassy parties with U.S. military officers, including Whalen. According to testimony at his trial, Wennerström gave the Soviets information on the U.S. defense system that included details of missiles, nuclear weapons, bombing sites and a lengthy report on his visit to a Strategic Air Command base where he was allowed to inspect nearly everything. He had also obtained a huge amount of classified material by bribing some of the officials he met during numerous trips to aircraft factories in the U.S. and Canada. "I had entrée everywhere," he testified. Wennerström's Soviet handlers told him not to bother with such "unnecessary" intelligence as data on Defense Department personnel—those matters were being taken care of by "an agent or agents" within the Pentagon.[52]

FBI agent Donald Gruentzel was conducting a damage assessment of the Wennerström case when he encountered Whalen's name during investigations into Wennerström's spying activities. At the same time, a counterintelligence source warned the FBI that there was a Soviet mole high up in the Pentagon. In late 1963 Gruentzel visited Whalen in his home to inquire whether Whalen had any knowledge about Wennerström and Edemski. The FBI put Whalen's house under surveillance and subpoenaed his bank records. Those documents revealed that Whalen, who had been deeply in debt, suddenly had come into an unexplained financial windfall in 1959. The FBI also placed an illegal wiretap on Whalen's home telephone, an action that nearly blew the Justice Department's case against Whalen in 1966.[53]

On September 22, 1964, an Army CIC agent telephoned Whalen and asked if he would come to a meeting at the Pentagon. By now Whalen was downing nearly a quart of liquor a day. The following day, after three or four drinks, Whalen arrived in time for the one o'clock meeting. He met with two FBI agents, Gruentzel and Paul Nugent, in a soundproof room near ACSI offices, where, unbeknownst to the FBI, the Army surreptitiously recorded their conversation. During the meeting Gruentzel confronted Whalen with his bank records and asked repeatedly if he had furnished information to the Soviets. Although Whalen identified Edemski's photograph, he denied that he had given Edemski any information. After the meeting, Whalen went home and got drunk.[54]

The next day Whalen met the agents at FBI headquarters

in Washington, where he underwent a polygraph exam. While Whalen was strapped to the polygraph machine, he thought that he was going to have another heart attack. "Just stop this," he told the agents. "I will tell you anything I can tell you, and let me sit down or lie down and rest somewhere." After Whalen rested for awhile, the agents continued the interview.[55]

"We were discussing at this point again, his finances," Gruentzel later testified, "as to why he had been in debt for such a long period of time, up until 1959, and during '59 and '60 the debts were erased. He had no debts, more money was put in the bank account, and [we] suggested the possibility that, maybe, this was the fruit of selling information to the Soviets. And, at this point, he just blurted out, 'O.k., you've got me over the barrel. I sold them the stuff.' "[56]

Two years later, on July 12, 1966, a federal grand jury indicted Whalen of acting as an agent of the USSR and conspiring to gather or deliver defense information to the USSR pertaining to "atomic weaponry, missiles, military plans for the defense of Europe, estimates of comparative military capabilities, military intelligence reports and analyses, information concerning the retaliation plans by the U.S. Strategic Air Command and information pertaining to troop movements."[57]

But Justice Department prosecutors had several difficulties with their case. First, there was the question of whether information about Whalen's finances had been obtained as a result of an illegal FBI wiretap. Second, there was the question of whether the FBI had advised Whalen of his rights during approximately thirty-six interrogations. Third, it was uncertain whether the court would allow the prosecutors to use confessions Whalen had made during the FBI interrogations. Finally, as in many cases involving espionage, there was concern that confidential sources and sensitive defense information would be exposed if the case went to trial in open court.[58]

Meanwhile, Federal Judge Oren Lewis issued a gag order forbidding the press from publishing any information about the confessions, even though that information had been discussed during a hearing in open court. Although there were numerous articles about the Whalen case in *The New York Times*, the *Washington Post*, and other media, the subject of Paperclip and Whalen's connection to the project never was revealed. No one ever reported what his job had been in the JCS. Witnesses who might have established the Paperclip connection and clarified other matters—such as the identity of Whalen's loose-lipped sources—never were called to testify. The witness list included Cone and JIOA officers Gardner and Lahodney. Although the JIOA name was mentioned in open court, no one reported what that agency's mission actually was. An Army press officer told *The New York Times* that he did not know what Whalen's duties had been in the JCS. In addition, the Army's press release concerning Whalen's background was misleading. Whalen was described simply as an officer in the Joint Chiefs of Staff agency, and the biography that the Army gave the press abruptly ended in 1955.[59]

Furthermore, no information was made public about Whalen's JIOA connections to both the State and Justice Departments. *The New York Times* quoted a State Department press officer, Robert McClosky, as saying that one of Whalen's JCS committee assignments (the Washington Liaison Group) involved updating the plans for the evacuation of U.S. citizens from any area of potential trouble. According to McClosky, that assignment was Whalen's only access to the State Department "that I am aware of." Yet, as has been shown repeatedly, the JIOA had close connections with both the State and Justice Departments. Included among the few JIOA documents available are memos signed by Whalen to both the Visa Department and the attorney general listing German and Austrian scientists who were recommended by the JIOA to be brought to the United States under Paperclip. State Department officials and the attorney general had approved their U.S. entry in part on the basis of JIOA Director Whalen's recommendation.[60]

In November 1966 U.S. Attorney C. Vernon Spratley announced that the Justice Department might not prosecute Whalen on espionage charges if the court suppressed a series of statements containing confessions that Whalen had given to the FBI. Judge Lewis warned government attorneys that "they can't rely on a confession alone." If Whalen claimed that he had made the statements involuntarily and if the government had no other evidence, "he will be set free regardless of how guilty he is," the judge added.[61]

Behind the scenes, Whalen cut a deal with the Justice Department. Whalen was concerned that if convicted of espionage, he would be stripped of his military benefits and his family would suffer as a result. Whalen agreed to plead guilty to a lesser charge if special legislation was passed guaranteeing his wife the survivor benefits accruing from his retired military status. This also meant that when Whalen died he could be buried alongside America's military heroes at Arlington Cemetery.[62]

Confronted with the lesser charge on December 17, 1966, Whalen told Judge Lewis, uncertainly, "Uh—I will plead guilty." Not satisfied with this answer, the judge explained the charges to Whalen in detail. At one point Whalen said he did not "understand the terminology" of the charges. "I'll put it in lower language," Lewis answered.[63]

"You are charged with conniving . . . to get secret documents pertaining to U.S. defense and giving them to the Russians to use against us. . . . Did you do that, Colonel?"

"Yes, sir," Whalen answered, betraying little emotion.[64]

After accusing Whalen of "selling me and all your fellow Americans down the river," Judge Lewis sentenced the man who had been at the helm of Paperclip while operating as a Soviet spy to fifteen years' imprisonment.[65]

13 Moon Walk in the Shadow of the Third Reich

I N the 1960s America's self-imposed goal was to beat the Russians into space. Vice President Lyndon Johnson noted the urgency of that mission in a 1961 report to President John Kennedy that states, in part: "In the crucial areas of our Cold War world, first in space is first, period. Second in space is second in everything."[1]

At NASA's George C. Marshall Space Flight Center in Huntsville, the German rocket group was working to carry out that mission by developing the powerful rockets needed to take man to the moon. The Germans had been transferred to NASA from the Army soon after the new civilian space agency was established. "We were the only group at that time that knew how to build long-range rockets," said Georg von Tiesenhausen, the team's official brainstormer, who had worked on a wartime plot to launch a rocket into New York City.[2]

The organization the Germans established at Marshall was almost an exact copy of the Peenemünde organization. "It had proved very efficient," said von Tiesenhausen. But it also meant that the Germans dominated the rocket program to such an extent that they held the chief and deputy slots of every major division and laboratory. And their positions at Marshall and the Kennedy Space Center at Cape Canaveral, Florida, were similar to those they had held during the war.[3]

- The Peenemünde team's leader, Wernher von Braun, became the first director of the Marshall Space Flight Center.
- Mittelwerk's head of production, Arthur Rudolph, was named project director of the Saturn V rocket program.
- Peenemünde's V-2 flight test director, Kurt Debus, was the first director of the Kennedy Space Center.

The American public was not told the full details about the Nazi pasts of NASA's new employees. And apparently, NASA officials did not even bother to check them out. James Kingsbury, former director of science and engineering at Marshall, said he knew about Rudolph's job at Mittelwerk, but he did not believe that NASA had obtained the Army's files on the Germans when they were transferred to the agency. "NASA really wouldn't have had reason to question anything in the Germans' records," he said.[4]

Other NASA officials say the Germans' Nazi pasts were not NASA's problem. The feeling was that "this was something that was all addressed and worked out years ago," recalled a high-ranking technical official who preferred to remain anonymous. He knew that one former Nazi party member, Richard Jenke, had problems during the war because his grandmother was Jewish. "He did show me one day a typewritten note signed by Adolf Hitler that said that, because of his good work for the Party, they would overlook his blood lineage."[5]

The Justice Department thought Kurt Debus's Nazi past violated U.S. immigration laws and held up his legal immigration for years because of his memberships in the SS, the

SA, and other Nazi groups. Questions also were raised when Debus violated security by sending messages to his girlfriend in Germany in code so that his wife would not find out. But the biggest problem was the wartime incident of Debus turning a colleague over to the Gestapo for making anti-Hitler statements. A security certificate signed by JIOA Deputy Director James Skinner noted that his value to the Army outweighed this example of ardent nazism. Skinner added that "any conscientious and patriotic, though short-sighted person might have done the same" as Debus. His immigration finally was approved after a new law went into effect December 1952 that no longer barred individuals who had belonged to Nazi organizations.[6]

Jewish groups did not forget the role the Germans had played in Hitler's Third Reich as easily as NASA did. Von Tiesenhausen recalled that "there were certain ethnic groups in the United States who were against us in principle. The ethnic prejudices operated throughout the time we had a von Braun team—it never ceased. Never." He blames Jews for being the force behind many of the Germans' forced retirements in the 1970s.[7]

Although their histories escaped scrutiny at NASA, there was criticism of the Germans' operating methods. Some American-born employees at Marshall viewed their tightly knit organization as a clique rather than a team. James Webb, NASA's second administrator, complained that the Germans were circumventing the system by attempting to build the Saturn V in-house at the center. Rocco Petrone, who became Marshall director in 1973, said that Webb felt the group needed to be more tightly managed. "There were a lot of very brilliant guys who had worked in an environment a little more loosely than you should on a tight program like Apollo," said Petrone. Von Braun also was criticized for thrusting himself into the limelight as the self-appointed spokesman on space exploration. At one point Webb told von Braun to stop accepting the hundreds of paid speaking engagements that were in direct violation of NASA employment regulations.[8]

The Germans themselves were aware of their detractors at NASA headquarters. "We were a very independent group, and some people didn't like that," said von Tiesenhausen. "You know when Washington hands out money, they always want to be in the loop." As an example, he describes von Braun's sales approach when he went to NASA headquarters in search of money. "He got us the funds we needed. And then he said, 'Okay, we are going to deliver. But in the meantime, don't bother us.' So this independence, a lot of people didn't like."[9]

The German influence at Marshall increased in the 1960s as new Paperclip recruits arrived as a result of the continuation of JIOA projects. A total of 267 individuals were brought in under Paperclip and National Interest in the 1960s, and an unknown number of others arrived under Project 63. The Paperclip recruits worked for NASA or at military installations including Edgewood Arsenal, Wright-Patterson Air Force Base, Fort Monmouth, and the Naval Ordnance Testing Station in China Lake, California. Seventy-eight others were employed under National Interest with defense contractors, universities, or private corporations, including Pennsylvania State University, the Massachusetts Institute of Technology (MIT), Bell Laboratories, RCA, CBS Laboratories, Martin Marietta, Convair, and Mobil Oil.[10]

In 1962 the JIOA was shut down as a cost-cutting measure after being in charge of Paperclip for seventeen years. Secretary of Defense Robert McNamara transferred the German scientist projects from the Joint Chiefs of Staff to the secretary of defense. The military wanted to continue the projects for a variety of reasons. First, the military custody procedures still allowed individuals to bypass the usual red tape when entering the country. Second, the foreign scientists under Paperclip could obtain security clearances more quickly than could non-project scientists, including Americans. Thus the project provided an immediate work force on classified jobs. Third, the projects saved the military a considerable amount of money. For example, a representative from the Navy reported that it would cost the Navy approximately $20,000 a year to send a scientist to an American university to obtain a doctorate, while it could recruit a German scientist who already had an advanced degree for only $1,200 in project expenses.[11]

Former JIOA Director Stone Christopher had retired from the Air Force by then, although he was working on another secret intelligence operation. In 1962 Christopher was hired to run Paperclip as a civilian. He said the project was still vital because it solved the acute shortage of scientists not only at NASA, but also among defense contractors involved in the space program. "Everybody was crying for physicists and engineers," Christopher said. "And Glen Martin, Westinghouse, General Electric people came into my office all the time asking me to help." At the time, U.S. companies also were placing employment ads in foreign newspapers and sending executives abroad on talent hunts.[12]

But the continuance of Paperclip angered some American-born employees at Marshall. A longtime administrator at Marshall said they complained about Paperclip because Germans were being hired instead of Americans. "And there were a few of the Germans who were not as well qualified because, indeed, they didn't even have degrees," he said. Furthermore, Paperclip recruits received preferential treatment over Americans at Marshall because the top officials were themselves German. "The 'Paperclip' people, when they would come to America, the first thing they would do would be usher them into Dr. von Braun's office. They immediately had an entrée to the big boy." Yet newly hired Americans with comparable experience were not given the same entrée to von Braun.[13]

While von Braun, Rudolph, and other early Paperclip recruits were hiding their Nazi pasts, the military was covering up the fact that the operation was still going on. The American public had been duped into believing that Paperclip had ended long ago. And the West German government had been told in 1958 that the U.S. had stopped recruiting German scientists in their own country. Therefore, anyone who tried to reveal any information about the project's existence was considered a threat.

The perpetuation of the coverup resulted in outright censorship of the press and the release of false information to the public in both the United States and West Germany. In one case in 1961, a West German reporter visited the Special Projects Team's office in Munich in search of information for a magazine article on West Germany's critical "brain drain," caused by the loss of scientists to employers in foreign countries. He did not know that this was the Paperclip operation. But he concluded that the office was engaged in an illegal recruiting program, because the team's officers were suspiciously tight-lipped and released minimal information.[14]

JIOA Director Navy Captain Earle Gardner thought the reporter's story would expose Paperclip and result in bad publicity. He told Army intelligence officers to make a statement in West Germany to the effect that the U.S. government, through its Special Projects Team office, "disseminates information" on U.S. job opportunities merely as a "public service." The reporter was denied access to figures on the number of scientists who recently had emigrated to America. Gardner said that information would only "whet the appetite of the reading public for additional disclosures for other periods," and then if the JIOA refused to disclose information, it "could convey the impression that we are trying to cover up."[15]

That example shows the mentality present in 1964 when historian Clarence Lasby submitted the manuscript for his book *Project Paperclip* to the military for clearance. It was Christopher who cleared Lasby's manuscript. "I went over that manuscript three times," Christopher told me. "I didn't think it was good to mention names like this fellow [State Department representative Samuel Klaus]." JIOA records show that Christopher also objected to Lasby's use of the words *exploitation* and *denial* because they might prove embarrassing for the U.S. government. When asked if he thought Lasby was aware that Paperclip was still in operation in the 1960s, Christopher said, "I would think so, he came into my office to see me."[16]

Lasby later recalled meeting an Air Force officer whom he thought was helpful, but no one was introduced to him as

being in charge of the project. He said he guessed that the
project had continued after 1952, but he did not mention that
in his book. Unlike today, Lasby had no way to force the
military to turn over classified records. "I had to rely on the
ambition and greed of a particular service to get records,"
Lasby said. "They were all so scared of everything." He expunged Klaus's name at the request of the State Department,
which refused to show him any documents. He received a
letter telling him to expunge the words *exploitation* and *denial*,
but he refused to do so. "I told them to go to hell and I used
it anyway," he said. Lasby did not see any JIOA files. Unknown to Lasby, the JIOA dossiers showing that Marshall
director von Braun had been in the SS, Kennedy Center director Debus had turned a colleague over to the Gestapo, and
Saturn manager Rudolph had worked at Mittelwerk were
locked up in a safe in Christopher's office.[17]

Meanwhile, by 1967 the Apollo moon project was under
way at NASA. But on January 27, tragedy struck as astronauts
Roger Chaffee, Virgil "Gus" Grissom, and Edward White sat
locked inside an Apollo capsule at the Kennedy Space Center.
At 6:31 P.M., there was a short circuit in defective wiring
beneath Grissom's pilot couch. Suddenly Grissom called over
the radio: "There's a fire in here." Six crewmen working near
the capsule began to tear at the escape hatch but were forced
to dash in and out of the smoke-filled room to breathe because
their emergency gas masks were the wrong type for the smoke
conditions in the room. Then the smoke grew so thick that it
hid the grisly scene of the three astronauts trapped inside the
burning space capsule.[18]

Ten days after the fatal fire Kurt Debus said: "We have
always adhered to the highest standards of safety." But as
director at the Kennedy Space Center, Debus was responsible
for checking out the capsule at the center and determining
whether to proceed with the test. "That was his responsibility
in the Kennedy Space Center," said former Paperclip specialist
Walter Haeussermann. It also had been Debus's responsibility
to see that emergency equipment was on hand. Not only were

"emergency fire, rescue and medical teams not in attendance," the Apollo Accident Board reported, "the emergency equipment located in the white room (at spacecraft level) and on the spacecraft work levels was not designed for the smoke condition resulting from a fire of this nature."[19]

The board castigated NASA's upper management and the capsule's contractor, North American Rockwell, for failing "to give adequate attention to certain mundane but equally vital questions of crew safety." The fire started when a spark from defective wiring ignited in the oxygen-filled chamber. But there were numerous other examples of sloppy workmanship and design, including a defective escape hatch. The Johnson Space Center in Houston had overseen the capsule design and Rockwell's work. Marshall had been responsible only for the launch vehicle, which was not mentioned in the report as being a problem.[20]

Ten months after the Apollo fire, von Braun's team had their first chance to see if their Saturn V moon rocket would fly. It was November 9, 1967—Arthur Rudolph's sixty-first birthday. As Saturn V program manager, Rudolph sat next to von Braun in the control room, watching the countdown to zero. "We wanted to go to the moon," said von Tiesenhausen. "If it's the last thing we do, we wanted to go to the moon. So we built the Saturn vehicle, a very expensive space vehicle." To accomplish that feat, the Germans first had to develop simpler models. And to do that, they had had to build weapons for Hitler and for the U.S. Army. One step after another led to the Saturn V. Now the giant rocket stood like a skyscraper struggling to break free from the clamps that held it upright on the launch pad at Kennedy Space Center. Then all 7.5 million pounds of thrust lifted the rocket off the earth with a deafening roar.[21]

On July 16, 1969, another Saturn V lifted astronauts into space. Four days later a lunar module called *Eagle* landed on the moon. The reaction of Huntsville residents that day was typical of the rest of the nation. The streets were empty as people watched the spectacular scene on television when Neil Armstrong and Edwin "Buzz" Aldrin walked on the moon.

"We've done it! We've hit the moon," the teenage daughter of one of the space scientists screamed as the celebration began. Later von Braun was carried on the shoulders of Huntsville residents amid ringing church bells and fireworks. Rudolph was showered with honors, including NASA's highest award, the Distinguished Service Medal, when he retired later that year.[22]

There are some who say it does not matter what crimes the Germans had committed, because they helped us get to the moon. Yet no one mentions the dead slaves who helped build the V-2, and whose ghosts still cry out for justice. We even have censored Dora survivors' point of view from our history books. Americans do not wish to be reminded of what Dora survivor Jean Michel said about the day that U.S. astronauts first walked on the moon: "I could not watch the Apollo mission without remembering that that triumphant walk was made possible by our initiation to inconceivable horror."[23]

Eli Pollach had worked on V-2s at Mittelwerk, yet no one helped him come to America after the war. Pollach was only seventeen years old when the SS rounded up the Jews of Hungary and sent him and his family to Auschwitz. Later, during an interview, his eyes filled with tears as his fingers gently touched a tattered photograph of his mother and father lying on the table before him. "This is all that is left of them," he said.[24]

At Auschwitz, Pollach's parents were ordered into the line that led to the gas chambers. He was loaded onto a train headed for Dora. "They called it the Sawatzki commando," he said of the work crew he was forced to join. "We had to go in the tunnels at six o'clock in the morning." He painted finished V-2s and helped load them onto boxcars in Mittelwerk's tunnels. "Some didn't come out because, you know, they died in there." Pollach was beaten by SS guards and he nearly starved to death. "I started getting fainting spells," he said. "So another inmate held me up, because once you fell down, either they left you there to die or they sent you to what they called the 'infirmary,' and that was the end of the line."[25]

After the war it took Pollach four years to get to America,

even though he had relatives living here. "So how did these people get here, with falsified documents and denying everything they did?" he asked. He said that going to the moon does not make up for twenty thousand dead Dora slaves. "They have a saying in Hebrew, if you need the thief, then you cut him off the gallows. But even if the United States needed these scientists, they should have reckoned a little bit for what they did."[26]

Still, the shadow of the Third Reich did cling to the Germans at Marshall. Just two weeks after the moon landing, von Braun confessed in a letter to an Army general that he had been a member of the SS. The letter to retired Major General Julius Klein discussed columnist Drew Pearson, who had revealed von Braun's SS membership decades earlier. It was written on von Braun's official stationery as director of Marshall and was marked "Personal and Sensitive."[27]

"It's true that I was a member of Hitler's elite SS. The columnist was correct," von Braun wrote to Klein. Then he admonished: "I would appreciate it if you would keep the information to yourself as any publicity would harm my work with NASA."[28]

That same year, West German prosecutors who were investigating crimes committed against Dora prisoners called on von Braun for a statement. In a general discussion about Mittelwerk, he told them that his younger brother Magnus "was engaged from approximately the fall, 1944 until the end of the war as a production engineer in Mittelwerk." Von Braun said he had visited Mittelwerk "approximately 15 times" and had been in the tunnels in 1943 while prisoners were quartered there. "I never saw a dead man, nor maltreatment nor a killing," he claimed, although he had heard "rumors" that prisoners had been hanged in the tunnels because of sabotage. The prosecutors then confronted him with the fact that several sabotage reports were found in Peenemünde files. "I cannot remember anything about it," he replied.[29]

None of the Paperclip group was called to testify when the West German case went to trial in 1971. But then key French witnesses like Jean Michel were not contacted either. "It was nothing but a coverup," Michel said recently. The court found that the Mittelwerk Prisoner Labor Supply office had requested that Dora prisoners be sent to work as slaves in the tunnels. Over a decade later Rudolph admitted to U.S. Justice Department prosecutors that it was he who had made those requests to the SS.[30]

Once America's goal of landing men on the moon was achieved, the politicians who controlled the goverment's purse strings found that public sentiment for space exploration had dwindled. The overwhelming interest was in the Vietnam War, protest marches, Martin Luther King's assassination, and riots in the streets. These pressing concerns crowded the astronauts' adventures in space off of the front pages of newspapers.[31]

In 1970, von Braun was reassigned to NASA headquarters in Washington. His transfer marked the beginning of the end of the German rocket team at NASA. "A lot of them got down in the dumps when von Braun left," recalled Alexander McCool, director of the Safety and Quality Assurance office at Marshall. After the Apollo program, von Braun worked on a project to send a man to Mars, but it fell flat. Congress was not interested.[32]

Since their Peenemünde days, the Germans always had enjoyed high-level protection. Now this "backcover," as the Germans called it, was gone. General Walter Dornberger had protected them from jealousies and undercutting at Peenemünde during the war. And the U.S. Army's backcover had included keeping secret the derogatory information in their files. "If the German group had stayed with the Army, they would probably have continued to be protected," the Marshall technical official observed.[33]

Even their unseen guardians in the Pentagon had closed up shop. Christopher left the project in 1966 because the interest in continuing Paperclip had waned. "I saw the thing was dying," he said. The projects were turned over to Astrid Kraus, assistant for research and development in the Department of Defense, while Army Colonel Neil ImObersteg ran two Special Projects Team offices in West Germany. "They picked up the pieces," Christopher said, as new recruits continued to arrive until around 1973. Then ImObersteg notified Kraus that the team's offices were going to be closed. "This has been an extremely enjoyable assignment for me," Im-Obersteg wrote in his farewell. "My best regards, and hoping we may meet again." The team's records, he said, would be burned.[34]

Things began to fall apart for the old rocket team in the early 1970s, when the Marshall Center's budget was drastically slashed and, as the Germans put it, the "Great Massacre" began. Following the civil service rule book, the nonveterans were the first to be cut, and those included the Germans. "So what happened for us . . . we got two options: either a reduction in grade, or getting out, retiring. That was the choice," said von Tiesenhausen. The Germans viewed the forced retirements and demotions as a deliberate attempt to eliminate the German influence at Marshall.[35]

Almost all of the top positions were cut with one sweep. Kurt Debus left NASA in 1974. Von Tiesenhausen, being younger than the others, was demoted a grade, but his job as assistant director of the Advanced Systems Department remained the same. He said he "made the best of it" and eventually received a NASA medal for exceptional service. Haeussermann, in charge of overall systems engineering, was told that his job was being cut and he did not qualify for any positions over a GS-12. "That was for me an offense," he said. Then his secretary was replaced by one who was less capable.[36]

Nevertheless, all of them retired with sizable pensions. Former NASA officials also point out that there were many more Americans than Germans who lost their jobs due to cutbacks. Rocco Petrone, who was director of Marshall at the time of the cutbacks, said that the center's organization was being restructured and the Germans had reached retirement age. "You have to remember, they had thirty years behind them," Petrone said. "They all came to talk to me individually and were so appreciative of what the country had done for them.

But they also understood that this time, their careers were coming to an end."[37]

When von Braun arrived in Washington in 1970 there were rumors that he was going to be named as NASA's next chief administrator. But there was still resentment toward von Braun's Nazi past in NASA headquarters and in the nation's capital. Politicians did not want to offend Jews by naming a former official of Hitler's regime to a high-ranking post in the U.S. government. "People said don't pay any attention to the rumors," said Dr. Charles Sheldon, former White House senior staff member of the National Aeronautics and Space Council. "Von Braun would never be given any political position. No one who had worked with Hitler and the Nazi government could be trusted."[38]

"And from then on, von Braun became a non-person," von Tiesenhausen recalled. Von Braun's dream of going to Mars was shelved. Nobody gave him assignments, nobody wanted anything from him. "You could see him wandering up these long corridors all by himself, up and down. Then he left. . . ."[39]

14

Trying to Open the Lid

I N the aftermath of the Watergate scandal, members of Congress began a series of investigations into the Nazis-in-America issue and past abuses of U.S. intelligence agencies. When these investigations began in 1974, Congresswoman Elizabeth Holtzman from New York was already a familiar face to most Americans. They had seen her tough questioning during the televised Nixon impeachment hearings. No sooner had President Nixon resigned than Holtzman was confronted with yet another difficult issue: she was told that there were Nazi war criminals living in the United States and that the U.S. government was covering it up.

"When they told me that there were Nazi war criminals in America, that the government had a list of these people and was doing nothing, my first reaction was incredulity because it made no sense to me," Holtzman recalled. "America fought

230

Hitler in World War II. Close to 200,000 Americans died in the process. Why would we give sanctuary to Nazi war criminals?"[1]

Holtzman raised that issue with immigration commissioner Leonard Chapman during a subcommittee hearing in April 1974. "He did admit to me that there was a list of alleged Nazi war criminals, and then when I asked, 'Well what are you doing about it?' I got hemming and hawing. So I asked to see the files myself, and it was clear that they were doing nothing."[2]

Over the next six years Holtzman conducted investigations, prodded her congressional colleagues, and hassled government agencies on the subject. In the process she received strong bipartisan support from colleagues on the House Judiciary Committee, including committee chairman Peter Rodino and Hamilton Fish. The eventual result was the 1978 passage of the "Holtzman Amendment" to the U.S. immigration law. The amendment provided a statutory basis to deport Nazi war criminals and to prevent their entry into the country as either immigrants or visitors. Until 1953 the Displaced Persons Act had barred from entry individuals who had engaged in persecution under the Nazi regime. A change in that law, however, had allowed even convicted Nazi war criminals, such as Otto Ambros, to enter the country. Holtzman's amendment closed that loophole. In addition to changing the law, Holtzman pressed the Carter administration to set up the Office of Special Investigations (OSI) in the Criminal Division of the Justice Department to investigate and prosecute cases involving Nazi war criminals. Finally there was a law and a prosecuting unit to do something about Nazis in America.[3]

Yet those accomplishments were not easily obtained. "Every one of those efforts involved a battle," Holtzman recalled. One battle involved the attempt to uncover information about Nazi scientists brought here under Paperclip. A tight lid of secrecy continued to surround the project. And no wonder. The American public believed that the project had ended in the late 1940s. No one knew that Paperclip had practically marched right into the congressional hearings.[4]

Nevertheless, disturbing questions did surface about Hubertus Strughold's Nazi past amid charges that government agencies and highly placed political officials were protecting him. While the Air Force touted him as the "father of American space medicine," Strughold was publicly identified as one of thirty-seven war crimes suspects who were under investigation by the U.S. Immigration and Naturalization Service (INS). His name was included on the list because of a letter written in 1958 by one Julian Bach to the editor of the *Saturday Review* concerning the Dachau experiments. But the 1958 investigation that followed quickly turned into a joke. INS made a discreet check with none other than the Air Force—the same military branch that helped cover up Strughold's past in the first place—and then dropped the investigation after being told that Strughold already had been "appropriately investigated."[5]

Soon after Strughold's name surfaced again in 1974, Holtzman received conflicting reports from INS when she inquired about the status of his case. In one instance, Holtzman obtained an INS status report noting that a regional INS office had been directed to cancel its investigation. Later, INS Director Chapman told Holtzman that the investigation into Strughold's background was still ongoing.[6]

A controversy ensued when INS closed the case following an inquiry on Strughold's behalf by his Texas congressman, Henry Gonzales, who complained to Chapman that Strughold's name had been released as a person under investigation. Gonzales said he had been informed by an "interested individual" that Strughold's background already had been thoroughly checked. "If he did have a suspect past," Gonzales wrote, "I do not believe he would have ever pursued his profession, let alone submit to extensive investigations required for the sensitive jobs that he held for our government." A few days later, Chapman reported back that inquiries to the military and other federal agencies had disclosed "no derogatory information" and therefore the INS considered the case closed.[7]

Then Strughold claimed in a New York newspaper that he had never even heard of the Dachau experiments until *after* World War II. That claim was disputed in a magazine article by journalist Charles Allen, which gave details of Strughold's attendance at a conference in 1942 at which the freezing experiments on Dachau prisoners were clearly revealed, causing a sensation among the scientists at the conference. After that revelation, U.S. immigration official Henry Wagner admitted to *The New York Times* that there was no evidence in Strughold's file that he had ever been asked directly whether he had known of the Dachau experiments on human beings.[8]

A General Accounting Office investigation in 1978 could have blown the lid off the entire Nazi issue, including Paperclip. The GAO is the investigating arm of Congress, and it has the authority to obtain documents and question witnesses. But the GAO allowed itself to be duped by government agencies instead of using its authority to conduct a thorough probe. The investigation focused on whether there had been a widespread government conspiracy to obstruct investigations of Nazi war criminals living in America. Although the GAO revealed that some government agencies had employed or utilized Nazis, the agency concluded that there had been no conspiracy to obstruct justice.[9]

But later the GAO was shocked to learn that government agencies had indeed deliberately withheld information from GAO investigators. As a result the GAO conducted another investigation in 1985. But that report was an outright whitewash. The GAO was informed of some of the major findings in this book, and the *Bulletin* article revealing the original JIOA coverup already had been published in April of that year. But GAO investigators said they were not interested in seeing the materials. The GAO's 1985 report not only ignored the published evidence, but it contained glaring errors, such as stating that Paperclip had ended in 1947(!), and parroted all of the false myths that have been trotted out through the decades. GAO investigator John Tipton later admitted in an interview that research for the report had been "superficial."[10]

The JIOA officers were not called to account for their actions at all. "The GAO should have looked at the problem with Paperclip where President Truman issued an executive order saying that Nazi war criminals were not supposed to be brought to this country—an order that we now know was flagrantly violated," Holtzman said. "If we have agencies of this government willing to deliberately overlook and violate presidential directives, if we have government agencies willing to deceive other government agencies in order to protect Nazi war criminals, then we have a very serious problem here."[11]

In 1974, while Holtzman was investigating Nazis, other congressional committees were uncovering a long history of other illegal activities by Army intelligence and the CIA. Strangely, the Nazi issue did not surface at all in those investigations, even though the intelligence agencies' use of Nazis was central to the subjects under investigation. For instance, one investigation uncovered the Army's illegal domestic spying activities. Yet no information surfaced to expose the tactics used by G-2 to suppress derogatory information about Paperclip.[12]

Another investigation did uncover the Army's LSD experiments at Edgewood. But the fact that Nazi scientists worked there under Paperclip was never disclosed in either congressional hearings or in an extensive investigation by the Army inspector general. That both the Army and CIA MK-ULTRA experiments stemmed from Nazi science was certainly relevant to understanding the early history of those secret projects.[13]

Although some information about the experiments was revealed, the question of rendering justice to the victims was another story. Regarding MK-ULTRA, Frank Olson's family finally learned that he had jumped from a hotel window after CIA agents slipped LSD into his drink. President Ford publicly apologized to the Olson family and signed legislation providing $750,000 to his survivors. But over a decade would pass before other MK-ULTRA victims would obtain anything resembling justice. On October 5, 1988, the CIA reached an out-of-court settlement with nine victims of Canadian psychiatrist Ewen Cameron's brainwashing techniques, which the CIA had funded. Cameron had subjected his patients to drug-induced "sleep therapy" for weeks at a time, gave them LSD, and administered electroshock therapy at up to seventy-five times the usual intensity, while forcing his patients to listen to recorded messages that played continuously for days at a time. The victims suffered permanent physical and mental damage as a result of the experiments.[14]

The Army's involvement in the psychochemical experiments that killed Harold Blauer also was revealed in 1975, along with evidence that the Army had covered it up. Yet it was not until 1987 that his daughter's lawsuit finally was settled in her favor in federal court. Even then, none of the doctors involved in the experiments were charged with committing a crime.[15]

The Nuremberg code pertaining to the rights of human subjects in experiments formed an issue in all of these cases. The report on an Army inspector general investigation of the Edgewood experiments discussed the Nuremberg guidelines in detail and judged that Edgewood doctors had violated the guidelines as well as the Army's own internal regulations. But in 1988 the CIA's lawyers ignored the Nuremberg guidelines by contending in court papers that "the doctrine of informed consent, as it is now understood, did not exist" when the Canadian experiments were conducted in the 1950s.[16]

Soldiers like James Stanley finally were informed in 1975 that they had been used as guinea pigs in psychochemical experiments at Edgewood. "When I received the Army's letter telling me this, I just stood in my living room and cried," Stanley recalled. But his happiness over having learned the truth would be short-lived.[17]

Army officials admitted during a House Armed Services Committee hearing in 1975 that at least one soldier had committed suicide and several others had been seriously injured as a result of the experiments. Yet the Army had never made any attempt to conduct follow-up tests on any of Edgewood's victims. After considerable congressional prodding, the U.S. Army Surgeon General, Lieutenant General Robert Taylor, promised committee members that all of the LSD victims would be located and given complete physical and psychological exams.[18]

As a result of lengthy congressional hearings and considerable media attention, the American public was left with the assumption that, at the very least, Edgewood's victims would be tested to determine if they had been hurt, and if so, would receive help. That assumption would prove false.

The Army did conduct a study of the LSD victims. And the National Research Council studied seven thousand other soldiers who had been given everything from nerve gas to PCP. But five years passed before the first study was completed, in 1980, and by then neither Congress nor the press was interested in the results. The studies were released quietly with no publicity whatsoever. No one seemed to care that they were a sham.[19]

Despite Taylor's pledge that 1,000 LSD victims would be located and given physicals, the LSD study shows that only 220 individuals—less than one-third of the total—actually were given physicals. One hundred others were merely sent forms. And 149 men flatly refused to participate in the study at all—over 8 percent of them saying they were suspicious of the Army's motives. One of them told the Army that he declined to participate out of "the fear [I] would be used again for test[s] of some sort or be doped and sign papers releasing the Army for these problems."[20]

Some of those who did participate said they were humiliated and outraged by the experience. Stanley, for instance, was told that he was going to be put up in a motel while given a physical at Walter Reed Army Hospital. "Instead I was taken to a psychiatric hospital and treated like a crazy person," Stanley said. "I was furious."[21]

Ken Loeh, who has been in and out of hospitals two dozen times since the experiments, broke down and cried over the phone when the subject of the follow-up exam came up during our conversation. "It's too painful to talk," he said. "I'll send you the information." A few days later, a package arrived in the mail. Inside were the tattered remnants of his life—the documentation of his experiments, the damaging effect on his health, and Taylor's testimony before Congress. Scrawled across that testimony, where Taylor promised that the soldiers would be helped, Loeh had written angrily, "Lies! Nothing but lies!"[22]

The LSD study has other serious flaws, not the least of which is the ethical question of whether it should have been overseen by the Army, which had conducted the Edgewood experiments in the first place. The study's author, Lieutenant Colonel David A. McFarling, who also conducted most of the physicals, leaves no doubt as to his personal views of the whole affair. Those views reflect the same cold war mentality that haunted Paperclip for decades. The real crux of the issue, according to McFarling, was that the presumed ends to which the Army LSD experiments were directed had justified the means. "It would have been grossly negligent of chemical warfare specialists not to have investigated LSD if only from a defensive standpoint," he argued. Maybe so, *but* was this study an appropriate place to discuss an issue that already had been investigated by Congress and the Army's inspector general?[23]

Even more disturbing, McFarling's study contains a six-page diatribe against the "cloak and dagger" manner in which the experiments had been portrayed in the press, repeats claims that the soldiers had been fully informed about the tests—a claim refuted by the Army's own inspector general—and asserts that the experiments had been medically supervised to insure the safety of the participants. McFarling also makes the outrageous and totally undocumented accusation against the very soldiers he was assigned to test. After pages of medical evidence, revealing that some men had suffered everything from grand mal seizures to suicide attempts, McFarling brushes off their complaints by stating that "some subjects may have consciously or subconsciously altered and manipulated their complaints for their own purposes, notably self-enrichment."[24]

A study conducted by the National Research Council raises equally disturbing questions, especially regarding protocol. The council did not deal with the issue of whether the soldiers had been harmed. It evaded that issue by investigating whether the chemical warfare agents and drugs other than LSD used on seven thousand soldiers at the base were capable of causing long-term damage to the soldiers' health. Even though the NRC revealed that several soldiers had been hurt during the tests—and even hospitalized—the council repeatedly said the available data was insufficient to determine the long-term effects of the experiments.[25]

This ambiguous conclusion should not be surprising. What the NRC report conveniently fails to tell the reader is that the project director for the entire study, Francis N. Marzulli, and several of the study's panelists and technical consultants had been employed at Edgewood or had been under contract to that base while the experiments were going on.

And all of them had connections to Paperclip. Project Director Marzulli worked at Edgewood in the 1950s. Panelist John J. O'Neill, now at Temple University Medical School, conducted chemical warfare research with Paperclip scientist Theodor Wagner-Jauregg when he worked at Edgewood in the 1950s. Four technical consultants also were directly connected to the base: James S. Ketchum, Joseph S. Wiles, Stephen Krop, and J. Henry Wills. Remember, it was Wills who had determined the effects of nerve gas on humans at Edgewood by examining captured records of the Nazi death camps.

If all that is not questionable enough, the NRC report is based in large part on Edgewood reports and published scientific literature written by the same men who conducted the experiments in the first place—hardly a group who would admit in published articles that their experiments had harmed anyone.[26]

For Stanley, however, the final insult was the U.S. Supreme Court's decision in his case. Stanley sued the government, claiming that he had suffered episodes of violence and memory loss as a result of the LSD experiments. But on June 25, 1987, the Supreme Court held that the government was not liable for injuries to servicemen when the injuries arose in the course of activities incident to their military service. In a scathing dissent Justice William Brennan cited the Nuremberg code, which the Army had flagrantly violated in the so-called interest of national security. "Having invoked national security to conceal its activities, the Government now argues that the preservation of military discipline requires that Government officials remain free to violate the constitutional rights of soldiers without fear of money damages," Brennan argued. "Soldiers ought not be asked to defend a Constitution indifferent to their essential human dignity."[27]

By 1980 the system to investigate and prosecute Nazis that Holtzman had worked to set up was in full operation. The Justice Department OSI's staff of historians and lawyers were investigating cases of Nazi war criminals who had lived openly in the United States for decades. Early that year, Harvard law student Eli Rosenbaum made a discovery that eventually would result in Arthur Rudolph's relinquishing his U.S. citizenship and leaving the country rather than contest charges that he had committed war crimes in Nazi Germany.

Rosenbaum was browsing in a Cambridge, Massachusetts, bookstore when he spotted Jean Michel's book *Dora*. "I was stunned," Rosenbaum recalled. "I had never seen camp Dora mentioned in any Holocaust literature." That oversight by Holocaust historians is one reason why French Resistance hero Michel decided to tell the horrifying story of how he and other Dora prisoners had been forced to work as slaves in Mittelwerk's tunnels. Then Rosenbaum read *The Rocket Team*, by Frederick Ordway and Mitchell Sharpe, which discussed Mittelwerk from the viewpoint of the Nazi rocket scientists who worked there. Rosenbaum was furious when he came across a passage that quoted Rudolph as saying he had cursed when he had to leave a New Year's Eve party in 1943 and go out into the cold weather to resolve a production problem at Mittelwerk.[28]

"I remember thinking, there were innocent people dying in

that hell hole, and here was Arthur Rudolph complaining that
he had to leave a nice warm party to go back to work," said
Rosenbaum. One of the first things Rosenbaum did after he
began working as an OSI attorney was to ask the unit's
then–deputy director Neal Sher if he had ever heard of Rudolph. He had not. But he authorized Rosenbaum to investigate.[29]

Over the next few years, the OSI quietly investigated the
Rudolph case, looking for evidence about what had happened
in that underground hell so long ago. The U.S. Army's secret
Dora war crimes case provided some of the evidence uncovered
by the OSI. Major Eugene Smith had died years earlier, but
his interrogations of Paperclip scientists at Fort Bliss had been
found. Unfortunately, that is not the case with another obvious
treasure chest of information. Remember (in chapter 4) how
the Air Force placed Mittelwerk director Georg Rickhey in
charge of forty-two boxes of Mittelwerk management records
at Wright Field? Perhaps it should not be surprising that those
records simply vanished without a trace.

By late 1982 OSI prosecutors felt they had proof that Rudolph had requisitioned and utilized slave laborers while serving as Mittelwerk's operations director. "In this case we have
not just the utilization of slave labor, which is a clear-cut war
crime under the Nuremberg laws," said Sher. "We have the
outright exploitation of slave labor . . . working under terrible
conditions."[30]

Rosenbaum, who directed the Rudolph investigation, com-
pares the case with that of Nazi Armaments Minister Albert
Speer, who was convicted and sentenced to twenty years' imprisonment by the International Military Tribunal for his role
in the utilization of slave labor. "If you look at what the IMT
said about Speer, most of it could easily be said about Rudolph
as well," Rosenbaum explained. "The IMT said that Speer
knew that concentration camp inmates were going to be used
as slave laborers to build his armaments. So did Rudolph.
Speer attended meetings that dealt with the capture and en-
slavement of more people and their use as slave laborers for

armaments production. So did Rudolph. In fact, Rudolph attended at least one meeting with the SS on that very subject, as did other high-ranking German scientists, including Wern- her von Braun. They discussed, among other things, the pos- sibility of bringing a large number of French citizens from France to work as slaves at Mittelwerk. And Rudolph, like Speer, requested—and received from the SS—ever larger numbers of concentration camp inmates to work for him."[31]

Another key part of the evidence against Rudolph was that the notorious Prisoner Labor Supply office at Mittelwerk was directly subordinate to him. That office worked directly with the SS labor allocation office to designate the number of pris- oners assigned to work in Mittelwerk's tunnels. SS officer Wilhelm Simon, convicted in the Army's Dora trial, headed that SS office. "Rudolph relied on Simon for, among other things, bringing an increased supply of slaves to work on V- 2 production," Rosenbaum said. Rudolph's subordinates in the Prisoner Labor Supply office also were responsible for determining the quantity of food the prisoners received—an amount so inadequate that thousands of prisoners starved to death.[32]

Rosenbaum also uncovered the evidence that civilian engi- neers subordinate to Rudolph had beaten or stabbed prisoners and had reported them as saboteurs to the SS. That resulted in some being hanged. Army records identify Rudolph's sub- ordinates, including his deputy, Karl Seidenstuecker, by name as abusing prisoners. As one witness at the Army trial put it, "practically all civilians who were working in the Prisoners' Labor Allocation" either ordered the punishment of prisoners or "carried out beatings on their own."[33]

The OSI found Rudolph living comfortably in retirement in San Jose, California. On October 13, 1982, and February 4, 1983, he was interrogated under oath by then–OSI director Allan Ryan, Jr., Deputy Director Sher, and Rosenbaum. In the meetings, the OSI attorneys examined the forms that Ru- dolph had filled out when he first arrived under Project Over- cast in 1945. He had joined the Nazi party in 1931, two years before the Nazi regime came into power, and was also a member of the SA. Rudolph told the OSI that he had participated in Nazi party meetings and processions, where he wore a Nazi arm band and paraded down the streets of Berlin.[34]

In 1943 Rudolph was working at Peenemünde when General Dornberger told him that he was going to Mittelwerk. "He just phoned me and said, 'You go with Sawatzki,' " Rudolph said. Sawatzki, who later was captured by U.S. Army troops at Nordhausen, became Rudolph's boss at the underground plant. Prisoners already were working and living in the tunnels when Rudolph arrived. Rudolph admitted to OSI that the prisoners were there for political reasons, not because they had technical skills. In Rudolph's view, they were "just bodies." Those "bodies" included a black American flyer named Johnny Nicholas, Jean Michel, Yves Beon and other members of the French Resistance, Hungarian Jews, including children, and Italian, Polish, and Russian POWs.[35]

When the OSI began to question Rudolph about the prisoners' living and working conditions, Rudolph first parroted the same story that he had told Smith in 1947—that he and other civilian engineers had worked under conditions identical to those of the prisoners. But Sher did not let him off the hook so easily.[36]

> "I worked twelve hours," Rudolph said.
> "Yeah, but you didn't—you didn't have to sleep in the tunnel, did you?" asked Sher.
> "No."[37]

Rudolph also admitted that the food was not the same for him and the prisoners, either. Rudolph ate his workday meals outside the tunnels, in a barracks cafeteria in which the prisoners were not allowed. Also, unlike the prisoners, Rudolph could eat his other meals at home.

"I want to show you a book," said Sher, as he placed *The "Dora"-Nordhausen War Crimes Trial* on the table. This was the U.S. Army prosecution team's grim account of the history of Mittelwerk-Dora, complete with photographs taken by the U.S. Army Signal Corps when Nordhausen was liberated. Sher turned to the page with two photographs of Dora's crematory. The caption under the photograph of the smoldering furnace noted that the prisoners' bodies "were in many cases emaciated to such an extent that the oven could take three or four at a time."[38]

    "Did you ever see it?" asked Sher, referring to the crematory.
    "From the distance, yes."
    "And you knew that prisoners who died at Mittelbau were cremated at the crematory. You knew that, didn't you?"
    (Rudolph nodded his head in agreement.)
    "Turn to the next page, Mr. Rudolph. You'll see pictures of prisoners who worked at Mittelwerk when they were liberated by the Allies." The photograph showed a truckload of dead prisoners whose bodies were nothing more than skeletons. "Do those people look like they were working under good conditions?"
    "No. Certainly not."
    "You know the figures are that nearly twenty thousand people died during your service at this facility?"
    "No."
    "Twenty thousand. Did that—would that surprise you?"
    "To me, yes."
    "You knew people were dying?"
    "Oh, yeah. I knew that."[39]

Rudolph said he had walked through the tunnels two or three times a day and had seen firsthand that conditions were bad for the prisoners. He also had visited Dora a couple of times to have a glass of schnapps with the SS commandant of the camp, Otto Foerschner, who was convicted of war crimes and hanged after the war. Rudolph admitted to Rosenbaum that he never had ordered his subordinates to cease abusing prisoners. This despite the fact that OSI had located a Mittelwerk directive in which Rudolph and other top-ranking civilians were instructed to order their subordinates to leave such punishment to the SS.[40]

Rudolph told OSI that Sawatzki had once threatened to put him in a concentration camp, but later in the interview he admitted that he had not taken Sawatzki's threat seriously; he figured Sawatzki needed him to get the rockets built on time. In the spring of 1944 Sawatzki was ill for a month, and when he returned, he was transferred to V-1 production. This left Rudolph completely in charge. "I was free of his darn interfering," Rudolph said. Yet, even then Rudolph did not make changes to help the prisoners. Instead he increased V-2 production schedules, which meant that more prisoners dropped dead from exhaustion. Rudolph said he did not try to lighten the prisoners' work schedules because, "I would be called on the carpet by Sawatzki even though I was not reporting to him anymore."[41]

> "We know, the world knows, it's part of—of history, that prisoners were forcibly taken from various concentration camps, Buchenwald, Auschwitz and others, and used as slave laborers to produce the V-2," said Sher. "You agree that that is true?"
>
> "That's true," said Rudolph.
>
> "It seems to me that you must have known that people were dying of disease and starvation and overwork. You must have known that."
>
> "Yes, I know that people were dying."[42]

Rudolph confessed that it was he who had asked the SS to send more prisoners to Dora in order to meet the labor demands of increased V-2 production schedules. When Sher asked him directly if he had requested that more forced laborers be brought down into that underground hell, Rudolph admitted, "Yes, I did." And he had dealt directly with SS officer Simon to make those requests. Rudolph said he had gotten the prisoners "from Dora, and I got them probably from Buchenwald or somewhere else."[43]

Rudolph thought Simon was a nice guy. After Simon's conviction at the Dora trial, Rudolph sent Simon's defense attorney a statement claiming that he and Simon had tried to improve conditions for the prisoners. Rudolph said he had told Simon that one prisoner was too sick to work and he was returned to the camp. The problem was, prisoners judged unfit to work were then shipped to Lublin extermination camp. The U.S. Army tribunal had rejected Simon's defense arguments along the same line and sentenced him to life imprisonment.[44]

One important issue in Rudolph's case is the prisoners' sabotage of the rockets. Numerous Dora survivors said they sabotaged rockets by urinating on wiring, removing vital parts, and loosening screws. "It was common practice," said Yves Beon, who sabotaged the rockets he worked on as a welder by making his welding appear sound when, in fact, the rocket parts were not welded at all. Beon believes that their sabotage efforts saved Americans' lives—that American troops landing at Normandy would have been killed if the rockets had functioned properly. "It would have been terrible for the Allies and for the American army," Beon said.[45]

"These prisoners, despite living under horrendous conditions, nevertheless attempted very courageously to sabotage this Nazi effort," Sher said in an interview. "Engineers would get involved because in order to find out who was the suspected saboteur, one would have to know, mechanically, how the rocket was being sabotaged. And reports were prepared and sent to the SS, and they would then find the saboteur. There are reported incidents of the saboteur being hung in very grotesque and slow fashion, and every slave laborer was ordered—ordered to watch the hanging."[46]

Sabotage reports were discussed in the U.S. Army's 1947 trial when Sawatzki's secretary, Hannelore Bannasch, testified that Mittelwerk management "passed on" sabotage reports and if anyone had signed them, it would have been Rudolph. Yet Rudolph told the OSI that he had not known that prisoners were sabotaging rockets.[47]

When the OSI concluded the interview, the attorneys gave Rudolph no indication when they would be back. Then, in late 1983, the OSI confronted Rudolph with the charges and some of the evidence. As a result Rudolph decided to relinquish his U.S. citizenship and leave the country. "He stated in an agreement formally, which he executed in my presence, in front of his lawyer and his daughter, that if these charges were brought into court he could not contest them," said Sher. Rudolph moved to Hamburg, West Germany, and currently is banned from entering the United States.[48]

"I think it's important that this government take a stand that Nazi war criminals are not wanted here," said Sher. "Particularly at a time when there are people, in very slick fashion, who claim the Holocaust never took place, who try to white-wash it and try to minimize what happened. I think that's very dangerous for the younger generation, and for history."[49]

The most disturbing example of that whitewash occurred in the late 1980s, in the aftermath of the Rudoph case.

15 Consequences

T HE shadow of an old V-2 rocket briefly touched the silver hair of some of the twenty-two men who strolled, chatting in English and German, to a three-tiered wooden stand. There they stood posing with a larger-than-life photograph of a blond, square-jawed Wernher von Braun while press cameras clicked and whirred. The huge engine nozzles of the Alabama Space and Rocket Center's (ASRC) Saturn V moon rocket loomed behind them.[1]

The event in Huntsville, Alabama, was billed as the fortieth anniversary of the old German rocket team's arrival in the U.S. under Paperclip. But a stinging irony lay in the timing of the April 1985 reunion, in that it was forty years to the month after American troops liberated the Dora slaves who also had helped build Hitler's infamous V-2 rocket. And in the shocking fact that two of the men being honored that day were under active OSI investigation for Nazi war crimes.[2]

Standing in the third row—the one wearing impenetrably dark glasses, the other wearing an open-necked shirt—were Guenther Haukohl and Dieter Grau. During World War II, Haukohl was Rudolph's subordinate at Mittelwerk as chief manager of installation and supervision of the manufacture of V-2s. Up to seven hundred prisoners worked as slaves in Haukohl's unit, under the supervision of a brutal capo named Georg Finkenzeller, who was convicted after the war of viciously beating prisoners.[3] The question of whether Haukohl had anything to do with prisoners being mistreated remains unanswered.

Grau, an engineer at Peenemünde, was sent by Wernher von Braun to Mittelwerk to find out why rockets produced at the underground factory were malfunctioning. During an inspection Grau found that prisoners who he said did not have a "positive attitude" had sabotaged the rockets. "They knew where they could tighten or loosen a screw, and this way try to interfere with the proper function of the missile," Grau said. Grau even told *Atlanta Weekly* in 1985 he had turned in a sabotage report on the prisoners.[4] But the question of whether Grau's report led to the prisoners being hanged also remains unanswered.

And those disturbing questions may never be answered. Patrick Richardson, a Huntsville attorney representing Haukohl and Grau, claimed that the Justice Department was on a Nazi "witch-hunt" and twice turned down OSI's request to interview the two men, in November 1985 and March 1986. A Cable News Network cameraman and I went to see Haukohl and Grau at their Huntsville homes for my CNN series broadcast in 1986. Haukohl refused to talk, and all Grau would say was, "I promised my lawyer I wouldn't make any further statements."[5]

From the morning shadows that lent an air of ambiguity to the ASRC's photographic session, the reunion moved to an indoor auditorium, where the near-darkness signaled a change of mood—a gathering of sinister forces, some from the distant past, some from the present. There in the auditorium, along with the old Germans themselves, were representatives of the forces that had helped create and perpetuate the lies that surrounded Paperclip and its spinoffs since 1945: the U.S. Army, NASA, and—a more recent addition—the empire built on zealotry and fraud by political extremist Lyndon LaRouche.[6]

After an hour-long slide show and briefing on the Army's latest weaponry, an ASRC public relations official set the ground rules for the press: there were to be no questions about Arthur Rudolph. But the questions were asked despite the gag attempt, and soon the air was filled with hostility and bitter comments about the OSI's handling of Rudolph's case. Retired Army Colonel Paul Towry, a former chief executive officer at Redstone Arsenal, lambasted the OSI, saying their investigations are "beginning to get out of hand."[7]

Then the press conference turned into a podium for the twisted paranoia and conspiracy theories of LaRouche. Marsha Freeman, Washington editor of *Fusion* magazine, a LaRouche mouthpiece, was introduced by the public relations officer and allowed to launch into a fifteen-minute attack on the OSI. "The witch-hunt against the leading space scientists of the United States is nothing less than a Soviet plot to destroy the military-scientific accomplishments of the U.S.," she said. Freeman concluded her tirade by asking for a congressional investigation and urging that the OSI be shut down. At that point the Germans in the audience cheered.[8]

The Huntsville gathering, with its bizarre mixture of adulation and paranoia, was a symptom of a gathering storm. For over forty years Paperclip had survived threats from within and without, kept on course by the firm determination that the ends justified the means, even if that meant breaking the law. Paperclip's dark secrets lay safely hidden in coverups, lies, and deceit. Now the Rudolph case had put a crack in the project's protective shell and threatened to expose all of those secrets.

An alliance quickly formed to close the gap and continue the coverup. It also resulted in the kind of Holocaust revisionism and whitewash that OSI Director Neal Sher had warned was taking place.

One figure in that alliance was Frederick Ordway, a former

NASA public relations official who was a close friend of Rudolph, Wernher von Braun, and other Paperclip scientists. Ordway publicly defended Rudolph, claiming that the Dora slaves had been "well fed." As evidence Ordway cited a letter by Milton Hochmuth, a former Army intelligence officer who had rounded up V-2s at Mittelwerk in 1945, in which Hochmuth says he remembers "being surprised at how well-fed . . . and in good health" he found the prisoners assigned to V-2 production.[9]

Ordway did not mention that Hochmuth also must have seen the dead bodies of six thousand Dora slaves lying on the ground, as former New York governor Hugh Carey and other American liberators did when they arrived on the same day as Hochmuth. "Everyone saw it," said Carey, who was then an eighteen-year-old Army sergeant. "We saw everything within a few minutes when we arrived at the site. It was horrible."[10]

Ordway also suppressed the most damaging evidence against his false claim—evidence he has had in hand for more than ten years: a taped interview with Dieter Grau conducted in 1971 for Ordway's book *The Rocket Team* (coauthored by Mitchell Sharpe). In describing the prisoners he saw during his wartime visit to Mittelwerk, Grau said, "the way they looked, they were not well fed at all and as far as I could see, had a tough time." Ordway conveniently left Grau's comments out of his book, which whitewashes Rudolph's activities at Mittelwerk.[11]

The LaRouche organization is another part of the alliance forged in response to the Rudolph case. The perennial presidential candidate's shadowy network has been described by the CIA as a "violence oriented" cult. The inner workings of a myriad of illegal money-funneling fronts and publications generally went unreported in the establishment press until hundreds of police raided LaRouche's Leesburg, Virginia, estate in 1986. In November 1988 LaRouche was convicted in a federal court in Alexandria, Virginia, of conspiracy to obstruct justice, mail fraud, and income tax evasion. According to the fifty-two-page indictment in that case, LaRouche personally instructed members to "use 'any means short of thievery and thuggery' to meet fund-raising quotas." But even his conviction for these crimes has not stopped LaRouche: in September 1990 he decided to run for Congress while still serving time in a federal penitentiary.[12]

The LaRouche group's virulent Nazi-style anti-Semitism also has been well documented. As the Anti-Defamation League's Irwin Suall put it, LaRouche is a "small time Hitler." The LaRouche group's idolatry of defense-related research, along with its smoke screen of wild allegations of anti-LaRouche conspiracies involving the Queen of England, the KGB, and even President Bush, make them a logical vessel for paranoia about the OSI's Nazi-hunting activities.[13]

LaRouche has long-standing ties with the Nazi scientists brought to the United States under Paperclip. One was Krafft Ehricke, a longtime member of the Fusion Energy Foundation and author of articles for *Fusion* magazine. Ehricke, who died in 1984, had been a tank commander in the Wehrmacht and an engineer at Peenemünde before working for the U.S. Army under Paperclip. Later Ehricke went to Bell Aircraft, where his old Peenemünde chief Walter Dornberger was vice president, and then joined the Convair division of General Dynamics, which built the Atlas missile. Another scientist with LaRouche ties was Konrad Dannenberg, who had been a rocket propulsion section chief at Peenemünde and was part of the original German rocket team brought to the United States in 1945. There is also rocket pioneer Hermann Oberth, who was brought to Huntsville under Paperclip in 1955. Oberth, it will be remembered, also smuggled his art treasures out of West Germany when he came here.[14]

Both Dannenberg and Oberth contributed to an anti-OSI rally held at LaRouche's heavily guarded estate in July 1985. The rally was held under the guise of being a tribute to Ehricke, with 450 military officers and scientists from West Germany and other countries in attendance. In his keynote address LaRouche claimed that the OSI was carrying out a "KGB-run

witch-hunt" against German scientists and accused the Justice
Department unit of commiting "treason." That rhetoric was
followed by Dannenberg's speech on the "lessons" of Peenemünde and the reading of a message from Oberth that
evoked the mystique of Nazi science.[15]

Dannenberg said he was "borne into this LaRouche affair"
when he was asked to honor Ehricke at the rally. "I have since
that time had only very very loose contacts with them," he
said. "I do not agree and go along with his [LaRouche's] basic
concept" or the aspects of LaRouche's operations that have
been in the news lately. "So in a way I have dissociated myself
from the group. On the other hand, of course, I certainly
appreciate that the group . . . supports Rudolph quite a bit.
I think they are doing a good job in that area."[16]

One highlight of the anti-OSI rally was a taped speech by
retired Major General John B. Medaris, Rudolph's old commander at Redstone Arsenal in Huntsville. In his speech, Medaris accused the OSI of waging an unconstitutional campaign
of "guilt by association" against German scientists. The old
Germans just "sit there now not knowing when somebody's
going to put them on the pillory for things of no consequence,"
Medaris said.[17]

Another featured speaker was the man who—apart from
LaRouche himself—cuts perhaps the oddest figure in the
whole spectrum of Rudolph's defenders. Friedwardt Winter-
berg, mentioned earlier as a high-priced candidate for Paper-
clip in 1959, is a German-born nuclear physicist at Nevada's
Desert Research Institute in Reno. In his speech at the
LaRouche rally Winterberg touched on a facet of LaRouche's
KGB–East German conspiracy theories by claiming that the
OSI's evidence against Rudolph had come from Communist
East Germany.[18]

Winterberg's ties to LaRouche go back to at least 1980,
when *Fusion* magazine published a controversial article by
Winterberg that explained how a hydrogen bomb is deton-
ated. A year later the Fusion Energy Foundation published
Winterberg's book *The Physical Principles of Thermonuclear*

Explosive Devices. Winterberg also writes for yet another LaRouche outlet, the *International Journal of Fusion Energy*, which bills itself as welcoming scientists whose articles are banned in established scientific journals "because of the ideological prejudice of journal referees."[19]

With Rudolph living in exile in Hamburg, Winterberg positioned himself with the press as Rudolph's public spokesman and defender. A great part of Winterberg's defense campaign consisted of sending reporters and congressmen reams of printed materials, much of it taken from some of the most virulently anti-Semitic publications in the country. One of those, *Spotlight*, is a weekly tabloid published by Liberty Lobby, an extreme right-wing group run by anti-Semite Willis Carto. Carto's notorious front group, Institute for Holocaust Review, was established for the sole purpose of denying the reality of the Holocaust.[20]

A lengthy pro-Rudolph article by Winterberg was featured in *Spotlight* on August 31, 1987. Medaris also chose to defend Rudolph in *Spotlight* by making the outrageous assertion that "even if you accept what the allegations have been, I cannot find any justice in bringing those kinds of charges against a man after 30-odd years—and certainly not when you consider he gave 30 years of very fine, dedicated service to this nation."[21] In other words, it is all right to use a mass murderer so long as he can help us get to the moon.

Winterberg sent reporters and congressmen *Spotlight* and other anti-Semitic materials with a cover letter written on letterhead stationery of the Office of the President of the state-funded Desert Research Institute, part of the University of Nevada system. Winterberg's letters reflected Holocaust revisionism at its worst, including false claims that Jews did not work at the V-2 rocket factory and slanderous assertions against famed Nazi hunter and concentration camp survivor Simon Wiesenthal. In a note to the World Jewish Congress, Winterberg suggested that Jews too can be Nazis. In a letter to Nevada senator Paul Laxalt, Winterberg claimed that Jews did not work at Mittelwerk and even cited as evidence an enclosed article from the Holocaust-denying magazine *Instauration*. Then he repeated an anti-Semitic slur against OSI Director Sher that he had read in *Instauration*.[22]

Winterberg also approached witnesses in an effort to get them to change their testimony about Rudolph. For example, he admitted in a letter to the *Bulletin of the Atomic Scientists* that he had questioned Hannelore Bannasch, a witness at the *Andrae* trial, after her OSI interrogation. Bannasch had testified under oath at the 1947 Army trial that if anyone had signed sabotage reports it would have been Rudolph. She confirmed that testimony in a 1983 sworn statement to the OSI. Suddenly, after a visit from Winterberg, Bannasch changed her entire story, claiming that Rudolph was innocent and that her original testimony had been "mis-translated."[23]

The line taken by Rudolph's defenders resulted in press coverage that reeked with Holocaust revisionism, perpetuating what Dora survivor Jean Michel described as the "monstrous distortion of history" that has "given birth to false, foul, and suspect myths." The U.S. Army's figure of at least twenty thousand prisoner deaths suddenly became five thousand, then four thousand, and in one United Press International story was reduced to four thousand slave laborers who "allegedly died." Rudolph's public statements were tinged with amnesia as he claimed that he "did not know the prisoners were dying." And since most reporters did not bother to interview Dora survivors, they were portrayed as being "well fed," while Rudolph was viewed as the real victim.[24]

Then NASA got into the act when the Marshall Space Flight Center held a "Wernher von Braun birthday reception" on March 25, 1987, honoring eighty-three former Paperclip specialists. Two of those honored—Grau and Haukohl—still were under active investigation by the Justice Department's Nazi-hunting unit. NASA's director, James Thompson, vowed to make the von Braun celebration an annual event and urged NASA employees to "rub elbows with these old guys—maybe some of their experience will rub off on us." NASA spokesman Bob Lessels said that Rudolph had not been invited to the party. Nevertheless, NASA's actions certainly raise questions as to the propriety of a federal agency holding public gatherings to honor men under investigation by the Criminal Division of the Justice Department.[25]

All of the activities tied to the Paperclip story in the 1980s—the Rudolph case and his defenders, the Alabama Space and Rocket Center and Marshall Center meetings, the OSI's investigations of other former Paperclip scientists—were carried out in an atmosphere in which the Reagan White House was sending out mixed signals about the OSI, Nazis, and even the Holocaust itself.

Former White House communications director Patrick Buchanan's views were the most unequivocal within the Reagan administration. Buchanan is well known for his attacks on OSI's prosecution of Nazi war criminals, and he has defended Nazis repeatedly and called for OSI's abolition in his syndicated columns and on television. Therefore it was logical that when Rudolph's colleagues sought an advocate within the administration, they went to Buchanan. In June 1985 former Paperclip scientist Eberhard Rees met with Buchanan to discuss the defenders' efforts to restore Rudolph's American citizenship. After the meeting Rees said that Buchanan had indicated he would support their cause.[26]

Others in the Reagan administration put out conflicting signals about the Holocaust and their commitment to the OSI. On the one hand, the administration claimed it supported OSI's mission to deport Nazi war criminals. On the other hand, in 1985 President Reagan laid a wreath at a war cemetery in Bitburg, West Germany, where Waffen SS troops were buried. And in October 1988 a nationwide school Holocaust history program was denied federal funding for the third straight year because of complaints by extreme right-wing factions in the U.S. Department of Education. Among the complaints was the claim by Dr. Christina Price, then from Troy State University in Alabama, that the Holocaust program was not "balanced" because "the Nazi point of view, however unpopular, is still a point of view and is not presented, nor is that of the Ku Klux Klan."[27]

Another controversy ensued over President Reagan's appointment of industrialist J. Peter Grace to chair a budget advisory committee, because of Grace's links to convicted Nazi war criminal Otto Ambros. Grace's chemical company had been employing Ambros as a technical advisor since his release from prison in Nuremberg in 1951. In the midst of bad publicity and an investigation by Congressman Tom Lantos of California, a Holocaust survivor, both Grace and Dow Chemical claimed that Ambros was no longer working for them. Ambros, however, admitted in an interview in 1986 that he is working for somebody in the United States, but he refused to say who. "I'm still working for U.S. companies but they don't want me to talk," he said. "There has been too much trouble with the press." Ambros said he works as a chemist developing new plastics and chemicals.[28]

Some of President George Bush's activities also raise serious questions about the OSI's fate under his administration. During Bush's 1988 presidential campaign several members of a volunteer ethnic coalition in Bush's campaign were exposed as Holocaust revisionists or members of Nazi or Fascist groups. Cochairman Jerome Brentar admitted that as a postwar officer in the International Refugee Organization in Germany he had helped hundreds of Nazis to emigrate to the United States, "whether [they were] in the Waffen SS or in the Wehrmacht." Other coalition members included Florian Galdau, a Romanian Orthodox priest who is the New York chief of the still-existing Iron Guard, Romania's pro-Nazi movement; Radi Slavoff, leader of a Bulgarian group formed by wartime members of the Nazi-aligned Bulgarian Legion; and former members of the Latvian SS and P-2 Lodge, an illegal Italian group that plotted to overthrow the Italian government in 1970 and install a dictator.[29]

In addition, on July 20, 1988, Bush attended a dinner in Detroit sponsored by the Captive Nations Committee and the American Friends of the Anti-Bolshevik Bloc of Nations, some of whose members are longtime agitators against OSI because of OSI's cases against East European Nazi collaborators. Even if Bush was unaware of their anti-OSI stance before the dinner, he certainly was made aware of it when outspoken OSI critic Bohdan Fedorak stated the groups' strong opposition to OSI in his introduction to Bush. "I'm sure that there was nothing derogatory in that type of remark," Fedorak said in an interview. "Otherwise, I'm sure that we would have heard it either from him [Bush] or from other people." According to Fedorak, Bush said nothing in the OSI's defense in his remarks at the banquet.[30]

Bush's background as a former CIA director poses a potential conflict should the OSI decide to deport a Paperclip scientist or other Nazi who had been on the CIA's payroll. The CIA's history certainly shows the agency's well-known propensity for protecting its own. In 1980, for instance, the OSI was forced to dismiss a denaturalization complaint against alleged Nazi war criminal Tscherim Soobzokov as a result of documents that suddenly appeared in his files *after* the OSI filed charges in 1979. The OSI complaint had charged that Soobzokov had concealed his membership in various Nazi organizations, including the Waffen SS, when he applied for a visa to enter the United States. The OSI was forced to dismiss its case when a "V-30 personal data form" and an "operations memorandum"—ostensibly showing that Soobzokov *had* disclosed what he was charged with concealing—mysteriously appeared in the CIA's files and in Soobzokov's possession. Interestingly, the State Department—the agency responsible for issuing Soobzokov's visa—had no record in its files of either document. Furthermore, when OSI attorneys initially reviewed the CIA's files on Soobzokov, no evidence of these materials had been found.[31]

"Given all this, some may conclude that the CIA may have manufactured this evidence to protect Soobzokov, long rumored to have been an employee of the Agency," Elizabeth Holtzman told her congressional colleagues in 1980.[32]

In looking at the whole story of Paperclip today, the project's most ominous legacy lies in the cold war philosophy of the intelligence officers who guided the project through the decades. Central to that Machiavellian belief is that the end justifies the means, no matter what the cost. It is a philosophy that is omnipresent in the late 1980s, most notably in Irangate. In both Paperclip and Irangate, a band of ideologues believed that their cause served a higher purpose than the laws that governed them.

None of the intelligence officers involved in Paperclip has ever been called to account before the American public, and many have even received promotions and honors for the activities reported in this book. The man at the helm of the original coverup schemes, JIOA Director Bosquet Wev, was promoted to the rank of rear admiral. He retired in 1957, having become commanding officer of the naval station in Norfolk, Virginia. The project's godfather in the late 1940s, Director of Intelligence Stephen Chamberlin, was promoted from major general to lieutenant general, assumed command of the Fifth Army in Chicago, and retired in 1951. Among those closest to the Germans, Army Air Forces Colonel Donald Putt eventually was promoted to the rank of lieutenant general in the U.S. Air Force. Putt retired in 1958, having held the position of military director of the Scientific Advisory Board to the Air Force Chief of Staff.[33]

JIOA Director William Whalen was incarcerated in the federal penitentiary at Lewisburg, Pennsylvania, in 1966 for his espionage activities, and was paroled just six years later. During his imprisonment Whalen thanked Judge Oren Lewis for saving his life, since he had almost died from alcoholism. His connection to Paperclip never was revealed. And some of the disturbing questions raised by that connection remain unanswered.[34]

The instigator of the European and Argentine conspiracies, EUCOM Director of Intelligence and Inter-American Defense Board chief Robert L. Walsh, was promoted to the rank of brigadier general and died in 1985. His deputy at EUCOM in 1947, Colonel Robert Schow, was named assistant director of the CIA in 1949. Schow took over as godfather to Paperclip in 1954, when he was promoted to major general and named assistant chief of staff for intelligence in Washington.[35]

The Inter-American Defense Board carried on business as usual with Latin American dictators, including Panamanian strongman Manuel Noriega until he was arrested in January 1990 and brought to the United States. In June 1986, at the same time that Noriega's drug- and gun-running operations were being exposed by a Senate subcommittee, Noriega attended an IADB ceremonial gathering in Washington to present a Panamanian award to U.S. Lieutenant General John Schweitzer, Walsh's modern-day predecessor as U.S. chairman of the IADB.[36]

Like the intelligence officers who brought them here, most of the older recruits out of the sixteen hundred Paperclip and the hundreds of others in Project 63 and National Interest have not been held to account for their activities either. And they also received awards and promotions. One scientist with disturbing links to Dachau experiments, Hubertus Strughold, was named chief scientist of the Aerospace Medical Division for the U.S. Air Force in 1961. He even received the Americanism Medal from the Daughters of the American Revolution, and in 1985 the Texas Senate declared June 15 of that year "Dr. Hubertus Strughold Day."[37]

French Resistance members and prisoners of war were used as slave labor at Peenemünde. Yet former Peenemünde general Walter Dornberger became vice president of Bell Aircraft Company and was never even questioned about his role in that deplorable affair. And this summer, when tourists converge on the Kennedy Space Center, all will pass by a portrait of former SS member Kurt Debus that hangs in the entrance in honor of Debus's service as the center's first director.[38]

Accused war criminal Arthur Rudolph lives in Hamburg, West Germany, collecting retirement checks from both the U.S. government and the German government. But at least he is barred from U.S. entry. "He is on watch lists, he cannot get a visa, and if he were found in the United States he would be subject to arrest," said OSI Director Sher.[39]

But the ban did not stop Rudolph's defenders from stepping up their campaign to bring him back to America. On November 26, 1988, former Paperclip recruit Walter Haeussermann sent President Reagan a letter asking that Rudolph be allowed to attend NASA's twentieth anniversary moon walk celebration in July 1989. Haeussermann admitted that the request for a one-time visit was a scheme to break the OSI. "We try whatever we can dream up," Haeussermann said. If Rudolph is allowed even one visit, "it would show, more or less, OSI has been overruled."[40]

NASA's moon walk celebration was held in July 1989, but Rudolph did not attend. His visa request had been turned down. In Huntsville, eight hundred Germans and Americans involved with Paperclip since 1945 attended a reunion in the Wernher von Braun Civic Center. The group's spokesman, Konrad Dannenberg, mentioned his exiled friend in his speech before the group. "We invited Rudolph to this celebration," Dannenberg said bitterly, "but circumstances did not permit him to be with us here today."[41]

As for the project that brought them here, no one reading this book should be surprised to learn that nothing has changed. The project is once again rearing its ugly head.

On August 10, 1989, the Pentagon quietly announced that there were exempted positions in Department of Defense installations that would be filled under the "program for utilization of alien scientists." The program is still run by the Research and Engineering Department, which took over Paperclip when the JIOA shut down in 1962.[42]

Thirteen of the new recruits work at NASA, including a world-renowned climatologist. "We don't beat the bushes to find them," said Robert Nance from NASA's Office of Policy. "We hire them in rare circumstances where their skills are so unique they can't be found in America, like work on teflon skins, or other specialists like we had with Wernher von Braun." The scientists at NASA work at Langly Research Center, Ames Research at Moffet Field, California, and Goddard Space Flight Center.[43]

NASA has the authority to employ up to 150 alien scientists, though Nance said they had to go through "immigration loops" to get them. As the case had been in the late 1950s, the program is viewed as a way to fill slots in a shrinking American labor force. "By the year 2000 there will be a third fewer American engineers and scientists available than there are now," Nance said. As a result he thought the program would play an even more important role in the future.[44]

Not surprisingly, the Pentagon will not talk about the program, and a spokesman claimed that he "couldn't find the policy." Suddenly Department of Defense officials became as tight-lipped as some intelligence officers who ran the operation had been. Former JIOA Director Benjamin Heckemeyer was close-mouthed about Paperclip in a telephone conversation in 1985. What little he did say, however, is a perfect summation of the whole sordid affair.

"Paperclip's a can of worms," he said and hung up the phone.[45]

Conclusion

I N late summer of 1990, as this book was being readied for publication, I was astonished to come across yet another disturbing account of the legacy left by Paperclip. After six years in exile in Hamburg, Arthur Rudolph arrived in Canada on July 1 to launch a smear campaign against the Office of Special Investigations, the Nazi-hunting Justice Department unit that had forced him to leave the United States. Incredibly, Rudolph had called on both old and newly recruited supporters in an audacious attempt to gain reentry to this country. The initial volley of Rudolph's campaign had been fired some months earlier at a gathering of former Paperclip rocketeers in Huntsville, Alabama. Ohio Congressman James Traficant promised the scientists in a speech that he would meet Rudolph at the U.S.-Canadian border and personally escort him across it. Rudolph's plans were cut short when he was met at the plane by Canadian Mounties and then put up for deportation hearings.[1]

On the stand, Rudolph glibly spun a revisionist history of Mittelwerk, reviving in particular the myth of its "well-fed" Jewish slaves. Even more appalling was the performance of Hugh McInnish, a U.S. Army–employed engineer who acted as Rudolph's "cocounsel" in the hearings. To complete the absurd picture, a platoon of home-grown Canadian Nazis—outfitted in full SS regalia—picketed alongside Rudolph's friends out on the streets of Toronto. Finally, on January 11, 1991, a Canadian court ruled that Rudolph was permanently barred from entering Canada because of his Nazi past.[2]

The events in Canada are a reminder not only of the enduring scars left by Paperclip but of the outdated cold war philosophy that the project embodied. That philosophy served as the underpinning for our national policy for nearly forty-five years. Only now, with the dramatic shift in world events that brought the cold war to an end, have the larger outlines of that policy and its often-tragic consequences become discernable. Only now can we begin to evaluate it with some degree of objectivity.

The central tenent of the cold war philosophy was perhaps never more succinctly stated than it was in a secret 1954 report prepared for the White House by a commission headed by former president Herbert Hoover. The report read, in part:

> It is now clear that we are facing an implacable enemy whose avowed objective is world domination. . . . There are no rules in such a game. Hitherto accepted norms of human conduct do not apply. . . . If the United States is to survive, long-standing American concepts of fair play must be reconsidered. . . . We must learn to subvert, sabotage and destroy our enemies by more clever, more sophisticated, more effective methods than those used against us.[3]

That view was accepted almost without question. Richard Bissell, then CIA chief of covert operations, told a CBS interviewer some twenty years later, "I think that's an excellent statement of the prevailing view, at least the view of those who'd had any contact with covert operations of one kind or another."[4]

In the decades since, U.S. intelligence agencies embraced that philosophy as justification for all manner of tactics—even those that violated America's own laws. Abroad it justified uncounted assassination plots and coups, the total number of which still remains secret. There were at least eight documented attempts to kill Fidel Castro, for example, and he claimed that there were more. At home the "anything goes" philosophy was at work in any number of illegal activities directed against American citizens. Under the guise of fighting communism the CIA conducted domestic drug experiments, the FBI infiltrated political groups, and the Army collected dossiers and spied on thousands of Americans exercising their right to free speech.

The Machiavellian attitude behind these operations was born when a World War II ally became a new enemy and the world axis shifted. To fight the Russians we turned to the men responsible for the horrors committed under Hitler and hired them to work as scientists, saboteurs, and spies. Over time these operations took on a life of their own. In particular, Paperclip expanded into Project 63 and Project National Interest and provided a convenient cover for still other covert operations. Over decades it became a chameleon of sorts, changing its size and shape to accommodate a succession of schemes in search of a place to hide from public scrutiny.

Under the protective blanket of cold war philosophy, no plot or person was too unsavory to bring into the fold. In the case of Paperclip, whatever crimes German specialists had committed in the past—joining the SS, torching a synagogue, conducting experiments on Dachau camp inmates—were, in the view of JIOA Director Bosquet Wev, dismissable as "picayune details."[5]

Anyone who doubts the pervasiveness of the cold war philosophy in the intervening decades need look no further than deposed Panamanian strongman Manuel Noriega, who remained on the CIA payroll for years despite evidence that his government was involved in drug trafficking, murder, rape, political corruption, and other crimes. Yet as late as May 1987 the head of the U.S. Drug Enforcement Agency was praising Noriega for his "personal commitment" in helping the DEA carry out its investigations in Panama.[6]

The mentality that governed Paperclip is essentially the same one that spawned the chain of secret ventures known collectively as "Irangate." The projects even bore fruit in strikingly similar ways. In both instances ideological zealots found ways to exclude from their inner circle those officials who bore legitimate responsibility for the policies that eventually were contravened. In Paperclip the JIOA's conduct caused State Department representative Samuel Klaus to note with gentlemanly suspicion, "I gathered . . . that there had been meetings of the group to which I had not been invited." Nearly forty years later, in the investigation of Irangate, Secretary of State George Shultz complained that he had been left "out of the loop."[7]

Not coincidentally, both cases also involved a band of ideologues who believed that their cause served a higher purpose than the policies in place. Who can forget secretary Fawn Hall's chillingly matter-of-fact assertion during the 1987 congressional hearings that "sometimes you have to go above the written law"?[8]

The flawed decision-making process that set into motion the Paperclips and Irangates of the last forty-five years have had a domino effect that often created as many problems as it solved. In direct defiance of President Truman's policy, the Paperclip masterminds brazenly had the German scientists' records changed to expunge evidence of war crimes and ardent nazism and secure permanent immigration status for them in the United States. Ostensibly that was done in the interest of national security. Once here, however, the scientists were given access to classified information—again, contrary to official policy—that revealed the inner-most workings of our defense system. As a result, it was not long before the very people brought here to ensure our security had themselves become a security risk.

Eventually some of the scientists took advantage of security lapses and left the country with classified material. German specialist Heinz Gartmann, for example, left Wright Field air base with turbojet rocket engine blueprints in his hand luggage. The full extent of the damage from incidents like that is still unknown. And what was the military's response when it was caught employing war criminals? Typically it was to try to hide its sins instead of atone for them, as Army intelligence did in sending Klaus Barbie to South America.[9]

Flash-forward again to Noriega (or any of the other U.S.-

supported Latin dictators whose short-term attractiveness has eventually turned into a liability). By the time we invaded Panama in 1989 there was no question in anybody's mind but that we had created a monster. "Our willingness to tolerate Noriega has in fact . . . put us in a position that is directly counter to the best interests of where we wanted to wind up," observed Senator John Kerry from Massachusetts.[10]

Operations like Paperclip are perhaps most indefensible on a moral level. Certainly no one can argue with the urgent postwar need to obtain German scientists' knowledge. Yet the way that was done seems unthinkable today. Was it really necessary to cover up Nazi crimes? Evade presidential policy? Harbor murderers? Change their records and then lie about it to other government agencies? Try to maintain the coverup even today?

The dispute over Paperclip isn't whether U.S. intelligence should have pursued a policy to protect American interests from the Soviets. Obviously the Russians represented a serious threat to our country's interests during most of the cold war period.

The argument here is over the means, not the ends, for there were alternatives to the decisions the JIOA officers made. For one thing, the German scientists could have been kept overseas and interrogated by scientists instead of by military officers. Indeed, for years after the war the U.S. high commissioner of Germany kept dozens of ex-Nazi scientists on the payroll—and under tight security—so that we could utilize their knowledge and expertise. Why the blind determination to bring war criminals here, in violation of our own laws, and essentially absolve them of their pasts?

Such activities seem even more incomprehensible in light of the fact that other pools of scientific talent were virtually ignored. The JIOA officers went to great lengths to help second-rate German technicians find jobs and a new life in America. Meanwhile, many American engineers who had suffered from layoffs in the defense industry went without jobs.

Survivors of the Holocaust also were overlooked. One such

survivor was Casimir Jobell, a Polish patriot, graduate engineer, and inventor who was forced to work as a slave laborer for the Henschel aircraft company and then emigrated to America after the war. He died working as a dishwasher in Boston.

For Jobell's daughter Miroslawa the events honoring German rocket scientists in Alabama in 1985 were particularly heart-rending. Why, she asked in a *Birmingham News* story, were specialists who served the Nazis "put on a pedestal" while men like her father who resisted "are hardly left being able to exist?"[11]

Why have we made heroes of men who assisted in one of the greatest evils in modern history? Some were unquestionably highly qualified scientists. Wernher von Braun, for example, was a brilliant man who contributed immeasurably to American missile and space programs. But he was also a Nazi collaborator. What price did we ultimately pay to tap the Germans' knowledge? The most common response is that it got us to the moon. But how do you balance that against murder?

Today, more is known than ever before of the wartime activities of the Paperclip scientists. Yet a number of them continue to be virtually deified by the military or by the communities in which they've settled. They're given medals and awards and glowing notations in history books. For someone who knows the true history of the medical experiments done in concentration camps, however, it is disquieting—to say the least—to drive by the official U.S. Air Force building in San Antonio named after Hubertus Strughold.

It's even more disturbing to see NASA and the state of Alabama hold annual events celebrating Wernher von Braun's birthday at which Guenther Haukohl and Dieter Grau, two scientists who are currently under Justice Department investigation for Nazi war crimes, are among the honorees—at taxpayers' expense!

Some think it is excessive, even obsessive, to continue investigating and prosecuting such men. However, former OSI director Allan Ryan, Jr., may have had a more accurate perspective: "To grant these people repose from the law . . . would mean that their thirty-five years of silence and our thirty-five years of inaction somehow atone for their awful crimes, and that justice is the result."[12] Already, in some cases justice delayed has meant justice denied, as the perpetrators have died.

Obviously the Paperclip story is not over. But the end of the cold war has given us an opportunity to cast off once and for all the kind of thinking that created and justified such operations. No matter how necessary intelligence activities may be, they cannot be allowed to operate unchecked, in secrecy and darkness, shielded from the democratic process of accountability.

Otherwise, in the end we become our own worst enemy. Edgewood already has provided us with a horrifying example of the true legacy of the cold war, which lies in the stories of James Stanley and other soldiers who were treated like laboratory rats. In essence we used Nazi science to kill our own people.

It is not necessary to violate America's laws to achieve our national goals. The era that gave rise to such flawed thinking is over. We may never be completely rid of the atrocities it spawned. But there is no reason to perpetuate them any longer.

GLOSSARY

AMHI	U.S. Army Military History Institute
BOL	Bolling Air Force Base History Office
CMH	Center for Military History
EA	Edgewood Arsenal
HI	Hoover Institute
HST	Harry S. Truman Library
INSCOM	U.S. Army Intelligence and Security Command
LC	Library of Congress
MAX	Maxwell Air Force Base History Office
NARS	National Archives and Records Service
NIH	National Institutes of Health
NSA	National Security Archives
OHS	Oregon Historical Society
ONH	Office of Naval History
OSI	U.S. Department of Justice Office of Special Investigations
WNRC	Washington National Records Center

NOTES

PROLOGUE

1. General Accounting Office, *Nazis and Axis Collaborators Were Used to Further U.S. Anti-Communist Objectives in Europe—Some Immigrated to the United States* (Washington, D.C.: Government Printing Office, 28 June 1985).

2. *Federal Register*, 10 August 1989.

3. Ambassador James Conant to Secretary of State, 13 July 1956, State Department "Operation Paperclip" microfiche, Civil Reference Branch, RG 59, NARS (hereafter cited as State fiche).

4. *U.S. v. Whalen*, CR 4360 (E.D. Va., 1966) (hereafter cited as *Whalen*).

5. One example was Soviet mole Donald Maclean's influence over which scientists were hired. See John Loftus, *The Belarus Secret* (New York: Alfred A. Knopf, 1982).

6. For a good overview of the Edgewood experiments see Colonel James R. Taylor and Major William Johnson, Inspectors General, "Research Report Concerning the Use of Volunteers in Chemical Agent Research," prepared for the Department of the Army, 21 July 1975 (obtained under the FOIA). See also *U.S. v. Stanley*, 483 U.S. 669 (1987) (hereafter cited as *Stanley*).

7. Linda Hunt, "U.S. Coverup of Nazi Scientists," *Bulletin of the Atomic Scientists*, April 1985, p. 24.

8. Traficant's speech at the Huntsville Holiday Inn, 12 May 1990, was sponsored by the Friends of Arthur Rudolph; for information on Traficant's Mafia ties see Dan Moldea, "Mafia and the Congressman," *Washington Weekly*, 19 April 1985.

9. Author interview with Elizabeth Holtzman.

CHAPTER 1: THE BEGINNING

1. For Navy mission history and activities see U.S. Naval Technical Mission in Europe, "Historical Data on NTME," and report summaries, RG 38, NARS; the Wagner description and Nazi records are in the Herbert Wagner JIOA dossier, RG 330, NARS. For general information see Clarence Lasby, *Project Paperclip* (New York: Atheneum, 1971).

2. Lasby, *Project Paperclip*.

3. For information about Wagner's entry date and avoidance of usual U.S. immigration procedure see the Immigration and Naturalization Service (INS) form in the Reinhard Lahde JIOA dossier, RG 330, NARS. Lahde was brought to the United States with Wagner. Wagner's Nazi records are in his JIOA dossier, RG 330, NARS.

4. Lasby, *Project Paperclip*.

5. Ibid.; John Gimbel, "U.S. Policy and German Scientists: The Early Cold War," *Political Science Quarterly*, 101 (1986). For CIOS history and OSS links see "Memorandum on the Establishment and Present Status of the Grey List Panel of the Combined Intelligence Objectives Subcommittee," 30 January 1945, entry 165, RG 226, NARS.

6. The report by John McArthur Harris, "Chemical Warfare Service," March to June 1945, is at AMHI.

7. Ibid.

8. For information on Ambros see the Nuremberg I. G. Farben case, *U.S. v. Krauch et al.*, M892, RG 238, NARS (hereafter cited as *Krauch*).

9. An overview of German science can be found in Leslie Simon, *German Research in World War II* (New York: John Wiley, 1947). OSS reports on German chemical warfare research are in RG 226, NARS.

10. For a comprehensive history of the early exploitation project see Ralph Osborne, "History of the Field Information Agency, Technical (FIAT)," Ralph Osborne file, AMHI. Statistics and an overview are in "Final Report of FIAT," 1 July 1947, 321.01-77(FIAT), RG 260, WNRC; and "Bi-Weekly Progress Report Number 1 for FIAT," 4 July 1945, GBI/FIAT/319.2, RG 260, WNRC. FIAT was established in July 1945 to wrap up CIOS responsibilties and oversee Paperclip in the European theater until 1947. Osborne was FIAT chief.

11. William Donovan to President Franklin Roosevelt, 1 December 1944, RG 226, NARS. For information on individuals used by the OSS see Stewart Alsop and Thomas Braden, *Sub Rosa: The OSS and American Espionage* (New York: Reynado Hitchcock, 1946). Allen Dulles's testimony as "Mr. B" is in House Committee on Expenditures in the Executive Departments, *National Security Act of 1947*, 80th Cong., 1st sess., H.R. 2319, 27 June 1947. This hearing was not made public until 1982, when the

Permanent Select Committee on Intelligence located the only existing transcript in CIA files during a committee review of CIA records. The original hearing was closed and the House's transcript was destroyed. See the introduction to the printed hearings for background.

12. President Franklin Roosevelt, "Memorandum for General Donovan," undated but stamped as received by Donovan's office on 18 December 1944, RG 226, NARS. Charles A. Bane, Office of the Secretariat, suggested to Donovan that Roosevelt's reply should be summarized to the OSS in Stockholm, "which first raised the question."

13. Pash's military career: Boris Pash file, HI; Boris Pash, *The Alsos Mission* (New York: Award House, 1969); U.S. Army Intelligence Center, *History of the Counter Intelligence Corps* (Fort Holabird, Md.: USAIC, December 1959), vol. 8, pt. 3, "CIC With the Alsos Mission," INSCOM. CIA "special operations" unit: from Senate Select Committee to Study Governmental Operations With Respect to Intelligence Activities, *Final Report*, bk. 4, 94th Cong., 2d sess., report no. 94-755 (Washington, D.C.: Government Printing Office, 1976), pp. 128–33 (hereafter cited as Senate Select Committee, *Final Report*, no. 94–755).

14. Samuel A. Goudsmit, *Alsos* (New York: Henry Schuman, 1947).

15. Ibid. Haagen's testimony is in *U.S. v. Brandt et al.*, M887, RG 238, NARS (hereafter cited as *Brandt*). Postwar job: Haagen's INSCOM dossier; French trial: in "2 German Doctors Sentenced," *The New York Times*, 15 May 1954.

16. Goudsmit, *Alsos*. Information about Hirt and chemical warfare experiments is in *Brandt*.

17. Alsos interrogation: in the Kurt Blome INSCOM dossier XE001248. Arrest reports: in Blome's Nuremberg arrest file, RG 238, NARS.

18. A comparison of the Allies' mustard gas with Tabun, Sarin, and Soman is in Taylor and Johnson, "Use of Volunteers in Chemical Agent Research." (Note: the classified chapter 9 of this report, "Intelligence Corps LSD Testing," was obtained under a separate FOIA request from INSCOM, "Project Derby Hat.")

19. A. K. Mills, "Investigation of Chemical Warfare Installations in the Munsterlager Area, Including Raubkammer," CIOS report no. 8, NIH.

20. Ibid.

21. Ibid. Identification of some detained individuals is found in "Final Report of FIAT"; Chemical Corps Historical Studies, "History of German Chemical Warfare in World War II," pt. 1, no. 2, RG 338, NARS; and Walter Schieber INSCOM dossier XE001005.

22. Author interview with retired U.S. Air Force Lieutenant General Donald Putt.

23. Putt interview; Donald Putt to Commanding General, AAF, "Report on Events and Conditions Which Occurred During Procurement of Foreign Technical Men for Work in the U.S.A.," 25 September 1945, located in the appendix of documents attached to Department of the Air Force, *History of the AAF Participation in Project Paperclip, May 1945–March 1947* (Wright Field, Ohio: Air Materiel Command, 1948), 4 vols., BOL (hereafter cited as *AAF Participation in Project Paperclip*). This history is valuable because its appendix contains AAF documents not found elsewhere concerning Paperclip, Wright Field, and the AAF Aero Medical Center.

24. Ibid.

25. Yaffa Eliach and Brana Gurewitsch, *The Liberators* (Brooklyn: Center for Holocaust Studies Documentation and Research, 1981).

26. Alexander's background and findings are in *Brandt*.

27. Eliach and Gurewitsch, *Liberators*.

28. *Brandt*.

29. Ibid.

30. Leo Alexander, "Neuropathology and Neurophysiology, Including Electroencephalography, in Wartime Germany," CIOS report L-170, found in *Brandt* records; Leo Alexander, "The Treatment of Shock From Prolonged Exposure to Cold, Especially in Water," CIOS report, USSR exhibit 435, International Military Tribunal, NARS.

31. Regarding Himmler's files see Alexander, "Treatment of Shock."

32. Ibid.

33. Ibid.; CIOS, "Aviation Medicine, General Medicine, Veterinary Medicine, Chemical Warfare," item nos. 24 and 25, file no. XXVII, WNRC.

34. Toftoy biography is from CMH. On Peenemünde generally see Lasby, *Paperclip*; Frederick Ordway and Mitchell Sharpe, *The Rocket Team* (Cambridge, Mass.: MIT Press, 1982); David Irving, *The Mare's Nest* (London: Panther Books, 1985); Walter Dornberger, *V-2* (New York: Viking, 1985); and Dieter Huzel, *From Peenemünde to Canaveral* (Englewood Cliffs, N.J.: Prentice-Hall, 1962).

35. Major Robert Staver letter to the author, 4 September 1985.

36. Author interview with retired Brigadier General James L. Collins. See also Linda Hunt, producer/reporter, "Nazi Coverup," a four-part series by the CNN Special Assignment I-Team, first broadcast in March 1986.

37. Ibid.

38. Author interview with Yves Beon.

39. Soldiers' reactions to Roosevelt's death are in the concentration camp film reel *Nordhausen*, a U.S. Army Signal Corps film, NARS.

40. Robert Staver letter to author; author interview with Herschel Auer-

bach. Auerbach located dental records of SS officers that were used later for identification purposes in *U.S. v. Andrae et al.*, M1079, RG 153 and RG 338, NARS (hereafter cited as *Andrae*). For a short history of Dora by war crimes staff see William Aalmann, *"Dora"-Nordhausen Labor-Concentration Camps and Information on the Nordhausen War Crimes Case*, prosecution staff booklet, in *Andrae*. For Dora survivors' perspective see Jean Michel, *Dora* (London: Weidenfeld and Nicolson, 1979); Jean Michel, *De L'Enfer Aux Etoiles* (Paris: Librairie Plon, 1985); and Yves Beon, *La planète Dora* (France: Éditions du Seuil, 1985). See also Linda Hunt, "Arthur Rudolph, NASA and Dora," *Moment*, April 1987; and Jósef Garliński, *Hitler's Last Weapons* (New York: Times Books, 1978).

41. Victor Bernstein, "I Saw the Bodies of 3000 Slaves Murdered by Nazis," *PM*, 17 April 1945.

42. Sworn Statement of Albin Sawatzki, 14 April 1945, prosecution exhibit, *Andrae*.

43. Information about the elusive forty-two boxes of documents and Rickhey's relationship with Beasley is in Rickhey's testimony, *Andrae*.

44. Osborne, "History of the Field Information Agency, Technical."

45. Carl Zeiss to USFET Headquarters, "Report on Evacuated Scientists From Carl Zeiss Jena," 17 July 1946, G-2 Paperclip "Top Secret" files, RG 319, WNRC.

46. See Wilhelm Eitel INSCOM dossier XE061886 and JIOA dossier, RG 330, NARS, for numerous statements regarding Eitel, especially the OMGUS memo to the S-2 Branch, 27 February 1949, and the Robert Haveman statement. For the fate of Jewish scientists see Bernt Engelmann, *Germany Without Jews* (New York: Bantam Books, 1984).

47. Ibid.

48. S. M. Hastings, "The NSWC/WOL Wind Tunnels," NSWC pamphlet, August 1979, ONH. For Navy mission history and activities see U.S. Naval Technical Mission in Europe, "Historical Data on NTME," and report summaries, RG 38, NARS.

49. Entry dates are in the Herbert Wagner JIOA dossier, RG 330, NARS.

CHAPTER 2: RULES OF THE GAME

1. U.S. Air Force Historical Office, "The Command and Project 'Paperclip,' " *History of the Air Research and Development Command*, vol. 1, chap. 9, 1954 (hereafter cited as *Air Research and Development Command*) (obtained from BOL under the FOIA).

2. Putt interview.

3. H. M. Mott-Smith to Navy Department, Bureau of Ordnance, 19 February 1945, G-2 Paperclip files, RG 319, WNRC.

4. Secretary of War Robert Patterson to Secretary, General Staff, 28 May 1945, G-2 Paperclip files, RG 319, WNRC.

5. Allied Control Authority, Control Council law no. 25, 29 April 1946. A copy of the law is in the G-2 Paperclip "Top Secret" files, RG 319, WNRC. Law no. 25 states that "senior officials or scientists who were members of the National Socialist German Workers' Party (NSDAP) or members of other Nazi organizations with more than nominal participation in its activities shall be removed and their replacement effected only by persons with suitable political records." Prohibited research included nuclear physics, poison gas, and rocket propulsion.

6. Telford Taylor, *Final Report to the Secretary of the Army* (Washington, D.C.: Government Printing Office, 15 August 1949).

7. AAF Headquarters, "Exploitation of German Specialists in Science and Technology in the U.S." in the appendix of *AAF Participation in Project Paperclip*.

8. War Department, Bureau of Public Relations, "German Scientists Brought to U.S.," 9 October 1945, G-2 Paperclip files, RG 319, WNRC.

9. JIC Charter/JCS 1569/1, CCS 334 JIC, 19 December 1942, sec. 6, RG 218, NARS.

10. "Basic Directive, JIOA," CCS 471.9, 1 May 1945, sec. 4, RG 218, NARS. A copy of the JIOA charter is located in the appendix of *AAF Participation in Project Paperclip*.

11. Lieutenant Colonel Monroe Hagood to Director of Intelligence, "Transfer of Escape and Evasion and P/W Interrogation Responsibility and Operations From Intelligence Group," 14 October 1946, G-2 Paperclip "Top Secret" files, RG 319, WNRC. For a history of the G-2 POW Branch see U.S. Army Intelligence Center and School, *The Evolution of American Military Intelligence* (Fort Huachuca, Ariz.: USAICS, May 1973); and Lloyd Shoemaker, *The Escape Factory* (New York: St. Martin's Press, 1990).

12. Assistant Secretary of War Robert A. Lovett to Major General Hugh J. Knerr, 4 October 1945, in the appendix of *AAF Participation in Project Paperclip*.

13. For project code names, lists of Gehlen's group, CPM/Navy and Hilger groups in the United States, travel schedules, U.S. agents who escorted them out of the country, a detailed description of facilities at Fort Hunt and Camp Ritchie, Cone memos, Hagood memos, including complaints of overworked staff, a discussion of MIS-X and MIS-Y activities, and other information on CPM Branch activities, see the G-2 Paperclip "Top Secret" files, RG 319, WNRC (declassified per author's FOIA request) and regular G-2 Paperclip files for the years 1945 and 1946, RG 319, WNRC.

For published sources on general POW interrogations at Fort Hunt see John H. Moore, *The Faustball Tunnel* (New York: Random House, 1978). Gehlen's views are in Reinhard Gehlen, *The Service* (New York: World Publishing, 1972).

14. Hilger's later trip to Washington is discussed in Raul Hilberg, *The Destruction of the European Jews* (Chicago: Quadrangle Books, 1961), pp. 703 and 707; and Christopher Simpson, *Blowback* (New York: Weidenfeld and Nicolson, 1988). On German intelligence in Russia see David Kahn, *Hitler's Spies* (New York: Macmillan, 1978).

15. For detailed reports, lists of names of both the rocket group and POWs, Backfire activities, statistics of three launches, and other information see the Backfire collection of documents in OMGUS/FIAT records, RG 260, WNRC. Launch statistics are also in a one-page summary of Backfire in the Hans Friedrich JIOA dossier, RG 330, NARS.

16. A memo concerning the attempt to interrogate Rudolph and mentioning Hans Lindenberg is in Arthur Rudolph INSCOM dossier AE529655.

17. Brigadier General George McDonald to Major General Hugh J. Knerr, 3 November 1945, in the appendix of *AAF Participation in Project Paperclip*; and Garliński, *Hitler's Last Weapons*.

18. McDonald to Knerr, 3 November 1945. "Memorandum on Dornberger," 2 October 1945, in the Walter Dornberger IRR dossier, RG 319, NARS. British POW ID cards: in the Walter Dornberger G-2 dossier, RG 319, WNRC.

19. Regarding Steinhoff see Bill Gross, "Pioneer Range Scientist Dies," *Missile Ranger*, 4 December 1987.

20. Author interview with Herbert Axster.

21. Qualification sheet noting "100% NAZI" in the Arthur Rudolph INSCOM dossier.

22. Background on Armin Stelzner is in *Basic Personnel Record*, Stelzner IRR dossier X8856123, RG 319, NARS.

23. Regarding Luftwaffe General von Rohden see General Carl Spaatz to Under Secretary of War Kenneth C. Royall, 18 December 1945; General George McDonald to General Spaatz, 13 February 1946; Assistant Secretary of War Howard C. Petersen to Commanding General, AAF, 27 February 1946, all in the appendix of *AAF Participation in Project Paperclip*.

24. Axster interview.

25. For several reports and memos regarding confrontations between Putt and Zobel, including problems caused by Putt's original promises to the group, see the appendix of *AAF Participation in Project Paperclip*.

26. Author interview with Ernst Eckert.

27. Captain Ransom K. Davis to Op-23 JIS, 5 March 1946 (CCS 471.9, 1 May 1945, sect. 4), RG 218, NARS.

28. Goudsmit, *Alsos*. Osenberg's files are in G-2 1918–51 files, RG 319, WNRC.

29. Goudsmit, *Alsos*.

30. USFET to Joint Chiefs of Staff, 17 July 1946, G-2 Paperclip "Top Secret" files, RG 319, WNRC.

31. On British spies see Loftus, *Belarus Secret*; and Alti Rodal, *Nazi War Criminals in Canada* (Ottawa: Canadian Government Inquiry on War Criminals, 1986).

32. JIOA to Joint Research and Development Board, 9 September 1947; and Joint Research and Development Board to JIOA, n.d., both in JIOA administrative files, RG 330, NARS. On 22 January 1946 Bush wrote President Truman about his objections to Paperclip and said, "The replacement of qualified American scientists and technicians, who are prevented by the military personnel policies from utilizing their skills, by imported German scientists and technicians seems to me decidedly unwise." Bush was afraid that the Germans would take jobs away from qualified American scientists. Truman replied on 24 January 1946: "I was morally certain that our home boys would not want any competition." Both letters are in the Paul G. Hoffman papers, HST.

33. Memo, Major General Leslie Groves to Director of Intelligence, 2 November 1946, JIOA administrative files, RG 330, NARS.

34. Carl Zeiss to USFET Headquarters, "Report on Evacuated Scientists From Carl Zeiss Jena," 17 July 1946, G-2 Paperclip "Top Secret" files, RG 319, WNRC; and JCS 1363/21, in SWNCC 257/17. See the SWNCC 257 series concerning the "Exploitation of German and Austrian Scientists." The Scholarly Resources' microfilm edition of the State-War-Navy Coordinating Committee (SWNCC) on Paperclip decisions is available at NARS.

35. Major George Collins, "Memorandum for Director JIOA," 9 August 1946, G-2 Paperclip "Top Secret" files, RG 319, WNRC.

36. See the SWNCC 257 series on microfilm at NARS.

37. German scientist project: see Rodal, *Nazi War Criminals in Canada*, pp. 327–42. Rodal also found evidence of U.S. and British intelligence establishing an "anti-Soviet spy network by smuggling known Nazi collaborators out of Eastern Europe without the Canadian government's knowledge" (p. 448). On the Australian government's participation in a British Commonwealth nations "cover-up which allowed Nazi war criminals to escape justice" see *The Australian*, 10 August 1985.

38. Rear Admiral Bosquet Wev file, ONH.

39. Author interview with Ida Klaus.

40. Samuel Klaus, "Memorandum to the Files," 24 April 1946 and 6 May 1946; and Samuel Klaus, "Memorandum for the Record, JIOA meeting June 11, 1946"—all in State Department microfiche (hereafter cited as State fiche), RG 59, NARS.

41. Memo, Samuel Klaus to Mr. Panuch, 20 June 1946, State fiche, RG 59, NARS.

42. U.S. Army biography of Major General Stephen J. Chamberlin, CMH.

43. For a discussion of the secretary of war's disapproval of retaining 558 POWs in United States see "Notes for Army-Navy Conference on Exploitation of Prisoners of War for Scientific and Intelligence Purposes," 5 April 1946, in G-2 Paperclip files, RG 319, WNRC.

44. Proposal to include those with "too-close" Nazi connections, SS, and General Staff specialists is included in "Exploitation of Prisoners of War," memo, in ibid.

45. Ibid.

46. Samuel Klaus, "Memorandum for the Files," 21 May 1946, memo regarding a JIOA meeting the same day, State fiche, RG 59, NARS.

47. On Chamberlin's request to Eisenhower for permission to include thirty intelligence specialists "within the 1000 German and Austrian specialists" see Major General Stephen J. Chamberlin to Chief of Staff, 30 July 1946, ID 383.7, in G-2 Paperclip "Top Secret" files, RG 319, WNRC.

48. Acting Secretary of State Dean Acheson, "Memorandum for the President," memo to Harry S. Truman, 30 August 1946; and SWNCC 257/22, in the SWNCC 257 series.

49. On the "Use of Paperclip as a Cover for Volunteer Foreign Specialists on Russian intelligence by This Division and CNI" and the five men at Fort Hunt, see Lieutenant Colonel H. B. St. Clair, Exploitation Branch, to Chief, Intelligence Group, 25 September 1946. On Hagood asking Chamberlin to take action to get three remaining men out of the United States, see Lieutenant Colonel Monroe Hagood to Director of Intelligence, 14 October 1946. Both documents are in G-2 Paperclip "Top Secret" files, RG 319, WNRC.

50. Acheson memo; and SWNCC 257/22.

CHAPTER 3: PEENEMÜNDE ON THE RIO GRANDE

1. Army Ordnance Department, Fort Bliss Rocket Project, "Report on Hermes Missile Project," RG 156, WNRC.

2. Captain Paul R. Lutjens, "Memorandum for the AC of S G-2, Intelligence Summary," 6 June 1947, G-2 Paperclip "Top Secret" files, RG 319, WNRC.

3. Ibid.; and Captain Paul R. Lutjens, "Memorandum for the AC of S G-2, Intelligence Summary," 20 June 1947, G-2 Paperclip "Top Secret" files, RG 319, WNRC.

4. Major Lyman G. White, "Paperclip Project, Ft. Bliss, Texas and Adjacent Areas," MID 918.3, 26 November 1947, G-2 Paperclip files, RG 319, WNRC.

5. *White Sands Missile Range* (Riverside, Calif.: Armed Services Press, 1987).

6. White, "Paperclip Project."

7. "Certain Paperclip personnel" quote is in Colonel R. F. Ennis to Commanding General, 17 April 1947, JIOA 1331, ID 400.112 Research, RG 330, NARS. On Gartmann, descriptions of documents, and "not taken accidentally" quote see "Secret" memo, Captain John P. Roth, EUCOM, to Chief, Technical Intelligence Section, AC of S, 8 April 1947; Lieutenant Colonel M. C. Taylor to Director of Intelligence, 14 April 1947; and Colonel R. F. Ennis to AAF Commanding General, 5 May 1947—all in G-2 Paperclip "Top Secret" files, RG 319, WNRC.

8. Information on Goethrup and Thiele is in the INSCOM dossier on "Operation MESA."

9. Lieutenant Walter Jessel, "Evidence of a Conspiracy Among Leading German 'Overcast' Personnel," 12 June 1945, OMGUS/FIAT, RG 260, WNRC.

10. Ibid.; Axster interview.

11. Axster interview. Hamill bio: in James McGovern, *Crossbow and Overcast* (New York: William Morrow, 1964).

12. Von Braun's SS membership: in Berlin Document Center reports and JIOA memo 691, 3 March 1947, in the Wernher von Braun INSCOM dossier. See also Wernher von Braun's FBI dossier. Von Braun's JIOA dossier is "missing" from the RG 330 files at the NARS. Anton Beier's SS records are noted in the Berlin Document Center report in Beier's JIOA dossier, RG 330, NARS.

13. For Debus's actions against a colleague see the Office of the Public Prosecutor case against Richard Craemer, Gestapo Headquarters, Berlin, in the Debus JIOA dossier, RG 330, NARS. Debus's SS membership records and witnesses who saw him in an SS uniform: in the Debus JIOA dossier and IRR dossier XE034033, RG 319, NARS.

14. Hamill's visit to Nordhausen is from McGovern, *Crossbow and Overcast*.

15. Army CIC cards with comments and a 27 May 1953 agent report are in Magnus von Braun INSCOM dossier C3001437. Von Braun Mittelwerk dates are from the Magnus von Braun interrogation, *Andrae* trial records.

16. Axster interview.

17. OMGUS Public Safety Branch, Investigation Section, "The Axster Couple," 25 March 1948; and OMGUS Public Safety Branch, Investigation

Section, "Sworn Statements," esp. those of Konrad Mommsen (18 December 1946 and 5 February 1948) and Gerhard Weise (undated but certified by Captain James Steward)—all in Herbert Axster's JIOA dossier, RG 330, NARS.

18. Axster interview.

19. OMGUS Public Safety Branch reports on Ilse Axster are in the Herbert Axster JIOA dossier, RG 330, NARS.

20. Stephen S. Wise to Secretary of War Robert Patterson, 14 April 1947, G-2 Paperclip files, RG 319, WNRC.

21. Ibid.

22. Ibid.

23. Secretary of War Robert Patterson to Stephen S. Wise, 8 May 1947, G-2 Paperclip files, RG 319, WNRC.

24. White, "Paperclip Project"; Herbert Axster JIOA dossier, RG 330, NARS; and Axster interview.

25. White, "Paperclip Project."

26. War Department, "Security Regulations for Project Paperclip," 28 August 1946, and "Code of Conduct," 12 April 1947, both in JIOA administrative files, RG 330, NARS.

27. White, "Paperclip Project."

28. Captain Paul R. Lutjens, "Memorandum for the AC of S, G-2, Intelligence Summary," 12 June 1947; and A. Lindenmayr letter, "Subject: Members of the German Scientists in the United States," April 1947, trans. Army CIC Agent George Ries—both in G-2 Paperclip "Top Secret" files, RG 319, WNRC.

29. Ibid.; Captain Paul R. Lutjens, "Memorandum to the AC of S, G-2," 24 July 1947, and "Memorandum for the Officer in Charge," 6 November 1947, in G-2 Paperclip "Top Secret" files, RG 319, WNRC.

30. Lutjens, "Memorandum," 6 November 1947.

31. Captain Paul R. Lutjens, "Memorandum for the AC of S, G-2, Intelligence Summary," 14 April and 6 June 1947, G-2 Paperclip "Top Secret" files, RG 319, WNRC.

32. Lutjens, "Memorandum," 20 June 1947.

33. Lutjens, "Memorandum," June 6 and 20, 1947.

34. Ibid.

35. Army Ordnance Department, "Hermes Missile Project."

36. Colonel Frank Reed to Colonel Clark, 24 January 1947, G-2 Paperclip files, RG 319, WNRC.

37. On von Braun's instructions to deliver a map to Dornberger's wife see cable S-5249, EUCOM General Clarence Heubner to AGWAR for General Chamberlin, 29 May 1947, in JIOA administrative files, RG 330, NARS. On the plot to bring documents to von Braun in the United States see

"Security Information," GID 73-0321, 1 July 1953, in the Wernher von Braun INSCOM dossier. On the Army's reaction to von Braun's denial of knowledge about documents: "Security Information," GID 73-0321, and Dornberger's letter in the Walter Dornberger G-2 dossier, RG 319, WNRC.

38. On the use of documents as a "bargaining lever" see Transmittal Slip, 66th CIC Group Headquarters, July 1953, in the Wernher von Braun INSCOM dossier.

39. The search for documents in Germany is described in Dornberger's letter in the Walter Dornberger G-2 dossier, RG 319, WNRC.

40. White, "Paperclip Project."

41. Extract of data is from FBI files as forwarded to the JIOA by A. Devitt Vanech, special assistant to the attorney general, on 21 February 1947, in FBI Extracts, Magnus von Braun's JIOA dossier, RG 330, NARS.

42. J. Edgar Hoover to Director of Intelligence, WDGS, 13 September 1947, G-2 Paperclip files, RG 319, WNRC.

43. Ibid.

44. Lieutenant Colonel Montie F. Cone, "Report," n.d., G-2 Paperclip files, RG 319, WNRC.

45. White, "Paperclip Project."

46. CIA, "German Scientists at Sukhumi, USSR," report to President Harry S. Truman, 31 October 1949, HST.

47. White, "Paperclip Project."

48. See examples of *Sponsoring Agency Security Reports* in individual dossiers.

49. Cone, "Report."

50. White, "Paperclip Project."

51. Cone, "Report."

CHAPTER 4: A HELL CALLED DORA

1. "Nazi Brains Help Us," *Life*, 9 December 1946, pp. 49–52; Herbert Shaw, "Wright Field Reveals 'Operation Paperclip,' " *Dayton Daily News*, 4 December 1946, p. 5; and *Newsweek*, 9 December 1946, pp. 68–69.

2. War Department, Public Relations Division, "Release," 27 November 1946, for release to the press on 4 December 1946, G-2 Paperclip files, RG 319, WNRC.

3. Ibid.

4. *AAF Participation in Project Paperclip*.

5. Accusations against Zobel are in *OMGUS Security Report*, 25 October 1946, in the Theodor Zobel INSCOM dossier B8003094 and Zobel's JIOA dossier, RG 330, NARS.

6. SS membership is in *Meldebogen* and sworn statement, 2 July 1947, in the Ernst Eckert JIOA dossier. The Berlin Document Center card showing Eckert's SS membership number, 6432691, is in Ernst Eckert INSCOM dossier D024720. Quotes are from Eckert interview.

7. Hermann Nehlson to Loewy, 17 October 1946, in *Andrae*, Preliminary Investigation file, roll 1.

8. Personal data sheets are in the Georg Rickhey JIOA dossier, RG 330, NARS.

9. Rickhey testimony, *Andrae*, transcript pp. 7524–59.

10. For example, the document Nehlson turned over to Smith was a management chart containing the names of Mittelwerk managers. See *Andrae*, Preliminary Investigation file, roll 1.

11. Ibid.

12. Patin Nazi party and SA membership: in *OMGUS Security Report*, 29 September 1948, in the Patin IRR dossier XE008256, RG 319, NARS. Relationship with Göring's nephew and others: in *Statements Made by Paperclip Specialist Albert Patin*, forwarded to the JIOA on 18 October 1948 by the Department of the Air Force, in the Albert Patin JIOA dossier, RG 330, NARS.

13. *Paperclip Specialist Albert Patin.*

14. See especially *Security Report of Sponsoring Agency*, 25 October 1946, stating that Patin "advises this command of attitude of other scientists," in the Albert Patin JIOA dossier, RG 330, NARS.

15. See *Basic Personnel Record*, in the Hermann Nehlson JIOA dossier, RG 330, NARS. See also Smith interrogation of Nehlson, in *Andrae*, Preliminary Investigation file, roll 1.

16. Hermann Nehlson to Loewy, 17 October 1946, in *Andrae*, Preliminary Investigation file, roll 1.

17. Ibid.

18. *OMGUS Security Report*, 19 June 1947, in the Hermann Nehlson JIOA dossier, RG 330, NARS.

19. Colonel Millard Lewis to Director of Intelligence, Exploitation Branch, 19 December 1946, in the Georg Rickhey IRR dossier, RG 319, NARS.

20. Major Eugene Smith to Air Provost Marshal, "Preliminary Investigation Regarding the Activities of Dr. Georg Rickhey," 23 May 1947, in *Andrae*, Preliminary Investigation file, roll 1.

21. Ibid.

22. Ibid.

23. Ibid.; Beon interview.

24. Smith interrogation of Hermann Nehlson.

25. Major Eugene Smith to Air Provost Marshal, "Investigation Re-

garding Activities of Dr. Georg Rickhey, Former Director-General of the Underground Mittelwerk Factory Near Nordhausen, Germany," 10 June 1947, in *Andrae*, Preliminary Investigation file, roll 1 (hereafter cited as Smith, "Activities of Dr. Georg Rickhey").

26. "Transcript of Conference of May 6, 1944 in the office of Director General Rickhey," 6 May 1944, OSI.

27. Smith, "Activities of Dr. Georg Rickhey."

28. Smith interrogation of Werner Voss, in *Andrae*, Preliminary Investigation file, roll 1.

29. Smith interrogation of Eric Ball, in *Andrae*, Preliminary Investigation file, roll 1.

30. "Special Order of Mittelwerk Factory Management," 22 August 1944, OSI.

31. Prisoner Labor Supply office is discussed in *People vs. Erwin Julius Busta and Ernst Sander*, Provincial Court of Essen, West Germany, 1971.

32. Smith interrogation of Arthur Rudolph, in *Andrae*, prosecution exhibit P-126.

33. Ibid.

34. Ibid.

35. Smith interrogation of Hans Friedrich, in *Andrae*, prosecution exhibit P-127.

36. Ibid.

37. Smith, "Activities of Dr. Georg Rickhey."

38. Ibid.

39. Ibid.

40. Georg Rickhey, "Report From Germany," n.d., in Georg Rickhey IRR dossier X8737323, RG 319, NARS.

41. Lieutenant Colonel William Berman to Chief, 7708 War Crimes Group, 17 June 1947, in Rickhey's IRR dossier, RG 319, NARS.

42. Lieutenant Colonel Clio Straight to War Department, 31 July 1947, in *Andrae*, Preliminary Investigation file, roll 1.

43. Cable, War Department to 7708 War Crimes Group, 7 August 1947, in *Andrae*, Preliminary Investigation file, roll 1. On von Braun's trip to Germany: Colonel R. F. Ennis to Executive, Intelligence Division, 11 February 1947, G-2 Paperclip files, 400.112, RG 319, WNRC.

44. Requests for documents: in cable S-1804, EUCOM Headquarters to WDGID, 4 August 1947, in *Andrae*, Preliminary Investigation file, roll 1. Congressman John Anderson and Rickhey family correspondence, including the "Gestapo" accusation: from *Andrae*, Preliminary Investigation file, roll 1, the Georg Rickhey IRR dossier, RG 319, NARS; the Rickhey JIOA dossier, RG 330, NARS; and the Rickhey G-2 dossier, RG 319, WNRC.

45. Charges are in *Andrae*, roll 5.

46. Wilhelm Simon testimony, *Andrae*.

47. Prosecution's opening statement, *Andrae*, transcript p. 35.

48. William Aalmann, *Dora* booklet, in *Andrae*.

49. Testimony of Georges Kassamatis and Rickhey are in *Andrae*. For testimony that Rickhey and Rudolph were on the distribution list to receive daily reports, see Leinweber testimony, *Andrae*, transcript pp. 4029–44.

50. Author interviews with Jean Michel and Beon; Sawatzki arrest reports, Army CIC reports on whereabouts, and memos from the War Crimes Group are in Albin Sawatzki INSCOM dossier XE185239.

51. Rickhey testimony, *Andrae*; and Wernher von Braun statement, defense exhibit D-38, also in *Andrae*.

52. Smith interrogation of Arthur Rudolph; and Rickhey testimony, transcript pp. 7560–82, both in *Andrae*.

53. Testimony about civilian engineers: in Kassamatis testimony, *Andrae*. Information on prisoner sabotage of rockets is from the Beon interview.

54. Testimony of Hannelore Bannasch, *Andrae*, transcript p. 7237.

55. Ibid.

56. Josef Ackerman and Cecil Jay testimony, *Andrae*, esp. transcript pp. 75–76.

57. George Finkenzeller testimony, in main trial, *Andrae*, transcript p. 6476. Finkenzeller's trial records are located on roll 16. For background on Guenther Haukohl see his IRR dossier, RG 319, NARS; Haukohl's JIOA dossier, RG 330, NARS; OSI interrogation of Arthur Rudolph, 13 October 1982 and 4 February 1983; and Hunt, "Nazi Coverup."

58. Kassimatis testimony, in *Andrae*, transcript pp. 1283–97.

59. Jean Michel testimony, in *Andrae*, transcript pp. 4153–213; Michel interview; and Hunt, "Arthur Rudolph, NASA and Dora."

60. Letter, Georg Rickhey to Colonel Peter Beasley, in the Rickhey JIOA dossier, RG 330, NARS. Information about Rudolph letter in Simon's defense: in OSI interrogation of Rudolph.

61. Colonel Montie Cone, "Office Memorandum," 5 March 1948, in the Georg Rickhey G-2 dossier, RG 319, WNRC.

CHAPTER 5: EXPERIMENTS IN DEATH

1. Robert J. Benford, *Report From Heidelberg* (Heidelberg, Germany: 1947). The administrative records of the AAF Aero Medical Center never have surfaced. Some original reports by German scientists that were translated at the center are located at the WNRC. Monthly status reports of research conducted at the center and lists of the center's Paperclip employ-

ees, including Ruff, Schaefer, and Becker-Freyseng, are in the appendix of documents attached to *AAF Participation in Project Paperclip*. The history's narrative never mentions the employees tried at Nuremberg.

2. Biography of Hubertus Strughold is in the Strughold JIOA dossier, RG 330, NARS.

3. *AAF Participation in Project Paperclip*.

4. Konrad Schaefer biography: in the Schaefer JIOA dossier, RG 330, NARS. The research paper "Durst and Durstbekampfung in Seenotfallen" that Schaefer delivered to the 1942 Nuremberg conference is found in Nuremberg doc. NO-401.

5. Ruff biography is in *Brandt*; Ruff and Strughold's publications are listed in the Strughold JIOA dossier, RG 330, NARS.

6. CNN West Germany News Bureau telephone interview with Siegfried Ruff, for author's "Nazi Coverup" series on CNN. Ruff's work at the AAF Center: AAF Aero Medical Center, "Monthly Status Report No. 6," 31 March 1946, in the appendix of *AAF Participation in Project Paperclip*.

7. Becker-Freyseng biography: from *Brandt*. His work at the AAF Center: in "Monthly Status Report" in the appendix of *AAF Participation in Project Paperclip*.

8. Karl Hoellenrainer testimony, *Brandt*, transcript pp. 10229–34 and 10508–44.

9. *Brandt*, NO-177, prosecution exhibit 133.

10. Ibid.; *Brandt*, NO-184, prosecution exhibit 132; and interrogation of Konrad Schaefer, M1019, RG 238, NARS.

11. *Brandt*, NO-185, prosecution exhibit 134. Becker-Freyseng admitted on the witness stand that he was the author of the letter signed by Schroeder; Hilberg, *Destruction of the European Jews*.

12. Hoellenrainer testimony, in *Brandt*.

13. Ibid.

14. Ibid.

15. Ibid.

16. *Brandt*, PS-1602, prosecution exhibit 44.

17. Weltz testimony, transcript p. 7188; NO-476, prosecution exhibit 40; NO-437, prosecution exhibit 42; NO-263, prosecution exhibit 47; and transcript pp. 6550 and 7199—all in *Brandt*.

18. Affidavit of Dr. Pacholegg, *Brandt*, transcript p. 15348.

19. *Brandt*, NO-220, prosecution exhibit 61.

20. *Brandt*, NO-402, prosecution exhibit 66.

21. Author telephone interview with Robert Benford. Benford considers Ruff to be his "close friend" and says he still is angry with Drew Pearson (and reporters in general) for keeping Ruff out of the United States. For documentation of requests to employ Schaefer, Ruff, and Becker-Freyseng

see Brigadier General Norris B. Harbold to Director of Intelligence, WDGS, 2 June 1946; and Harbold to Director of Intelligence, 14 June 1946—both in JIOA administrative files, RG 330, NARS.

22. Benford interview; and Army CIC arrest warrants, Nuremberg defendant case files, RG 238, NARS.

23. Author interview with Theodor Benzinger; interrogation of Theodor Benzinger, 20 September 1946, M1019, RG 238, NARS; and *Brandt*, NO-224, NO-401, and prosecution exhibit 76.

24. "Sworn Statement of Theodor Hannes Benzinger," U.S. Department of Justice, Office of Special Investigations, 22 November 1983 (given to the author by Benzinger). The best source of information on Benzinger's Paperclip activities is the Theodor Benzinger INSCOM dossier XE073663; see also the Benzinger JIOA dossier, RG 330, NARS.

25. Interrogation of Hermann Becker-Freyseng, 24 September 1946, M1019, RG 238, NARS.

26. Ibid.

27. Prosecution's opening statement, *Brandt*, transcript pp. 12–24. For a published account of the Nuremberg trials that is valuable for atmospheric details see Victor Bernstein, *Final Judgment* (London: Latimer House, 1947). Bernstein's news stories in *PM* also contain information not found elsewhere, particularly regarding the American liberation of Dachau, Nordhausen, and other camps where he was on the front line with combat troops. See also Alexander Mitscherlich and Fred Mielke, *Doctors of Infamy* (New York: Henry Schuman, 1949).

28. *Brandt*.

29. Ibid.

30. Taylor, *Final Report*, pp. 300–304; Hilberg, *Destruction of the European Jews*.

31. Beiglboeck testimony, in *Brandt*, transcript pp. 8970, 8921, and 8978.

32. Final Pleas, *Brandt*, roll 37–38.

33. Hoellenrainer testimony, *Brandt*.

34. Ibid.

35. Ibid.

36. Ibid.

37. Ruff defense document book, exhibit 4; Schaefer defense document book, exhibit 1; Schroeder defense document book, exhibit 6—all in *Brandt*, roll 35.

38. Ruff defense document book, *Brandt*, exhibit 10, roll 35.

39. *U.S. vs Stanley*, 483 U.S. 669 (1987) (hereafter cited as *Stanley*).

40. *Brandt*, transcript pp. 11504–5.

41. Ruff testimony, *Brandt*, transcript p. 6558.

42. John Bullard and T. A. Glasgow oral history interview with Major General Harry Armstrong, April 1976, Brooks Air Force Base, MAX.

43. Benford interview.

44. Schaefer lists Nuremberg trial information in *Basic Personnel Record* and *Biographical and Professional Data* forms; and *Security Certificate From the JIOA*, 28 April 1950, signed by JIOA Director Daniel Ellis, in the Konrad Schaefer JIOA dossier, RG 330, NARS.

45. Captain Seymour Schwartz to Directorate of Intelligence, Headquarters USAF, 27 March 1951, JIOA administrative files, RG 330, NARS.

46. Taylor, *Final Report*.

47. Department of the Air Force, *German Aviation Medicine: World War II*, 2 vols. (Washington, D.C.: Government Printing Office, 1950).

48. Ibid., vol. 1, pp. 12–51. Becker-Freyseng is identified as the author of this chapter in an obscure reference on p. 51, noting that the chapter was based on material "meticulously compiled by the last chief of the aeromedical section [Becker-Freyseng] attached to the Chief des Sanitats-wesens der Luftwaff [Schroeder]."

49. Ibid.

CHAPTER 6: ESCAPE FROM JUSTICE

1. Complaints against the Axsters are in the Herbert Axster JIOA dossier, RG 330, NARs.

2. List of names, denazification information, and correspondence on Greenhouse are located in: records of U.S. Occupation Headquarters, OMGUS Civil Affairs Division, Public Safety Branch, RG 260, WNRC (hereafter cited as Greenhouse files).

3. Denazification law: in OMGUS booklet, "Military Government Regulations: Title 24 Important German Legislation," 22 April 1946, JIOA administration files, RG 330, NARS.

4. Lieutenant Colonel Clarence Howe, "Semi-Monthly Trend Report," report to the Deputy Director of Intelligence, 20 August 1947, RG 319, WNRC.

5. James F. Tent, *Mission on the Rhine* (Chicago: University of Chicago Press, 1982); and Lucius Clay, *Decision in Germany* (Garden City, N.Y.: Doubleday, 1950).

6. Ibid.

7. Delbert Clark, "Nazis Sent to U.S. as Technicians," *The New York Times*, 4 January 1947.

8. For problems recruiting see Lieutenant Colonel Edward Sheley, As-

sistant Chief of Air Staff–2 to CPM Branch MIS, 16 May 1946, G-2 "Top Secret" Paperclip files, RG 319, WNRC.

9. Commander C. R. Welte, "July Report, Exploitation Division," memo to the JIOA director, 5 August 1947, JIOA administrative files, RG 330, NARS.

10. General Lucius Clay to AGWAR, cable CC-1671, 20 September 1947, JIOA administrative files, RG 330, NARS.

11. OMGUS, IA and C Division, to Chief of Staff, "Political Clearance of German Scientists Presently in the U.S.," and supporting documents, August 1947, OMGUS Civil Affairs Division, RG 260, WNRC. Stephen S. Wise to Secretary of War Robert Patterson, 14 April 1947, G-2 Paperclip files, RG 319, WNRC.

12. OMGUS, IA and C Division, to Chief of Staff, "Denazification of Scientists Desired for Operation Paperclip," and supporting documents, 6 February 1945, OMGUS AG files, RG 260, WNRC.

13. Hans Zeigler's Nazi membership information is in Berlin Document Center reports and *Meldebogen*; a sworn statement by Hans Zeigler dated 28 October 1947; and Captain Jack James, "Report on Denazification Procedure," memo to the Office of Military Government of Bavaria, 13 April 1946—all in the Hans Zeigler JIOA dossier, RG 330, NARS.

14. Rudolf Thauer's Nazi membership information, his *Fragebogen*, and his denazification court information are in the Thauer G-2 dossier, RG 319, WNRC.

15. Nuremberg doc. NO-401.

16. On Kamm see memo, Colonel L. Williams, Acting Chief, Intelligence Group, to Commander in Chief, EUCOM, 11 June 1947. On Sielaff see Colonel Laurin L. Williams, "Subject: Denazification of Ernst Sielaff," memo to the chief of Navy intelligence, 29 July 1947. Both are in the G-2 Paperclip files, 400.112 Research, RG 319, WNRC.

17. Letter, Dr. Heinz Fischer to Colonel Donald Putt, 25 June 1946; memo, Colonel Harold Watson to Commanding General, AAF, 13 July 1946; and memo, Lieutenant Colonel Monroe Hagood to Assistant Chief of Air Staff–2, 22 July 1946—all in JIOA administrative files, RG 330, NARS.

18. Denazification court decision, 12 August 1947, and police and witness reports are in the Emil Salmon JIOA dossier, RG 330, NARS.

19. See memo, Air Materiel Command to Director of Air Force Intelligence, 28 April 1950, asking JIOA to reopen the case to secure a new sentence "sufficiently mitigated" to allow Salmon's immigration, in the Salmon JIOA dossier, RG 330, NARS.

20. *OMGUS Security Report*, 19 April 1949; and memo, Colonel Daniel Ellis to Director, Intelligence Division, 11 May 1950—both in the Emil Salmon JIOA dossier, RG 330, NARS.

21. Major General Robert L. Walsh biography: from U.S. Air Force.

22. Information on individuals is in the Greenhouse files.

23. Author interview with Albert Losche.

24. General background: in Greenhouse files; and Army CIC agent B. C. Harness, "Personality Report," 3 January 1949, in Karl Herrnberger INSCOM dossier XE253550.

25. Heinz Schmalschlaeger background: in Army CIC report, 1 March 1956, in Schmalschlaeger INSCOM dossier F8085185.

26. Background of Abels and Striedter: in Arnold Silver, CI Section, "Information on Greenhouse Personnel Needed for Denazification," memo to the Office of the Deputy Director of Intelligence, EUCOM, 27 August 1947, in the Greenhouse files.

27. Fischer's status: G. F. Corrigan, Denazification Analyst, "Status of Denazification Cases of German Nationals of Interest to Intelligence Agencies," memo to Theo Hall, Chief, Public Safety Branch, 27 April 1948, in the Greenhouse files. Regnath background is in "Interrogation of Franz Regnath," Headquarters, Third Army, Interrogation Center report, M1019, NARS.

28. Major Thomas Grant, ODI, EUCOM, "Request for Amnesty From Denazification for Certain German Nationals," memo to Colonel W. L. Fagg, Office of the Deputy Director of Intelligence, EUCOM, and Theo E. Hall, 13 October 1947, in the Greenhouse files.

29. Colonel W. L. Fagg to ODI, EUCOM, 7 November 1947, Greenhouse files.

30. Theo Hall, OMGUS, Public Safety Branch, to ODI, EUCOM, 13 October 1947, Greenhouse files.

31. Ibid.; Major General Robert Walsh to Public Safety Branch, 20 November 1947, Greenhouse files.

32. Albert Schweizer, Civil Administration Division, "Denazification of German Nationals Formerly Employed on Intelligence Project," memo to OMGUS, 1 June 1948, Greenhouse files.

33. "Personality Report," Army CIC agent B. C. Harness, 3 January 1949, in Herrnberger's INSCOM dossier.

34. Robert Bruce, OMGUS, "Denazification of German National Formerly Employed on Intelligence Project," memo to the Office of the Military Governor, 6 May 1948, Greenhouse files.

35. Eviction order: see memo, Peter Vacca, OMGUS, to Office of the Director of Intelligence, OMGUS, 2 April 1947, Heinz Schmalschlaeger INSCOM dossier.

36. House hearings "On the Need for Screening Displaced Persons for Entry Into the U.S." 80th Cong., 2d sess., August 2, 5, and 6, 1948.

37. Petersen, *American Occupation*.

38. OMGUS to Chief of Staff, cable CC-2102, October 1947, ODI, OMGUS, RG 260, WNRC.

CHAPTER 7: THE DOSSIERS

1. JIOA meeting is from Samuel Klaus, "Memorandum for the File," 27 February 1947, State fiche, RG 59, NARS.

2. Ibid.; for Hilldring complaints about JIOA see Samuel Klaus, "Memorandum for the Files," 26 February 1947, State fiche, RG 59, NARS.

3. Ibid.

4. Ibid.

5. Lieutenant Colonel Montie Cone to JIOA, memo regarding 146 reports, 8 May 1947, JIOA administrative files, RG 330, NARS.

6. Memo discussing von Braun is in JIOA Director Thomas Ford to USFET, 3 March 1947, JIOA administrative files, RG 330, NARS.

7. Samuel Klaus, "Meeting," 5 June 1946, State fiche, RG 59, NARS.

8. On JIOA expunging information see Samuel Klaus, "Memorandum to Secretary JIOA, Regarding Meeting of February 27, 1947," 5 March 1947; on Rickhey see Samuel Klaus, "German Scientist Program," 17 July 1947—both in State fiche, RG 59, NARS.

9. Author interview with retired Army Colonel Montie Cone. See also Hunt, "Nazi Coverup."

10. Hunt, "U.S. Coverup of Nazi Scientists"; JIOA Director Bosquet N. Wev to Major General Stephen J. Chamberlin, 2 July 1947, G-2 Paperclip files, RG 319, WNRC.

11. Ibid.

12. For Wev and Cone's complaints to congressmen see Samuel Klaus, "Memorandum," 9 July 1947, State fiche, RG 59, NARS.

13. Memo, Samuel Klaus to Mr. Eddy, 13 March 1947; Samuel Klaus, "German Scientist Program," 17 July 1947—both in State fiche, RG 59, NARS.

14. Robinson biography: House Committee on Expenditures in the Executive Departments, *State Department*, Subcommittee hearings, 80th Cong., 2d sess., March 10 and 12, 1948.

15. Author interview with Samuel Cummings; and Rebecca Wellington letter to author.

16. Hans Giesecke's JIOA dossier, RG 330, NARS; and microfilm investigative records of Portland Bund, OHS.

17. Colonel R. F. Ennis, "Press Release on Project Paperclip," correspondence, Public Relations Division, 20 February 1947; and letter, Major

General F. L. Parks to Colonel George Eyster, 21 May 1947—both in G-2 Paperclip files, RG 319, WNRC.

18. Cone interview; AFS complaints to Truman: in "Our Scientists Say, 'Send Nazis Home,' " *Washington Daily News*, 24 March 1947. UPI story: USFET to General Parks, War Department, cable SX-2691, 27 February 1947, in JIOA administrative files, Cables, RG 330, NARS. Regarding Axsters: Delbert Clark, "Nazis Sent to U.S. as Technicians," *The New York Times*, 4 January 1947.

19. Pearson story about Krauch: in cable, War Department, Intelligence Division, WDGS, 11 March 1947, JIOA administrative files, RG 330, NARS. See also "Outline for Briefing General Eisenhower on German Scientists Exploitation Program," 11 March 1947; and "The High Points of Conference on Paperclip," meeting held on March 11 and 12, 1947, between General Chamberlin and the chief of staff, the secretary of war, and the assistant secretary of war, with Lieutenant Colonel Hagood briefing—both from G-2 Paperclip files, RG 319, WNRC.

20. Key sources on Army intelligence domestic spy operations are in Senate Committee on the Judiciary, *Report on Military Surveillance of Civilian Politics*, 93d Congress, 1st sess., 1973; Senate Committee on the Judiciary, *Military Surveillance*, hearings 93d Congress, 2d sess., 1974; Senate Committee on the Judiciary, *Army Surveillance of Civilians: A Documentary Analysis*, 92d Cong., 2d sess., 1972; and Senate Select Committee to Study Governmental Operations with Respect to Intelligence Activities, *Final Report*, no. 94-755. For an overview of military intelligence domestic spy operations see Frank J. Donner, *The Age of Surveillance* (New York: Alfred A. Knopf, 1980).

21. Cone interview; and Tyler Abell, ed., *Drew Pearson Diaries* (New York: Holt, Rinehart and Winston, 1974).

22. Seymour Nagan, "Top Secret: Nazis at Work," *New Republic*, 11 August 1947; and memo, "Subject: Seymour Nagan," 11 August 1947, G-2 Paperclip files, RG 319, WNRC.

23. Regarding AFS: Colonel R. F. Ennis to Public Relations Division, 3 March 1947; and report by Edward Wetter, chief of the Chemical and Biological Warfare Section, Scientific Branch ID, "Public Meeting on Biological Warfare," 5 March 1947—both in G-2 Paperclip files, 400.112 Research, RG 319, WNRC.

24. JIOA Deputy Director Walter Rozamus to Chief, Exploitation Branch, 17 October 1947, JIOA administrative files, NARS. For more on Adolf Thiel see his JIOA dossier, RG 330, NARS.

25. Major General Robert LeGrow Walsh bio is from the U.S. Air Force; Major General Robert Schow bio is from CMH; Brigadier General William Fagg bio is from the U.S. Air Force.

26. JIOA Governing Committee Minutes of Meeting, 14 November 1947, G-2 Paperclip "Top Secret" files, RG 319, WNRC.

27. Hunt, "U.S. Coverup of Nazi Scientists"; and JIOA Deputy Director Walter Rozamus to Exploitation Branch, 18 November 1947, JIOA administrative files, RG 330, NARS.

28. Anton Beier's Berlin Document Center SS card, *Meldebogen*, and other reports are in Beier's JIOA dossier, RG 330, NARS.

29. Hunt, "U.S. Coverup of Nazi Scientists"; JIOA Deputy Director Walter Rozamus to Captain Francis Duborg, ONI, 28 November 1947, JIOA administrative files, RG 330, NARS.

30. Herman Kursweg's *OMGUS Security Reports*, signed by Colonel C. F. Fritzsche, 10 July 1947; and 16 February 1948, are in Kursweg's JIOA dossier. Willi Heybey's *OMGUS Security Report*, signed by Colonel C. F. Fritzsche, 16 February 1948; and Heybey's SA membership, noted in *Meldebogen*, are in Heybey's JIOA dossier. Ernst Winkler's *OMGUS Security Report*, signed by Colonel Robert Schow, 18 November 1946; and by Colonel W. L. Fagg, n.d., and Winkler's SA and other Nazi memberships, noted in *Meldebogen*, are all in his JIOA dossier, RG 330, NARS.

31. Hunt, "U.S. Coverup of Nazi Scientists"; and memo, Lieutenant Colonel Montie F. Cone to JIOA, 28 November 1947, JIOA 4079, JIOA administrative files, RG 330, NARS.

32. Ibid.; Guenther Haukohl's *OMGUS Security Report*, signed by Colonel C. F. Fritzsche, 27 October 1947 and 10 February 1948, are in Haukohl's IRR dossier, RG 319, and his JIOA dossier, RG 330, NARS. Hans Friedrich statements about Hitler are in Affidavit, 14 May 1947, in Friedrich INSCOM dossier XE222767.

33. Hunt, "U.S. Coverup of Nazi Scientists"; and JIOA Director Bosquet N. Wev to Director of Intelligence, EUCOM, 4 December 1947, JIOA 4102, JIOA administrative files, RG 330, NARS.

34. Ibid.

35. Memo, Robert W. Bruce, Office of Military Government (for Hess) to Commanding General, EUCOM, 12 May 1948, G-2 "Top Secret" Paperclip files, RG 319, WNRC.

36. Ibid.; Heinrich Kliewe's *OMGUS Security Report*, 11 February 1948, says that Kliewe "was an ardent Nazi. Records available to this headquarters indicate that subject is likely to become a security threat to the United States." The *OMGUS Security Report*, biography, and memos about the controversy over denazification are in Kliewe INSCOM dossier H8049883.

37. Ibid.

38. Anton Beier's *OMGUS Security Report*, signed by Colonel C. F. Fritzsche, 30 September 1947 and 12 February 1947, are in Beier's JIOA

dossier. Ernst Eckert's *OMGUS Security Report*, signed by Colonel C. F. Fritzsche, 10 February 1948, is in Eckert INSCOM dossier D024720. Information on Friedrich Wazelt is in *Security and Immigration Dossier Check Sheet*, signed by M. B., 14 February 1950, in Wazelt's JIOA dossier, RG 330, NARS.

39. Hunt, "U.S. Coverup of Nazi Scientists"; Wernher von Braun's *OMGUS Security Report*, signed by Colonel C. F. Fritzsche, 18 September 1947 and 18 September 1948, are in von Braun's FBI file and INSCOM dossiers D8022816 and XE185780.

40. Hunt, "U.S. Coverup of Nazi Scientists"; and Herbert Axster's *OMGUS Security Report*, signed by Colonel C. F. Fritzsche, 18 September 1947 and by Colonel W. L. Fagg, 12 May 1948, are in Axster's JIOA dossier, RG 330, NARS.

41. Wilhelm Eitel's *OMGUS Security Report*, signed by Colonel W. L. Fagg, 7 September 1948, and AEC comments, from *Security Report by Sponsoring Agency*, 16 April 1948, are in Eitel's JIOA dossier and INSCOM dossier XE061886.

42. Wilhelm Eitel's *HICOG Security Report*, signed by Colonel Charles Adams, 25 November 1948, is in Eitel's INSCOM dossier.

43. For friends' statements see files in the Ernst Eckert JIOA dossier, RG 330, NARS, and INSCOM dossier DO24720. Theodor Zobel's JIOA dossier, RG 330, NARS and INSCOM dossier B8008094.

44. Information on Busby and his tactics is in House Committee on Expenditures in the Executive Departments, *State Department*.

45. Busby discusses the Chicago Police Department in ibid. The "red squad" is discussed in Donner, *Age of Surveillance*.

46. House Committee on Expenditures in the Executive Departments, *State Department*; Representative McCormack quote is from *Congressional Record*, 15 May 1952, p. 5266.

47. Ned Brooks, NBC radio script, 25 March 1948, in JIOA administrative files, RG 330, NARS.

48. Busby speech is in *Congressional Record*, 25 March 1948; he repeats the charges in *Congressional Record*, 15 May 1952.

49. On Robinson quitting: *Congressional Record*, 15 May 1952; Klaus interview; and Lasby, *Project Paperclip*.

50. Hoover meeting: Lieutenant General S. J. Chamberlin to Major General George McDonald, 11 May 1948; and Assistant Secretary USAF to Secretary USAF, 13 May 1948—both in G-2 Paperclip files, RG 319, WNRC.

51. Ibid.

52. JIOA Director Daniel Ellis to JIOA Screening Panel, JIOA 3473, 2 September 1949, G-2 Paperclip files, RG 319, WNRC.

CHAPTER 8: CIA DIRTY TRICKS IN THE "NATIONAL INTEREST"

1. CIA-OPC cases are in State/National Interest Cases (NIC), JIOA administrative files, RG 330, NARS.

2. Procedures for admittance notes that the ninth proviso is used if they are "inadmissible" under U.S. law. See JIOA Director Daniel Ellis to Navy, Air and Army Chiefs of Procurement, JIOA memo 2758, 16 November 1950, JIOA administrative files, RG 330, NARS. The CIA "hundred persons act" is sec. 7 of the CIA act of 20 June 1949, 50 USC 403h.

3. Rodal, "Nazi War Criminals in Canada," chap. 7 and notes.

4. For an example of JIOA's sales pitch see JIOA Director Daniel E. Ellis to Dr. Ernest Hollis, U.S. Office of Education, 31 January 1950, JIOA administrative files, RG 330, NARS. Company lists are in JIOA post-1952 administrative files (declassified per author's FOIA request), RG 330, NARS.

5. JIOA Director to Chief, Special Procurement Section, Intelligence Division, 17 October 1949, G-2 Paperclip files, RG 319, WNRC.

6. Most CIA-OPC cases were "sponsored" by State, but the military did sponsor some of them—for example, Air Force cases involving Soviet defectors. See NIC files, JIOA administrative files, RG 330, NARS.

7. Memo, John Russell, U.S. Office of Education, to College and University Administrators, 28 March 1950, JIOA administrative files, RG 330, NARS.

8. Robert Rice, University of North Carolina, to Colonel Laurin Williams, WDGS, 13 February 1948, G-2 Paperclip files, 400.112 Research, RG 319, WNRC; and report by Wilhelm Krauledat, Intelligence Branch, U.S. Army, 26 July 1947, in Adolf von Hoermann's JIOA dossier, RG 330, NARS.

9. Leonard Alberts's Nazi memberships: see Berlin Document Center report, 2 September 1947; and counterespionage activities, Humphries's quote, and other reports, especially a summary of the investigation from Bechtel Corporation records—all in Alberts's IRR dossier EZO12128, RG 319, NARS, or his JIOA dossier, RG 330, NARS.

10. Ibid.

11. For fake ID cards and other information on Langfeld see Goerz Langfeld INSCOM dossier XE208037; "Hitler's Agent Ensconced in Westchester," *New York Herald Tribune*, 1 August 1940 identifies Langfeld as being seen at the home of Nazi agent.

12. For a summary of Grace-Ambros history see Joe Conason, "The Corporate State of Grace," *Village Voice*, 12 April 1983.

13. *Krauch*; and Nuremberg document NI-4830.

14. British report and quotes are in Senate Committee on Military Affairs, Subcommittee hearings, 79th Cong., 1st sess., 1945, pursuant to S. Res. 107 and 146, *Elimination of German Resources for War*, pt. 10, p. 1276.

15. Josiah DuBois, *The Devil's Chemists* (Boston: Beacon Press, 1952). See also Joseph Borkin, *The Crime and Punishment of IG Farben* (London: Andre Deutsch Ltd., 1979); references to JIOA objectives lists are in Otto Ambros INSCOM dossier XE021877; and W. R. Grace on JIOA company lists are in JIOA post-1952 administrative files, RG 330, NARS.

16. For lists of Edgewood Arsenal contracts with W. R. Grace and dozens of other companies and universities see "Index to Classified Edgewood Arsenal Records," in U.S. Army custody, WNRC.

17. Hunt, "Nazi Coverup."

18. Example of Wisner CIA report is in Herbert Axster's JIOA dossier, RG 330, NARS. CIA-OPC complicity with Nazi war criminals is discussed in Loftus, *Belarus Secret*, and Simpson, *Blowback*. OPC history: in Senate Select Committee to Study Governmental Operations With Respect to Intelligence Activities, *Final Report*, no. 94-755.

19. Memo, General Stephen Chamberlin to Frank Wisner, 18 February 1948, G-2 Paperclip files, 400.112 Research, RG 319, WNRC.

20. Regarding State accelerating visas see JIOA Director Bosquet Wev to Navy, Army, Air Intelligence Divisions, JIOA memo 891, 17 March 1948, in G-2 Paperclip files, 014.33, RG 319, WNRC. For results of the meeting with H. L'Heureux see JIOA Deputy Director C. Welte to JIOA Director, 1 June 1948, G-2 Paperclip files, 014.32 Research, RG 319, WNRC.

21. For discussions of the second clause in National Interest policy, involving aliens other than Germans employed in civilian agencies, "in consideration of exceptional services," see JIC 282/38, JIC memo 285; further discussion on defining the second part of the policy clause is in CCS 334 (G12-44) S. 10—both in RG 218, NARS. Author interview with retired Army Colonel Bernard Geehan. For CIA counsel's comments on CIA hundred persons act see House Committee on the Judiciary, *Efficiency of the INS*, 96th Cong., 1st sess., 31 October 1979.

22. "Mikolajczyk Got Secret Unit's Aid," *The New York Times*, 4 November 1947.

23. For Poles: regarding Jan Kolendo see JIOA Director R. D. Wentworth to H. L'Heureux, JIOA memo 3038, 27 July 1949, and regarding Lieutenant General Izydor Modelski see JIOA Director Daniel Ellis to L'Heureux, JIOA memo 3857, 22 September 1949, both in JIOA administrative files, State/NIC, RG 330, NARS. For Italians, especially Secondo Campini, see Brigadier General Walter Agee to JIOA, 3 May 1950, JIOA

administrative files, AF/NIC, RG 330, NARS. Peter Pirogov, *Why I Escaped* (London: Harvell Press, 1950); and Pirogov records, JIOA AF/NIC files, esp. letter, Deputy Attorney General Peyton Ford to JIOA Deputy Director James Skinner, 8 December 1950, regarding how the Internal Security Act held up Pirogov's admission under normal process "by reason of his membership in the two Soviet youth organizations," JIOA administrative files, RG 330, NARS.

24. JIOA Deputy Director Walter Rozamus to H. L'Heureux, JIOA memo 3535, 21 October 1947, JIOA administrative files, 383.7 Immigration, RG 330, NARS. Finn proposal and correspondence of Donovan, Gruenther, Kennan, and others are in P and O 091.714 TS (sec. 1, case 1), RG 319, NARS. JIOA records on Finns are in JIOA administrative files, State/NIC, RG 330, NARS. See box 26 for personal immigration information on all Finns, including Kurt Saarela, who jumped ship in Norfolk, Virginia, in 1947.

25. Letter and attached proposal, Alpo Marttinen to General William Donovan, 29 February 1948 in P and O 091.714 TS (sec. 1, case 1), RG 319, NARS.

26. Ibid. For later Finn arrivals see State/NIC files in JIOA administrative records, boxes 26 and 33—for lists, entry dates, and a JIOA conference with State in 1950 regarding Finns illegally residing in the United States.

27. For Army CIC reports and other information on Papkow see Alexander Papkow INSCOM dossier F8011971.

28. Robert Bishop and E. S. Crayfield, *Russia Astride the Balkans* (New York: McBride, 1948).

29. Ibid.

30. Information on Manicatide: in NIC files, JIOA administrative files, RG 330, NARS. Court sentence noting Manicatide by name is in "Rumanians Sentence 82 in Treason Trial," *The New York Times*, 20 November 1946.

31. CIA activities in Italy were first disclosed in Representative Otis Pike, "Special Supplement: The CIA Report the President Doesn't Want You to Read," *Village Voice*, February 16 and 22, 1976. See also William Corson, *The Armies of Ignorance* (New York: Dial Press, 1977); and Simpson, *Blowback*.

32. Balabanoff case: discussed in Minutes of JIOA Governing Committee Meeting, 20 October 1947, G-2 Paperclip files, RG 319, WNRC.

33. Ibid. Regarding Saraget, de Gespardi, and general information on the split see *The New York Times*, January 6–9 and 12, 1947 (regarding Balabanoff speaking), and 14 January 1947. See also "Denounces Communists," *The New York Times*, 23 December 1947, for an example of

Balabanoff assailing the "fascist tactics" of Communists in the American press.

34. Steven Rearden, *The Formative Years* (Washington, D.C.: Office of the Secretary of Defense, Historical Office, 1984), p. 281; General Stephen Chamberlin to Frank Wisner, 19 February 1948, G-2 Paperclip files, 400.112 Research, RG 319, WNRC.

35. Lucius Clay, *The Papers of General Lucius D. Clay*, ed. Jean Edward Smith (Bloomington: Indiana University Press, 1974).

36. Ibid., pp. 568–69 (telegram).

37. Rearden, *Formative Years*; and Richard Freeland, *The Truman Doctrine and the Origins of McCarthyism* (New York: Alfred A. Knopf, 1972).

38. Rodal, "Nazi War Criminals in Canada."

39. Wev quote is in Minutes of JIOA Governing Committee Meeting, 11 February 1948, G-2 Paperclip files, 400.112 Research, RG 319, WNRC.

40. "Looming war" comment: in JIOA Liaison Officers' Conference, 20 July 1950, G-2 "Top Secret" Paperclip files, RG 319, WNRC. Paperclip policy limiting procurement is SWNCC 257/33.

CHAPTER 9: THE ARGENTINE CONNECTION

1. Milton Bracker, "Quislings Receive Argentine Refuge," *The New York Times*, 27 March 1949.

2. On Eichmann see Wisliceny affidavit, 29 November 1945, Office of U.S. Counsel for Prosecution of Axis Criminality, *Nazi Conspiracy and Aggression*, vol. 8 (Washington, D.C.: Government Printing Office, 1946–48), p. 610. Braden-Peron conflicts: in Gary Frank, *Juan Peron v. Spruille Braden: The Story Behind the Blue Book* (Lanham, Md.: University Press of America, 1980). See also Silvano Santander, *Juan Domingo Peron y Eva Duarte, agentes del nazismo en las Argentina* (Buenos Aires: Editorial Antygua, 1955).

3. Frank, *Juan Peron vs. Spruille Braden*; and Santander, *Juan Domingo Peron y Eva Duarte*.

4. Ibid.

5. SANACC 257/36.

6. For Walsh history with the IADB see "IADB Yearbook 1952."

7. Noriega-IADB story was reported by the Associated Press, 12 June 1986. Noriega bestowed the Panamanian medal on Lieutenant General John Schweitzer, chairman of the U.S. delegation to the IADB.

8. *The Inter-American Defense Board* (Washington, D.C.: IADB, 1987).

9. Milton Bracker, "Peron Decorates General Ridgway, Aides; Awards May Stir Congressional Questions," *The New York Times*, 15 July 1949; "Seven U.S. Generals Honored," *The New York Times*, 1 September 1948.

10. For Stroessner visit see "IADB Yearbook 1953." Stroessner's background and Paraguay: in Scott Anderson and Jon Anderson, *Inside the League* (New York: Dodd, Mead, 1986). For Ovando visit see "IADB Yearbook 1961"; for Ovando-Barbie connection see Magnus Linklater, Isabel Hilton, and Neal Ascherson, *The Nazi Legacy* (New York: Holt, Rinehart and Winston, 1984).

11. Quote is from "IADB Yearbook 1953."

12. For a discussion of policy see Inter-American Military Cooperation Act, 23 June 1947, H.R. 3836, 80th Cong., 1st sess. On Barbie see Linklater, Hilton, and Ascherson, *Nazi Legacy*.

13. Ladislas Farago, *Aftermath* (New York: Simon and Schuster, 1974); and *Inter-American Defense Board*.

14. Milton Bracker, "Anti-Peron Group Pushes Nazi Issue," *The New York Times*, 25 July 1949.

15. Department of State, "Consultation Among the American Republics With Respect to the Argentine Situation," memorandum, February 1946, otherwise known as the "Blue Book," RG 59, NARS. This is a State Department–FBI investigation of Argentina's collaboration with Nazis during World War II that Braden used against Peron during elections. See Frank, *Juan Peron vs. Spruille Braden*.

16. Farago, *Aftermath*; and *Inter-American Defense Board*.

17. Heinz Conradis, *Design for Flight: The Kurt Tank Story* (London: MacDonald, 1960).

18. Memo, Secretary of State to U.S. Political Adviser on German Affairs, 19 September 1947, 862.542/9-1947, RG 59, NARS.

19. Conradis, *Design for Flight*; letter, Society for the Prevention of World War III to Under Secretary of State Robert Lovett, 16 April 1948, 862.20235/4-1648, RG 59, NARS.

20. Conradis, *Design for Flight*.

21. Ibid.; "Peron Pushes Industry," *The New York Times*, 9 February 1951.

22. See attachments to memo, JIOA Director Daniel Ellis to Robert Spalding, Intelligence Adviser, Department of State, 10 July 1951, JIOA administrative files, RG 330, NARS.

23. Memo, Robert Murphy to Secretary of State, 18 December 1948, JIOA administrative files, RG 330, NARS.

24. See Ellis to Spalding, including attachments.

25. Schulze is discussed in SANACC 257/28; Gruber and HICOG group are discussed in JIOA Director Daniel Ellis to O. L. De Barenguer Cesar,

Brazilian Embassy, 9 February 1951, JIOA memo 263, in JIOA administrative files, RG 330, NARS.

26. "Austrian Scientists," IRR dossier, RG 319, NARS.

27. Walter Schreiber's bio and connections to the Reich Research Council are from Alexander Hardy, "The Case of Walter Schreiber," memorandum, 17 February 1952, in Schreiber's JIOA dossier, RG 330, NARS.

28. Ibid. Ding-Schuler quote is from Nuremberg doc. NO-257.

29. Schreiber's Antifa training: CIC investigation report, 15 December 1949; and Hardy, "Case of Walter Schreiber"—both in the Walter Schreiber JIOA dossier, RG 330, NARS.

30. Minutes of Schreiber's press conference, 19 November 1948, and CIC interrogation of Karl Buesing, 3 December 1948, are in ODI subject file, RG 260, WNRC. For CIA interrogation of Schreiber and other sources see CIA, "Background and Procedures Used in the Preparation of Defendants for Confessions," memo, n.d., John Marks files, NSA.

31. Brigadier General Otis Benson, Jr., to Commanding General, Air University, 4 June 1951, in JIOA administrative files, RG 330, NARS.

32. Hardy, "Case of Walter Schreiber"; and Dr. Leo Alexander to Dr. John Conlin, February 1952—both in the Walter Schreiber JIOA dossier, RG 330, NARS.

33. INS Boston, "Statement of Janina Iwanski," 27 February 1952, in the Walter Schreiber JIOA dossier, RG 330, NARS.

34. Armstrong quote is in memo, Dr. Edward Young, Physicians Forum, February 1952, in the Walter Schreiber JIOA dossier, RG 330, NARS.

35. Finletter release: in Schreiber's JIOA dossier, RG 330, NARS.

36. Benson is quoted in memo, Dr. Gaylord Anderson to the Association of Schools of Public Health, 6 February 1952, in Schreiber's JIOA dossier, RG 330, NARS.

37. JIOA Director Colonel Benjamin W. Heckemeyer to Major General Robert L. Walsh, Chairman, U.S. Delegation IADB, JIOA memo 238, 12 February 1952, in JIOA administrative files, Miscellaneous Correspondence, RG 330, NARS. For meeting of 12 February 1952 to honor Reyes see "IADB Yearbook 1952" and "IADB Yearbook 1955."

38. For Reyes meetings see Headquarters, USAF to USAIRA Buenos Aires, cable AFOIN-52571, 14 February 1952, and letter, Walsh to Argentine Air Attaché, 28 February 1952; Walsh quote is in letter, Walsh to Reyes, 17 March 1952—all in the Walter Schreiber JIOA dossier, RG 330, NARS.

39. Schreiber later worked in Paraguay, according to the *International Herald Tribune*, 21 February 1983; for details of Schreiber's departure for Buenos Aires see letter, JIOA Director Colonel Benjamin Heckemeyer to

James Riley, U.S. Immigration, 19 June 1952, in JIOA administrative files, RG 330, NARS.

40. Multhopp's Nazi party membership and biography are from Agent Report, signed by Sergeant Cornelius Walsh, 22 December 1949, in Hans Multhopp's INSCOM dossier; and "Martin Company Claims Plane Can Fly From Pentagon," *Washington Post*, 14 April 1964.

41. On Glenn Martin, Republic Aviation, Kurt Tank, and the ABMA recruiter see memo, Colonel Harlan Holman to Assistant Chief of Staff, G-2, 29 August 1957, in ACSI post-1952 Paperclip files, RG 319, WNRC (declassified per author's FOIA request).

CHAPTER 10: SPIES, SPOOKS, AND LSD

1. Seymour Hersh, *Chemical and Biological Warfare: America's Hidden Arsenal* (New York: Doubleday, 1969).

2. Taylor and Johnson, "Use of Volunteers in Chemical Agent Research."

3. Author interview with James Stanley.

4. Ibid.

5. Ibid.

6. Author interview with Seymour Silver.

7. Captain Seth Palagi, "Report of Denazification Procedure," 29 October 1947; and *OMGUS Security Report*, 25 December 1947—both in the Kurt Rahr JIOA dossier, RG 330, NARS.

8. Lieutenant F. E. Van Sickle, "Memorandum for Post Intelligence," 23 March 1948; Trurnit accusation: CSGID to EUCOM, cable WAR-87364, 30 September 1947—both in the Kurt Rahr JIOA dossier, RG 330, NARS.

9. Colonel John Wood, *Security Report by Employing Agency*, 29 March 1948, in the Hans Trurnit INSCOM dossier D184062; and Silver interview.

10. Theodor Wagner-Jauregg's background is from his JIOA dossier, RG 330, NARS; and Silver interview.

11. Information on Friederich Hoffmann: INSCOM dossier 215327144.

12. "The History of Captured Enemy Toxic Munitions in the American Zone, European Theater, May 1945 to June 1947," Office of the Chief of Chemical Corps, Headquarters, EUCOM; and Silver interview.

13. J. H. Wills and I. A. DeArmon, *Medical Laboratory Special Report No. 54* (Army Chemical Center, November 1954).

14. "The Army's Human Guinea Pigs," *Freedom*, August 1979.

15. Ibid.

16. National Research Council, *Possible Long-Term Health Effects of*

Short-Term Exposure to Chemical Agents, 3 vols. (Washington, D.C.: National Academy Press, 1984); see vol. 2, p. 36, for mustard experiments. Tabun reference: in L. Wilson Greene, "Psychochemicial Warfare, A New Concept of War," Army Chemical Center report, August 1949.

17. Greene, "Psychochemical Warfare."

18. John Marks, *The Search for the Manchurian Candidate* (New York: McGraw Hill, 1980).

19. Memo, Colonel Patrick Fokers to Major P. M. Wilson, FIAT, 14 September 1948, in Walter Reppe INSCOM dossier D60608.

20. Interrogation of Karl Tauboeck, September 20 and 21, 1945, M1019, RG 238, NARS; and Tauboeck INSCOM dossier XE187079.

21. Ibid. Tauboeck's CIA connection is from CIA Inspector General Report, 1951, in John Marks files, NSA.

22. Marks, *Manchurian Candidate*.

23. Ray Treichler's position at Edgewood is noted in "Edgewood Arsenal Quarterly Historical Report," 17 March 1958 and May 1958 (obtained under the FOIA). Hoffmann's CIA connections are in his INSCOM dossier; other individuals' CIA connections are noted in Marks, *Manchurian Candidate*.

24. Silver interview.

25. Ibid.

26. Ibid.; "Trip Reports," in Friederich Hoffmann's INSCOM dossier.

27. Friederich Hoffmann, William A. Mosher, and Richard Hively, "Isolation of Trans-Δ^6-Tetrahydrocannabinol From Marijuana," *Journal of the American Chemical Society*, 20 April 1966; author interview with James Moore; and Marks, *Manchurian Candidate*.

28. See "Bluebird/Artichoke" documents in G-2 "Top Secret" Paperclip files, RG 319, WNRC; and Van Sim, "Trip Report," February 1956 (obtained under the FOIA).

29. Lieutenant Colonel David McFarling, "LSD Follow-up Study Report," U.S. Army Medical Department, 1980 (obtained under the FOIA).

30. Stanley interview.

31. Information on interrogation teams: in "Project Derby Hat" INSCOM dossier. On the Thornwell case see *Thornwell v. U.S.*, 471 F. Supp. 344 (D.D.C., 1979); and Thornwell INSCOM dossier HE05255.

32. Minutes of JIOA Liaison Officers Meeting, 15 November 1949, G-2 "Top Secret" Paperclip files, RG 319, WNRC.

33. William Safire, "The German Problem," *The New York Times*, 2 January 1989.

34. JIOA Liaison Officers Meeting, 15 November 1949.

35. Army officer quote on Schieber and nerve gas reference are in Schieber INSCOM dossier D231194.

36. Schieber discusses his Armaments Supply Office activities in "Interview with Walter Schieber," Nuremberg doc. NO-1298, 8 February 1947, and Nuremberg doc. PS-104; arrest report is in Schieber INSCOM dossier.

37. Released from prison reference is in Agent Report I-421, 7970 CIC Group, 9 September 1949; Lieutenant Colonel Merellat Moses to 7970 CIC Group, 23 March 1948; and cable, Lieutenant Colonel M. C. Taylor to OMGUS, 26 April 1948—all in the Walter Schieber INSCOM dossier.

38. French attempt: Agent Report I-421, 9 September 1949; spy suspect and arms: Agent Report, 19 December 1949; CIC agent quote: Special CIC Agent Richard Scutt, Agent Report I-421, 14 December 1949—all in Walter Schieber INSCOM dossier.

39. Blauer information is from records of his daughter's lawsuit, *Barrett v. U.S.*, 660 F. Supp. 1291 (S.D.N.Y., 1987) (hereafter cited as *Barrett*). Martin Lee and Bruce Shlain, *Acid Dreams* (New York: Grove Press, 1985), p. 38; Amedeo S. Marrazzi, "Trial of EA 1298 at New York State Psychiatric Institute," report to Edgewood's scientific director, 15 January 1953; report, Sidney Maltiz, Acting Principal Research Psychiatrist, New York State Psychiatric Institute, to Van Sim, 16 February 1956; and Van Sim, "Trip Report," February 1956—all in *Barrett*.

40. Statistics on experiments: from National Research Council, *Possible Long-Term Health Effects*.

41. Taylor and Johnson, "Use of Volunteers in Chemical Agent Research."

42. Ibid.

43. National Research Council, *Possible Long-Term Health Effects*, vol. 2, pp. 52–53, 64, 65, and 67–68.

44. Ibid., p. 248 (dioxin), 135, 156, and 163. CS experiments: "Operation Black Magic," Edgewood Arsenal report, January–May 1959.

45. *Bonner v. U.S.*, CIV 81-16 3 (E.D.N.C., 1981) (hereafter cited as *Bonner*). A complete report of Bonner's experiment is contained in Stuart Karger, "Incapacitating Dose of CAR 302,668 in Man, and Efficacy of Physostigmine as an Antidote," Edgewood Arsenal Technical Memorandum 114-20, August 1968.

46. Jim Santori, "Private War of Ken Loeh," *Southern Illinoisan*, 20 December 1981.

47. Ibid.

48. Reference to grand mal seizures is in McFarling, "LSD Follow-up Study," pp. 2 and 35; other effects are noted in National Research Council, *Possible Long-Term Health Effects*.

49. *Bonner*.

50. McFarling, "LSD Follow-up Study" (suicide attempts), pp. 21 and 53.

51. For Army denials see *Loeh v. U.S.*, CIV 77-2065-B (S.D. Ill., 1977).

52. Stanley interview.

CHAPTER 11: PIPELINE TO THE ALAMAC HOTEL

1. Contract terms with Alamac Hotel is in "Minutes of JIOA Liaison Officers Meeting," 26 February 1951, G-2 Paperclip files, RG 319, WNRC. The Alamac Hotel is now a condominium complex.

2. Detailed statistical reports are in JIOA post-1952 administrative files, RG 330, NARS.

3. For a copy of a Project 63 flyer with contract information see State fiche, RG 59, NARS. Policy: JCS 1363/75, RG 218, NARS.

4. Special Projects Team reports are in ACSI post-1952 Paperclip files, RG 319, WNRC.

5. Author interview with retired Army Master Sergeant George Meidlein.

6. Information on Neumaier, Ulm, Lohninger, and other Austrians is in "Austrian Scientists," IRR dossier, RG 319, NARS.

7. Ernest Richter, Special Projects Team, trip report to ACSI, 16 April 1957, ACSI post-1952 Paperclip files, RG 319, WNRC.

8. Information on Krejci-Graf and Kress: see "Austrian Scientists."

9. Memo, Colonel Lewis Perry to ACSI, 6 July 1951, JIOA administrative files, RG 330, NARS.

10. Ibid.

11. Houdremont was tried in Nuremberg, case 10, *U.S. v. Krupp et al.*, M896, RG 238, NARS. Quote is from Minutes of JIOA Liaison Officers Meeting, 2 February 1951, G-2 Paperclip files, RG 319, WNRC.

12. Minutes of JIOA Liaison Officers Meeting, 2 February 1951.

13. Ibid. On Kamptner see AC of S report, USFA Headquarters, 29 August 1950, in Kamptner INSCOM dossier XE271686.

14. Minutes of JIOA Liaison Officers Meeting, 2 February 1951.

15. Blome information: Hunt, "U.S. Coverup of Nazi Scientists." Original Alsos interrogation: Kurt Blome INSCOM dossier XE001248.

16. Hunt, "U.S. Coverup of Nazi Scientists." Blome court decision: *Brandt*.

17. Hunt, "U.S. Coverup of Nazi Scientists." Fort Detrick interrogation: Blome's INSCOM dossier.

18. For copies of contracts see Kurt Blome's INSCOM dossier and his JIOA dossier, RG 330, NARS.

19. Memo, Dr. J. B. Koepfli to State Department, 6 April 1951. See

also J. B. Koepfli to Frederich Nolting, 14 January 1952, regarding the JIOA misrepresenting contracts and CIA and State comments about the JIOA's "dubious" recruiting methods, including an "ex–diamond merchant from LA"; all are from State fiche, RG 59, NARS.

20. For a Project 63 flyer see State fiche, RG 59, NARS.

21. Complaints by Helmut Ruska are in memo, Carl Nordstrom, Chief Scientific Research Division, HICOG, to JIOA Director Benjamin Heckemeyer, 7 December 1951, JIOA administrative files, RG 330, NARS. Buss complaints: Wilhelm Buss IRR dossier EE392034, RG 319, NARS.

22. Cable, John McCloy, HICOG, to Secretary of State, 21 February 1952, State fiche, RG 59, NARS.

23. Karl Weber, CIA Frankfurt, to Marshall Chadwell, CIA Washington, CIA memo S/C (4-5-6), OSI (7-8), 20 February 1952, State fiche, RG 59, NARS. But the West German government could not have been too happy with the CIA either; see Alistair Horne, *Return to Power* (New York: Praeger, 1956), pp. 121–23, for a short but fascinating account of a CIA-backed guerrilla unit that was caught operating in West Germany with a "liquidation" list that included top West German government officials.

24. Memo, Karl Weber to P. G. Strong, March 18, 1952, State fiche, RG 59, NARS.

25. *Air Research and Development Command.* See also Colonel U. P. Williams, "Alleged Recruitment Program," memo to the ACSI, 23 November 1956, noting the value of continuing Paperclip and an estimated 420,000 engineering school graduates in Russia, ACSI post-1952 Paperclip files, RG 319, WNRC.

26. Geehan interview.

27. Ibid.

28. Ibid.

29. Ibid.

30. *Air Research and Development Command.*

31. For information on Herbert Alfke see CIA Biographic Register, July 1952; and memo, CIA, Liaison Division, to Director of Intelligence, U.S. Air Force, 23 August 1952—both in the Alfke JIOA dossier, RG 330, NARS.

32. See Ampatco file, JIOA administrative files, RG 330, NARS.

33. Information on Klein: Lieutenant Colonel Eugene Cook to JIOA Director, 1 June 1950, memo noting that Klein "has been dropped from the list for security reasons," JIOA administrative files, RG 330, NARS.

34. Wuensch's U.S. entry is noted in cable, HICOG to 66th Army CIC, March 1950, in Guido Wuensch IRR dossier XE187525, RG 319, NARS.

35. Anne Burger biography and biological warfare job description: memo, C. F. Berrens, Naval Medical Research Institute, to Chief of Naval

Operations, 27 November 1950, JIOA administrative files, Navy Escape Clause, RG 330, NARS. Erich Traub biography is in Traub's JIOA dossier, RG 330, NARS.

36. Traub's trip to Turkey is discussed in Alsos interrogation of Kurt Blome, Blome INSCOM dossier XE001248.

37. Author interview with retired Air Force Colonel Stone Christopher.

38. Ibid.

39. Geeham interview; records on Oberth's U.S. entry are in ACSI post-1952 Paperclip files, RG 319, WNRC.

40. Axster interview.

41. *Air Research and Development Command*; Ernst Czerlinsky Berlin Document Center report, 1 June 1953 contract, and *Basic Personnel Record for German Specialists* listing NSDAP, SS, SA, and other organizations are in Ernst Czerlinsky IRR dossier XE301737, RG 319, NARS.

42. Biographies are in Horst Gerlach's and Fritz Klaiber's ACSI dossiers, ACSI post-1952 Paperclip files, RG 319, WNRC.

43. Biographies are in Eduard Wulkow's and Hermann Donnert's ACSI dossiers, ACSI post-1952 Paperclip files, RG 319, WNRC.

44. Osenberg signed a certificate transferring Pfeiffer to Kiel on 13 April 1944, in Albert Pfeiffer INSCOM dossier.

45. Christopher interview. For an example of polygraph questions see Hans Dolezalek INSCOM dossiers XI574906 and I13B488.

46. Christopher interview.

47. JIOA 1957 list, JIOA post-1952 administrative records, RG 330, NARS (declassified per author's FOIA request).

48. Messerschmitt use of slave laborers is described in Benjamin Ferencz, *Less Than Slaves* (Cambridge, Mass.: Harvard University Press, 1979); Messerschmitt denazification: "Messerschmitt Fined as Nazi," *The New York Times*, 27 May 1948.

49. Ferencz, *Less Than Slaves*; *The New York Times*, April 3 and 5, 1963.

50. Wilhelm Wessel biography: Wessel's ACSI dossier, in ACSI post-1952 Paperclip files, RG 319, WNRC; Otto Cerny information is in memo, Mrs. Hedemarie Cerny to Andrew Loehr, Special Projects Team, 19 September 1956, in Cerny INSCOM dossier GE009781.

51. Lists of Fort Monmouth recruits, Josef Parth's ACSI dossier, and Hans-Joachim Naake's ACSI dossier are in ACSI post-1952 Paperclip files, RG 319, WNRC.

52. Ivan Simitch, "Memo for the Record," 8 July 1953; Hans Ziegler, "Memo for the Record," 14 August 1953; and Ivan Simitch, "Memo for the Record," 14 August 1953—all in ACSI post-1952 Paperclip files, RG 319, WNRC.

53. Olaf Guzmann statement and Major Lewis Saxby, "In the Matter of CWO Ivan Simitch and Mr. and Mrs. Guzmann," 18 January 1954, are in the Guzmann ACSI dossier, ACSI post-1952 Paperclip files, RG 319, WNRC.

54. Ibid.

55. Ibid.

56. Colonel Frank Moses, "Memorandum," 11 November 1953, in the Olaf Guzmann ACSI dossier, ACSI post-1952 Paperclip files, RG 319, WNRC.

57. American Chemical Society complaint: memo, Herbert Schon to Colonel Kight, Army Press Desk, 21 November 1956; and memo, Colonel U. P. Williams to ACSI, 23 November 1956—both in ACSI post-1952 Paperclip files, RG 319, WNRC.

58. Ambassador James Conant to Secretary of State, 13 July 1956, State fiche, RG 59, NARS.

59. ACSI Deputy Director General Robert Schow to JIOA, 26 July 1956; and U. P. Williams, AC of S, to CRD, 26 November 1956—both in ACSI post-1952 Paperclip files, RG 319, WNRC.

60. Christopher interview. For Christopher correspondence on name change to Project DEFSIP see memo, JIOA Director Stone Christopher to Army, Navy, Air Force Intelligence Chiefs, 26 March 1957, JIOA post-1952 administrative files, RG 330, NARS.

61. Walter Sullivan, "Soviet Launches Earth Satellite," *The New York Times*, 5 October 1957.

62. Colonel Benjamin Heckemeyer to ACSI Deputy Director General Robert Schow, 1 November 1957, in ACSI post-1952 Paperclip files, RG 319, WNRC.

CHAPTER 12: WHAT PRICE TREASON?

1. Whalen biography is from ACSI, "The William H. Whalen Case," ACSI Case Summary, 1968, in William Whalen INSCOM dossier B1009214.

2. Whalen's relationship with Edemski and Edemski's biography are in Whalen's INSCOM dossier.

3. Quote is from Eugene Stapleton, "Memorandum for the DOI," 1 September 1970, Whalen's INSCOM dossier.

4. ACSI, "Whalen Case"; U.S. Army Intelligence Command, "Summary of Information," memo, 27 August 1970, in Whalen's INSCOM dossier. Information on Whalen's finances is in *Whalen* trial records.

5. ACSI, "Whalen Case."

6. Walter Sullivan, "Soviet Launches Earth Satellite," *The New York Times*, 5 October 1957; and *The New York Times*, 14 September 1959.

7. Author interview with Rocco Petrone.

8. Whalen's biography: in ACSI, "Whalen Case"; information on other officers is from JIOA post-1952 administrative files, RG 330, NARS, and ACSI post-1952 Paperclip files, RG 319, WNRC.

9. Author interview with retired Army Colonel Robinson Norris.

10. Colleagues' descriptions of Whalen with sources' names deleted: Agent Report, 1 June 1965; 902d Intelligence Corps Group, "Memo for the Record," 1 November 1964; and Agent Report, 8 December 1964—all from Whalen's INSCOM dossier.

11. JIOA to Special Projects Section, U.S. Army, Europe, 7 November 1957, in Hans Longosch's ACSI dossier, ACSI post-1952 Paperclip files, RG 319, WNRC.

12. Statistics and information on where recruits worked are in JIOA post-1952 administrative files, RG 330, NARS.

13. Popodi biography is in INSCOM dossier GE012017; Nowatny information is in "Austrian Scientists."

14. See especially "Request for BDC and Wast Check," 7 November 1958, in Gorges INSCOM dossier HE031272.

15. "Complaint Made by Telefunken to the U.S. Charge d'Affaires in Bonn Concerning an Offer of Employment Extended to a Telefunken Employee," unsigned memo, 26 November 1959, in JIOA post-1952 administrative files, RG 330, NARS.

16. Quotes are from *Bild-Zeitung*, in the Hans Goslich ACSI dossier, ACSI post-1952 Paperclip files, RG 319, WNRC.

17. Memo, Major George Lanstrum, ACSI, to Major Lewis Saxby, Special Projects Section, Frankfurt, 22 November 1957, in the Hans Goslich ACSI dossier, ACSI post-1952 Paperclip files, RG 319, WNRC.

18. Max Frankel, "U.S. Refuses to Yield Rights: Soviet Asks Talk," *The New York Times*, 28 November 1958; and Osgood Caruthers, "Gromyko Warns of 'Big War' Peril in Berlin Dispute," *The New York Times*, 26 December 1958.

19. Jack Raymond, "President Bars Troop War in Europe But He Declines to Rule Out a Nuclear War," *The New York Times*, 12 March 1959.

20. ACSI, "Whalen Case."

21. ACSI, "Damage Assessment in the Case of Whalen," April 1965, in Whalen's INSCOM dossier.

22. ACSI, "Administrative Investigation Concerning the Assignment of Lt. Colonel William Henry Whalen," memo, 1 February 1965, in Whalen's INSCOM dossier.

23. ACSI, "Damage Assessment."

24. Whalen's memos to the State Department are in JIOA post-1952 administrative files, RG 330, NARS.

25. Lists and statistics: ibid.

26. For Winterberg listings see Brigadier General Richard Collins, "Disposition Form: Alien Specialists Interested in Employment in the United States," 5 January 1959; and memo, Brigadier General Richard Collins to ACSI, Special Projects Section, 9 January 1959—both in ACSI post-1952 Paperclip files, RB 319, WNRC.

27. Letter, Knut Lossbom to Hans Dolezalek, 3 August 1953; *Alien Personal History Statement*, 25 August 1953, in Dolezalek's INSCOM dossier XE574904.

28. Sandy McPherson, "Top German Scientist Washed Dishes in City," *Calgary Herald*, 5 May 1959; "German Immigrant to Get New Start at Local Firm," *Huntsville Times*, 6 May 1959; and "Rocket 'Expert' Says He Wasn't," *Huntsville Times*, 10 May 1959. The personnel office at Brown Engineering confirmed Wigand's 1959 employment.

29. Rossmann INSCOM dossier XE574904; see also letter, G. A. Little to Major Lewis Saxby, 31 October 1952, on Rossmann not qualifying for immigration, in Rossmann's ACSI dossier, ACSI post-1952 Paperclip files, RG 319, WNRC.

30. Memo regarding intelligence meeting and enclosure no. 1 identified as being JIOA, 1 March 1960, in ACSI post-1952 Paperclip files, RG 319, WNRC.

31. ACSI, "Damage Assessment."

32. Stapleton, "Memorandum."

33. Memo, Colonel Graham Schmidt to Director, Security Plans and Programs, Office of the Assistant Secretary of Defense, March 1965, in Whalen's INSCOM dossier.

34. ACSI, "Damage Assessment."

35. Statement on "William Henry Whalen" was submitted to the American Embassy by Walter Mueller, 20 May 1963, State Department document referral from Whalen's INSCOM dossier.

36. ACSI, "Whalen Case."

37. Ibid.

38. Norris and Christopher interviews.

39. Hans Zeigler to JIOA Director Earle Gardner, 9 August 1960; E. M. McDermott to Security Control Officer, Fort Monmouth, Department of the Army, August 1960; and JIOA Director Earle Gardner to ACSI, 31 October 1960—all in JIOA post-1952 administrative files, RG 330, NARS.

40. Ibid.

41. JIOA Director Earle Gardner to Director of Intelligence, 8 August 1960; and JIOA Director Earle Gardner, "Memorandum for the Record," 5 August 1960—both in JIOA post-1952 administrative files, RG 330, NARS.

42. Norris interview; lists of recruits are in *Personnel Employed Under DEFSIP Contracts*, in JIOA post-1952 administrative files, RG 330, NARS.

43. Ibid.

44. ACSI, "Whalen Case."

45. U.S. Army Intelligence Command, "Summary"; and ACSI, "Damage Assessment."

46. ACSI, "Whalen Case"; and *Whalen*.

47. Ibid.

48. Agent Report, 9 February 1966, in Whalen's INSCOM dossier.

49. *Whalen*; and ACSI, "Whalen Case."

50. ACSI, "Whalen Case."

51. Ibid.

52. Information on Wennerström is in Fred Graham, "Retired Pentagon Officer Is Seized as Spy for Soviets," *The New York Times*, 13 July 1966; H. K. Ronblom, *The Spy Without a Country* (New York: Coward-McCann, 1965); and Thomas Whiteside, *An Agent in Place* (New York: Viking, 1966).

53. *Whalen*.

54. Ibid.

55. Ibid.

56. Testimony of Gruentzel is in ibid.

57. Grand Jury Indictment is in ibid.

58. Ibid.

59. Ibid.; E. Kenworthy, "Officials Say FBI Agents Shadowed Spying Suspect From 1959 to 1961," *The New York Times*, 14 July 1966; and Army press release, in Whalen's INSCOM dossier.

60. Kenworthy, "FBI Agents Shadowed Spying Suspect"; memos to State and Justice Departments signed by Whalen are in both JIOA post-1952 administrative files, RG 330, NARS, and ACSI post-1952 Paperclip files, RG 319, NARS.

61. "U.S. May Not Prosecute Whalen on Spy Charges," *Washington Star*, 14 November 1966.

62. Information on plea bargain is in memo, JAG Special Assistant Conrad Philos to Attorney General, 12 December 1966, in Whalen's INSCOM dossier.

63. "Whalen Pleads Guilty to Defense Secret Plot," *Washington Post*, 17 December 1966.

64. Ibid.

65. *Whalen*.

CHAPTER 13: MOON WALK IN THE SHADOW OF THE THIRD REICH

1. Joseph Trento, *Prescription for Disaster* (New York: Crown, 1987).

2. Michael Jennings interview with Georg von Tiesenhausen.

3. Ibid.

4. Michael Jennings interview with James Kingsbury.

5. Michael Jennings interview with Marshall Space Flight Center technical official.

6. Debus's immigration problems: 12 February 1953, INS files; James H. Skinner, *Security Certificate From the JIOA*, 16 June 1950, all in Kurt Debus JIOA dossier, RG 330, NARS.

7. Von Tiesenhausen interview.

8. Peter Cobun, "A Footnote Is Enough," *Huntsville Times*, 8 August 1976; Trento, *Prescription for Disaster*; and Petrone interview.

9. Von Tiesenhausen interview.

10. Statistics are in JIOA post-1952 administrative records, RG 330, NARS.

11. Special Projects Team, "Cost Estimates and Evaluation," memo, 31 August 1964, JIOA post-1952 administrative records, RG 330, NARS.

12. Christopher interview.

13. Michael Jennings interview with Marshal Space Flight Center administrator.

14. JIOA Director Earle Gardner to Director of Intelligence, 5 April 1961, JIOA post-1952 administrative records, RG 330, NARS.

15. JIOA Director Earle Gardner to ACSI, 5 April 1961; and Colonel Clarence Nelson to Chairman, JIOA, 3 April 1961—both in JIOA post-1952 administrative records, RG 330, NARS.

16. Christopher interview; memo on meeting between ACSI representative Henry Milne and Colonel Stone Christopher, 23 November 1964, JIOA post-1952 administrative records, RG 330, NARS.

17. Author interview with Clarence Lasby; Lasby, *Project Paperclip*.

18. Accident investigation reported in *The New York Times*, and the *Washington Post*, 10 April 1967. Trento, *Prescription for Disaster*.

19. Ibid.; Michael Jennings interview with Walter Haeussermann.

20. Von Tiesenhausen interview.

21. Trento, *Prescription for Disaster*; von Tiesenhausen interview.

22. Pat Naute, "Apollo Success Brings Rejoicing for Huntsville," *Birmingham News*, 22 July 1969.

23. Michel, *Dora*.

24. Author interview with Eli Pollach.

25. Ibid.

26. Ibid.

27. Letter, Wernher von Braun to Major General Julius Klein, 2 August 1969, OSI.

28. Ibid.

29. Transcript of the interrogation of Wernher von Braun, 7 February 1969, German Embassy, New Orleans.

30. Author interview with Jean Michel, *People v. Busta and Sander*, Provincial Court of Essen, West Germany, 1971.

31. Trento, *Prescription for Disaster*.

32. Michael Jennings interview with Alexander McCool.

33. Marshall technical official interview.

34. Christopher interview; Neil ImObersteg to Astrid Kraus, 17 February 1967, JIOA post-1952 administrative records, RG 330, NARS. Paperclip was canceled by DOD directive 70-7, 24 March 1970. Individuals recruited up to that time continued to arrive until around 1973.

35. Von Tiesenhausen interview.

36. Haeussermann interview.

37. Petrone interview.

38. Cobun, "A Footnote Is Enough."

39. Von Tiesenhausen interview.

CHAPTER 14: TRYING TO OPEN THE LID

1. Holtzman interview.

2. Ibid.

3. Ibid.; Public Law 95-549.

4. Holtzman interview.

5. Bach letter in *Saturday Review*, 9 August 1958, is in the Hubertus Strughold file, OSI. Memo, Representative Elizabeth Holtzman to INS Commissioner Leonard Chapman, 10 June 1974.

6. Holtzman memo to Chapman.

7. Representative Henry Gonzales to INS Commissioner Leonard Chapman, 25 June 1974; and INS Commissioner Leonard Chapman to Representative Henry Gonzales, 12 July 1974—both in Strughold OSI file.

8. Charles Allen, "Hubertus Strughold, Nazi in USA," *Jewish Currents*, December 1974; and Ralph Blumenthal, "Anti-Nazi Drive a Year Later: No U.S. Legal Moves Are Taken," *The New York Times*, 23 November 1974.

9. General Accounting Office, *Widespread Conspiracy to Obstruct Probes*

of Alleged Nazi War Criminals Not Supported by Available Evidence—Controversy May Continue (Washington, D.C.: Government Printing Office, 15 May 1978).

10. Letter, Representative Peter Rodino, Chairman, House Committee on the Judiciary, to Comptroller General Charles Bowsher, 17 May 1982, notifying him that "government agencies misled GAO and Congress." See also CBS, "60 Minutes," 16 May 1982; Loftus, *Belarus Secret*; GAO, *Nazi and Axis Collaborators*; and author interview with John Tipton.

11. Holtzman interview.

12. Senate, *Final Report*, no. 94-755.

13. House Committee on Armed Services, *Military Hallucinogenic Experiments*, hearings, 94th Cong., 1st sess., 8 September 1975.

14. For the Olson family's reaction see "Family Blames CIA in Death," *Washington Post*, 11 July 1975; and Lee Hockstader, "Victims of 1950s' Mind-Control Experiments Settle with CIA," *Washington Post*, 5 October 1988.

15. U.S. Army, "Inquiry Into the Facts and Circumstances Surrounding the Death of Mr. Harold Blauer at the New York State Psychiatric Institute and Subsequent Claims Actions," inspector general report (obtained under the FOIA); and *Barrett*.

16. Taylor and Johnson, "Use of Volunteers in Chemical Agent Research"; and Lee Hockstader, "Victims of 1950s' Mind-Control Experiments," *Washington Post*, 5 October 1988.

17. Stanley interview.

18. House Committee on Armed Services, *Military Hallucinogenic Experiments*.

19. McFarling, "LSD Follow-up Study."

20. Ibid.

21. Stanley interview.

22. Ken Loeh correspondence with author. Loeh applied for veterans benefits in the 1950s. In correspondence between the Army and a Veterans Administration official, the Army first denied that Loeh had participated in the experiments and then refused to reveal the identity of the chemical agent used because the name was classified.

23. McFarling, "LSD Follow-up Study."

24. Ibid.

25. National Research Council, *Possible Long-Term Health Effects*.

26. Ibid. Some of the most revealing documents obtained under the FOIA from Edgewood are lists of individuals who either worked at Edgewood or were under contract from 1945 to 1970. These lists contain the names of dozens of well-known scientists who became department heads at such major universities as Harvard, MIT, Stanford, Maryland, Tulane, and

others across the country. See also the footnotes of NRC studies for their published work on experiments at Edgewood.

27. *Stanley.*
28. Author interview with Eli Rosenbaum; Michel, *Dora*; Ordway and Sharpe, *Rocket Team.*
29. Rosenbaum interview.
30. Author interview with OSI Director Neal Sher.
31. Rosenbaum interview.
32. Ibid.; *Andrae* trial record.
33. *Andrae.*
34. OSI interrogation of Arthur Rudolph.
35. Ibid.
36. Ibid.
37. Ibid.
38. Ibid.; and Aalmans, *"Dora"-Nordhausen War Crimes Trial.*
39. OSI interrogation of Arthur Rudolph.
40. Ibid.
41. Ibid.
42. Ibid.
43. Ibid.
44. Ibid.
45. Beon interview.
46. Sher interview.
47. Bannasch testimony, *Andrae.*
48. Sher interview. See also Arthur Rudolph–OSI agreement, 28 November 1983, OSI (obtained under the FOIA).
49. Sher interview.

CHAPTER 15: CONSEQUENCES

1. Michael Jennings, "Shadows Touch State's Surviving Rocketry Pioneers," *Birmingham News*, 27 April 1985. The author attended this event with a West German TV crew whose story aired the day of President Reagan's visit to Bitburg Cemetery.
2. For author's CNN report on Grau and Haukohl see Hunt, "Nazi Coverup."
3. Haukohl's biography is in his JIOA and INSCOM dossiers; estimate of seven hundred prisoners is from Georg Finkenzeller's testimony in *Andrae*. See also "Kommando" list showing Finkenzeller and Schochel as being capos in Haukohl's detail, in *Andrae*, prosecution exhibits; Finkenzeller's separate trial is in *Andrae*, roll 16.

4. Rudolph discusses Grau's visit to Mittelwerk in OSI interrogation of Rudolph; Grau quotes are from a 17 June 1971 taped interview with Dieter Grau by Frederick Ordway and David Christensen (obtained by the author under the FOIA from OSI); and *Atlanta Weekly*, 26 May 1985.

5. UPI, "Lawyer Refuses 'Witchhunt' Interviews," 7 March 1986; and Hunt, "Nazi Coverup."

6. For background on LaRouche see Dennis King, *Lyndon LaRouche and the New American Fascism* (New York: Doubleday, 1989); *Extremism on the Right* (New York: Anti-Defamation League of B'nai B'rith, 1983); Anti-Defamation League of B'nai B'rith, "The LaRouche Network: A Political Cult," *ADL Facts*, Spring 1982; and Dennis King and Ronald Radosh, "The LaRouche Connection," *New Republic*, 19 November 1984. With the exception of King and a handful of others, the press ignored LaRouche's activities for a decade. For reporters' problems when covering LaRouche: Dennis King affidavit regarding death threats, 7 June 1984, in *LaRouche et al. v. National Broadcasting Company*, 479 U.S. 818 (1986); and Patricia Lynch, "Is Lyndon LaRouche Using Your Name?" *Columbia Journalism Review*, March–April 1985. Author's experiences as a result of a *Bulletin of the Atomic Scientists* story are reported in Investigative Reporters and Editors Award submission forms, 1986.

7. Author's notes of meetings. This gag attempt was brazen. After *Birmingham News* reporter Michael Jennings and I began asking questions about Rudolph, we were ordered to the front of the auditorium. The West German TV crew videotaped the event from the back of the room. The crew's photographer, who was born in Israel, told the author that a representative of the space museum said he was glad to see them because the American press was "a pain in the neck when it came to the Nazi issue." The West German crew was not amused.

8. Author's notes. Marsha Freeman reported in "News Briefs," *Fusion*, May–June 1985, that "one Linda Hunt" attended the event. For LaRouche members' attack on the author's *Bulletin* coverup story see *New Solidarity*, 23 March 1985.

9. Referring to Ordway, Rudolph told the OSI, "I consider him a friend," in OSI interrogation of Rudolph; letter, Milton Hochmuth to Frederick Ordway, 19 November 1984, in the author's personal collection. For an example of Ordway's defense of Rudolph see Ordway letter and the author's response in *Bulletin of the Atomic Scientists*, December 1985.

10. Author interview with former New York governor Hugh Carey.

11. Ordway and Sharpe, *Rocket Team*; and Grau tape interview.

12. "Violence oriented" quote is from CIA memorandum, 15 July 1976, in Dennis King affidavit, *LaRouche v. NBC*; Caryle Murphy, "LaRouche Indicted on Tax, Mail Fraud Charges in Va.," *Washington Post*, 15 October

1988; and Kent Jenkins, Jr., "From Prison Cell, LaRouche Raises $221,000 for House Race," *Washington Post*, 2 June 1990.

13. The ADL's Irwin Suall called LaRouche a "small time Hitler" on NBC's "First Camera," March 1984. For evidence of LaRouche's anti-Semitism see judge's decision dismissing Larouche's libel action against the ADL, in *U.S. Labor Party et al. v. Anti-Defamation League of B'nai B'rith*, No. 79-11470 (N.Y. App. Div., 1980):

> Plaintiffs [LaRouche group] have linked prominent Jews and Jewish organizations both in this country and abroad with the rise of Hitler, Nazis and Fascism, the international drug trade, and a myriad of purported conspiracies that have bedeviled the United States and the world at large, including a conspiracy to assassinate the U.S.L.P. leader, Lyndon LaRouche. At a minimum, under the fair comment doctrine, the facts of this case reasonably give rise to an inference upon which the A.D.L. can form an honest opinion that the plaintiffs are anti-Semitic. (p. A-13)

14. Krafft Ehricke bio is in his ACSI dossier, ACSI post-1952 Paperclip files, RG 319, WNRC. For Ehricke and Fusion Energy Foundation connections see *Fusion*, March–April 1985; Konrad Dannenberg authored a lengthy article, "From the First Large Guided Missile to the Space Shuttle: A Pictorial History," also in *Fusion*, March–April 1986.

15. Dannenberg and Oberth's participation and information on anti-OSI LaRouche rally is in Nancy Spannaus, "Space Pioneer Honored," *New Solidarity*, 21 June 1985; and Marjorie Hecht, "Schiller Meet: Drop OSI, Start Crash SDI Effort," *New Solidarity*, 24 June 1985.

16. Michael Jennings interview with Konrad Dannenberg.

17. For Medaris message at LaRouche rally see Spannaus, "Space Pioneer Honored"; and Hecht, "Schiller Meet"; *Birmingham News*, 5 May 1985.

18. Spannaus, "Space Pioneer Honored"; and Hecht, "Schiller Meet."

19. Friedwardt Winterberg, "The MIRV Concept and the Neutron Bomb," *Fusion*, October 1980; and AP, "Magazine to Publish H-Bomb Description," 3 September 1980; Winterberg letter regarding LaRouche's candidacy for president is in *Fusion*, March 1980; and Friedwardt Winterberg, *The Physical Principles of Thermonuclear Explosive Devices* (New York: Fusion Energy Foundation, 1981). Information on Winterberg writing for the *International Journal of Fusion Energy* is in "The Leonardo Project," *Fusion*, March–April 1986.

20. For information on *Spotlight* and Willis Carto see *Extremism on the Right*. As example of the notorious anti-Semitism of *Spotlight* and Carto see *Mermelstein v. Institute for Historical Review*, CIV 356-542 (Calif. Sup. Ct.),

the case of Auschwitz survivor Mermelstein against Carto and others who claimed that no Jews were gassed in gas chambers at Auschwitz.

21. "German Rocket Scientist Used, Discarded by Ungrateful U.S.," *Spotlight*, 31 August 1987; Medaris quote is from "America Sacrifices Integrity," *Spotlight*, 8 July 1985. See also Medaris's attack on the OSI in "General Says OSI is Unconstitutional," *Executive Intelligence Review*, 9 August 1985.

22. Winterberg letters to the World Jewish Congress, 14 December 1985; to Eli Rosenbaum, 20 May 1985 and 2 January 1986; and to Senator Paul Laxalt, 22 July 1985 (enclosing the January 1985 issue of *Instauration*), all in author's collection; and *Spotlight*, 31 August 1987. Note: for extensive documentation on the sad fate of Jews at Mittelwerk/Dora see *Andrae*, especially the hospital reports listing the number of Jews who died, the cause of death, the number of those worked to death, and the number judged too weak to work who were then sent by train to Lublin for extermination.

23. Winterberg admitted to having interrogated Bannasch in a letter to Len Ackland, editor of the *Bulletin of the Atomic Scientists*, 8 April 1985. Winterberg discusses contacting some Dora survivors in Thomas Franklin, "Witnesses Without Testimony," *Huntsville News*, 6 April 1987. "Thomas Franklin" is an alias used by Hugh McInnish, an Army employee in Huntsville who frequently writes pro-Rudolph articles for the *Huntsville News* under an alias.

24. Michel, *Dora*; for an example of "alleged" deaths see UPI, "Supporters Challenging Agency's Allegations," 1 November 1985; Rudolph quotes are from John Hubner's articles, "The Unmaking of a Hero" (29 September 1985) and "The Americanization of a Nazi Scientist" (6 October 1985), both in *San Jose Mercury News*. Hubner was one of the few reporters who did interview Dora survivors.

25. Linda Hunt, "NASA's Nazis," *The Nation*, 23 May 1987.

26. For Buchanan meeting with Rees see UPI, 15 October 1985.

27. Ed Vulliamy, "Holocaust Project Funds 'Eliminated' by Ideology?" *Washington Post*, 4 October 1988.

28. Hunt, "Nazi Coverup."

29. Russ Bellant, *Old Nazis, the New Right and the Reagan Administration* (Cambridge, Mass.: Political Research Associates, 1988); "Bush Campaign Committee Contains Figures Linked to Anti-Semitic and Fascist Backgrounds," *Washington Jewish Week*, 8 September 1988; and "Head of Latvian Group Quits Over Link to SS," *The New York Times*, 4 November 1988. Brentar quote is from David Lee Preston, "Bush Backer Helped Many Nazis Enter U.S.," *Detroit Free Press*, 10 September 1988.

30. "Bush Campaign Committee"; and Michael Jennings interview with Bohdan Fedorak. For East European groups' anti-OSI activities see

The Campaign Against the U.S. Justice Department's Prosecution of Suspected Nazi War Criminals (New York: ADL, June 1985).

31. *Congressional Record*, 3 December 1980.

32. Ibid.

33. Rear Admiral Bosquet Wev biography is from the ONH; Major General Stephen Chamberlin biography is from the CMH; Lieutenant General Donald Putt biography is from the U.S. Air Force.

34. Letter, William Whalen to Judge Owen Lewis, in *Whalen*.

35. General Robert L. Walsh biography is from the U.S. Air Force; General Robert Schow biography is from the CMH.

36. On Noriega see the testimony of Jose Blandon, Senate Subcommittee on Terrorism, Narcotics and International Communications, hearings, 100th Cong., 2d sess., February 8, 9, 10, and 11, 1988. For Noriega bestowing a medal on Schweitzer see AP report, 12 June 1986.

37. On Strughold see U.S. Air Force, news release, 11 June 1985.

38. Dornberger information is in *Current Biography Yearbook* (New York: H. W. Wilson Company, 1965).

39. Sher interview.

40. Haeussermann interview.

41. Author notes on 19 July 1989 meeting.

42. *Federal Register*, 10 August 1989.

43. Author interview with Robert Nance.

44. Ibid.

45. Author telephone conversation with retired Army Colonel Benjamin Heckemeyer.

CONCLUSION

1. Congressman Traficant's speech at the Huntsville Holiday Inn, May 12, 1990.

2. Author interview with Canadian Justice Department prosecutor Donald MacIntosh, who explained that, under Canadian law, nonlawyers were permitted to act as counsel at the hearing.

3. Bill Moyers, *The Secret Government* (Washington, D.C.: Seven Locks Press, 1988), p. 42.

4. Ibid.

5. Hunt, "U.S. Coverup of Nazi Scientists."

6. Letter, DEA Administrator John Lawn to General Manuel Noriega, 27 May 1987, published in Senate Committee on Foreign Relations, hearings before the Subcommittee on Terrorism, Narcotics and International Communications, 100th Cong., 2d sess., 1988.

7. Samuel Klaus, "Memorandum for the Files," 21 May 1946, State fiche; Moyers, *Secret Government*.

8. Moyers, *Secret Government*, p. 7.

9. Captain John P. Roth, EUCOM, to Chief, Technical Intelligence Section, A C of S, 8 April 1947, G-2 Paperclip "Top Secret" files, RG 319, WNRC.

10. Senate Committee on Foreign Relations, hearings on Noriega before the Subcommittee on Terrorism, Narcotics and International Communications, 100th Cong., 2d sess., 1988, p. 149.

11. Michael Jennings, "Daughter of Inventor Questions Father's Twist of Fate," *Birmingham News*, 11 November 1984.

12. Allan A. Ryan, Jr., *Quiet Neighbors* (New York: Harcourt Brace Jovanovich, 1984), p. 339.

SELECTED BIBLIOGRAPHY

BOOKS AND ARTICLES

Allen, Charles. "Hubertus Strughold, Nazi in USA." *Jewish Currents*, December 1974, pp. 5–11.

Alsop, Stewart, and Thomas Braden. *Sub Rosa: The OSS and American Espionage*. New York: Reynado Hitchcock, 1946.

Anderson, Scott, and Jon Anderson. *Inside the League*. New York: Dodd, Mead, 1986.

Bellant, Russ. *Old Nazis, the New Right and the Reagan Administration*. Cambridge, Mass.: Political Research Associates, 1988.

Benford, Robert J. *Report From Heidelberg*. Heidelberg, Germany: privately printed, 1947.

Beon, Yves. *La planète Dora*. France: Éditions du Seuil, 1985.

Bernadac, Christian. *Les Médicins maudits*. France: Éditions France-Empire, 1967.

Bernstein, Victor. *Final Judgment*. London: Latimer House, 1947.

———. "I Saw the Bodies of 3000 Slaves Murdered by Nazis." *PM*, 17 April 1945, p. 1.

Bishop, Robert, and E. S. Crayfield. *Russia Astride the Balkans*. New York: McBride, 1948.

Borkin, Joseph. *The Crime and Punishment of I. G. Farben*. London: Andre Deutsch, 1979.

Bower, Tom. *The Paperclip Conspiracy*. Boston: Little, Brown, 1989.

The Campaign Against the U.S. Justice Department's Prosecution of Suspected War Criminals. New York: Anti-Defamation League of B'nai B'rith, June 1985.

Clay, Lucius. *Decisions in Germany*. Garden City, N.Y.: Doubleday, 1950.

———. *Papers of Lucius D. Clay*. Edited by Jean Edward Smith. Bloomington: Indiana University Press, 1974.

319

Comptroller General of the United States, General Accounting Office. *Nazis and Axis Collaborators Were Used to Further U.S. Anti-Communist Objectives in Europe—Some Immigrated to the United States.* Washington, D.C.: Government Printing Office, 28 June 1985.

————. *Widespread Conspiracy to Obstruct Probes of Alleged Nazi War Criminals Not Supported by Available Evidence—Controversy May Continue.* Washington, D.C.: Government Printing Office, 15 May 1978.

Conason, Joe. "The Corporate State of Grace." *Village Voice*, 12 April 1983, pp. 1, 10–19.

Conradis, Heinz. *Design for Flight: The Kurt Tank Story.* London: MacDonald, 1960.

Corson, William. *The Armies of Ignorance.* New York: Dial Press, 1977.

Department of the Air Force. *German Aviation Medicine: World War II*, vols. 1 and 2. Washington, D.C.: Government Printing Office, 1950.

————. *History of AAF Participation in Project Paperclip, May 1945–March 1947.* Wright Field, Ohio: Air Materiel Command, 1948.

U.S. Air Force Historical Office. "The Command and Project 'Paperclip.' " *History of the Air Research and Development Command.* Chap. 9, vol. 1, 1954. (Declassified per author's FOIA request.)

Donner, Frank J. *The Age of Surveillance.* New York: Alfred A. Knopf, 1980.

Dornberger, Walter. *V-2.* New York: Viking, 1958.

DuBois, Josiah. *The Devil's Chemists.* Boston: Beacon Press, 1952.

Eliach, Yaffa, and Brana Gurewitsch. *The Liberators.* Brooklyn, N.Y.: Center for Holocaust Studies Documentation and Research, 1981.

Engelmann, Bernt. *Germany Without Jews.* New York: Bantam Books, 1984.

Extremism on the Right. New York: Anti-Defamation League of B'nai B'rith, 1983.

Farago, Ladislas. *Aftermath.* New York: Simon and Schuster, 1974.

Ferencz, Benjamin. *Less Than Slaves.* Cambridge, Mass.: Harvard University Press, 1979.

Forrestal, James. *The Forrestal Diaries.* Edited by Walter Mills. New York: Viking, 1951.

Frank, Gary. *Juan Peron vs. Spruille Braden: The Story Behind the Blue Book.* Lanham, Md.: University Press of America, 1980.

Freeland, Richard. *The Truman Doctrine and the Origins of McCarthyism.* New York: Alfred A. Knopf, 1972.

Garliński, Józef. *Hitler's Last Weapons.* New York: Times Books, 1978.

Gehlen, Reinhard. *The Service.* New York: World Publishing, 1972.

Gimbel, John. "U.S. Policy and German Scientists: The Early Cold War." *Political Science Quarterly*, 101 (1986), pp. 433–451.

Goudsmit, Samuel. *Alsos.* New York: Henry Schuman, 1947.

Hersh, Seymour. *Chemical and Biological Warfare: American's Hidden Arsenal.* New York: Doubleday, 1969.

Hilberg, Raul. *The Destruction of the European Jews.* Chicago: Quadrangle Books, 1961.

Hoffmann, Friederich, William A. Mosher, and Richard Hively. "Isolation of Trans-Δ^6-Tetrahydrocannabinol From Marijuana." *Journal of the American Chemical Society,* 20 April 1966, p. 1832.

Horne, Alistair. *Return to Power.* New York: Praeger, 1956.

Hubner, John. "The Americanization of a Nazi Scientist." *West* magazine (*San Jose Mercury News*), 29 September 1985, pp. 6–34.

———. "The Unmaking of a Hero." *West* magazine (*San Jose Mercury News*), 6 October 1985, pp. 6–11, 22–30.

Hunt, Linda. "Arthur Rudolph, NASA and Dora." *Moment,* April 1987, pp. 32–36.

———. "NASA's Nazis." *The Nation,* 23 May 1987, p. 671.

——— (executive producer and reporter). "Nazi Coverup." CNN Special Assignment I-Team series, four parts. First broadcast in March 1986.

———. "U.S. Coverup of Nazi Scientists." *Bulletin of the Atomic Scientists,* April 1985.

Huzel, Dieter. *From Peenemünde to Canaveral.* Englewood Cliffs, N.J.: Prentice-Hall, 1962.

The Inter-American Defense Board. Washington, D.C.: IADB, 1987.

Irving, David. *The Mare's Nest.* London: Panther Books, 1985.

Jennings, Michael. "Shadows Touch State's Surviving Rocketry Pioneers." *Birmingham News,* 27 April 1985, p. 1.

Jennings, Michael, and Kent Faulk. "Lines Drawn on Issue of Rudolph." *Birmingham News,* 4 November 1984, p. 1.

Kahn, David. *Hitler's Spies.* New York: Macmillan, 1978.

King, Dennis. *Lyndon LaRouche and the New American Fascism.* New York: Doubleday, 1989.

Lasby, Clarence. *Project Paperclip.* New York: Atheneum, 1971.

Lee, Martin, and Bruce Shlain. *Acid Dreams.* New York: Grove Press, 1985.

Linklater, Magnus, Isabel Hilton, and Neal Ascherson. *The Nazi Legacy.* New York: Holt, Rinehart and Winston, 1984.

Loftus, John. *The Belarus Secret.* New York: Alfred A. Knopf, 1982.

Marks, John. *The Search for the Manchurian Candidate.* New York: McGraw-Hill, 1980.

McGovern, James. *Crossbow and Overcast.* New York: William Morrow, 1964.

Michel, Jean. *De l'enfer aux etoiles.* Paris: Librarie Plon, 1985.

———. *Dora.* London: Weidenfeld and Nicolson, 1979.

Mitscherlich, Alexander, and Fred Mielke. *Doctors of Infamy*. New York: Henry Schuman, 1949.

Moore, John H. *The Faustball Tunnel*. New York: Random House, 1978.

Moyers, Bill. *The Secret Government*. Washington, D.C.: Seven Locks Press, 1988. (This is an adaptation of Moyers's PBS programs "The Secret Government" and "Essay on Watergate.")

National Research Council. *Possible Long-Term Health Effects of Short-Term Exposure to Chemical Agents*, vols. 1–3. Washington, D.C.: National Academy Press, 1982, 1984, 1985.

Ordway, Frederick, and Mitchell Sharpe. *The Rocket Team*. Cambridge, Mass.: MIT Press, 1982.

Pash, Boris. *The Alsos Mission*. New York: Award House, 1969.

Petersen, Edward. *The American Occupation of Germany: Retreat to Victory*. Detroit: Wayne State University Press, 1977.

Pike, Representative Otis. "Special Supplement: The CIA Report the President Doesn't Want You to Read." *Village Voice*, February 16 and 22, 1976.

Pirogov, Peter, *Why I Escaped*. London: Harvell Press, 1950.

Rearden, Steven. *History of the Office of the Secretary of Defense*. Vol. 1, *The Formative Years*. Edited by Alfred Goldberg. Washington, D.C.: Historical Office of the Secretary of Defense, 1984.

Rodal, Alti. *Nazi War Criminals in Canada*. Ottawa: Canadian Government Commission of Inquiry on War Criminals, 1986.

Santander, Silvano. *Juan Domingo Peron y Eva Duarte, agentes del nazismo en las Argentina*. Buenos Aires: Editorial Antygua, 1955.

Santori, Jim. "Private War of Ken Loeh." *Southern Illinoisan*. 20 December 1981, p. 33.

Shoemaker, Lloyd. *The Escape Factory*. New York: St. Martin's Press, 1990.

Simon, Leslie. *German Research in World War II*. New York: John Wiley, 1947.

Simpson, Christopher. *Blowback*. New York: Weidenfeld and Nicolson, 1988.

Speer, Albert. *Inside the Third Reich*. New York: Macmillan, 1970.

Taylor, Telford. *Final Report to the Secretary of the Army*. Washington, D.C.: Government Printing Office, 1949.

Tent, James F. *Mission on the Rhine: Reeducation and Denazification in American-Occupied Germany*. Chicago: University of Chicago Press, 1982.

Trento, Joseph. *Prescription for Disaster*. New York: Crown, 1987.

U.S. Army Intelligence Center. *History of the Counter Intelligence Corps*. Vol. 8, pt. 3, "CIC With the Alsos Mission." Fort Holabird, Md.: USAIC, December 1959. (From INSCOM.)

U.S. Army Intelligence Center and School. *The Evolution of American Military Intelligence*. Fort Huachuca, Ariz.: USAICS, May 1973.

U.S. Chief Counsel for Prosecution of Axis Criminality. *Nazi Conspiracy and Aggression*. Washington, D.C.: Government Printing Office, 1946–48.

U.S. Congress. House. Committee on Armed Services. *Military Hallucinogenic Experiments*. Hearings. 94th Cong., 1st sess., 8 September 1975.

U.S. Congress. House. Committee on Expenditures in the Executive Departments. *National Security Act of 1947*. 80th Cong., 1st sess., 27 June 1947.

———. Committee on Expenditures in the Executive Departments. *State Department*. Subcommittee hearings. 80th Cong., 2d sess., March 10 and 12, 1948.

U.S. Congress. House. Committee on the Judiciary. *Alleged Nazi War Criminals*. 95th Cong., 1st sess., 1977.

U.S. Congress. Senate. Committee on Military Affairs. *Senate Resolutions 107 and 146*. Subcommittee hearings. 79th Cong., 1st sess., 1945.

U.S. Congress. Senate. Committee on the Judiciary. *Army Surveillance of Civilians: A Documentary Analysis*. 92d Cong., 2d sess., 1972.

———. Committee on the Judiciary. *Report on Military Surveillance of Civilian Politics*. 93d Cong., 1st sess., 1983.

U.S. Congress. Senate. Select Committee to Study Governmental Operations With Respect to Intelligence Activities. *Final Report*. Bks. 1–6. 94th Cong., 2d sess. Washington, D.C.: Government Printing Office, 1976.

White Sands Missile Range. Riverside, Calif.: Armed Services Press, 1987.

LEGAL CASES

Barrett v. U.S., 660 F. Supp. 1291 (S.D.N.Y., 1987). See numerous Edgewood Arsenal documents, especially L. Wilson Greene, "Psychochemical Warfare, a new Concept of War," Army Chemical Center report, August 1949.

Bonner v. U.S., CIV 81-16 3 (E.D.N.C., 1981). See report on experiment in Stuart Karger, "Incapacitating Dose of CAR 302,668 in Man, and Efficacy of Physostigmine as an Antidote," Edgewood Arsenal Technical Memorandum 114-20, August 1968.

LaRouche et al. v. National Broadcasting Company, 479 U.S. 818 (1986).

Loeh v. U.S., CIV 77-2065-B (S.D. Ill., 1977).

Thornwell v. U.S., 471 F. Supp. 344 (D.D.C., 1979).

U.S. v. Stanley, 483 U.S. 669 (1987).

U.S. v. Whalen, CR 4360 (E.D. Va., 1966).

U.S. Labor Party et al. v. Anti-Defamation League of B'nai B'rith, No. 79-11470 (N.Y. App. Div., 1980).

WAR CRIMES TRIAL RECORDS

People v. Busta and Sander, Provincial Court, Essen, West Germany, 1971. Transcript of the interrogation of Wernher von Braun at the German Embassy, New Orleans, for the Provincial Court, Essen, West Germany, 7 February 1969.

The trial records noted below are on microfilm at NARS.

U.S. v. Andrae et al. (Dora), M1079, RG 153 and RG 338.
U.S. v. Brandt et al. (Medical Case), M887, RG 238.
U.S. v. Krauch et al. (I. G. Farben), M892, RG 238.
U.S. v. Krupp et al. (Industrialists), M896, RG 238.
U.S. v. Weiss et al. (Dachau), M1174, RG 153 and RG 338.
U.S. v. von Weizsaecker et al. (Ministries), M897, RG 238.
Nuremberg War Crimes Trial Interrogations, M1019, RG 238.

Interrogations of special interest: Otto Ambros, Hermann Becker-Freyseng, Theodor Benzinger, Kurt Blome, Reinhard Gehlen, Eugen Haagen, Eduard Houdremont, Willy Messerschmitt, Werner Osenberg, Franz Regnath, Julius Reppe, Siegfried Ruff, Konrad Schaefer, Walter Schieber, Gerhard Schrader, and Karl Tauboeck. See also the subject files on Procurement of Foreign Labor, Japanese-German Cooperation, Secret Weapons, and Notes on German Weapons.

NO L-170 (*Brandt*), Leo Alexander, "Neuropathology and Neurophysiology, Including Electroencephalography, in Wartime Germany," CIOS report.
USSR Exhibit 435 (*IMT*), Leo Alexander, "The Treatment of Shock From Prolonged Exposure to Cold, Expecially in Water," CIOS report.
NO-401 (*Brandt*), "Report on a Scientific Conference on 26 and 27 October 1942 in Nurenberg on Medical Problems Arising From Distress at Sea and Winter Hardships." Gives the names of ninety-five participants in the conference, speakers, and topics of speeches. File includes copies of speeches. See especially Konrad Schaefer, "Thirst and Measures to Combat it in Cases of Sea Distress."
NO-619 (*IMT*), "2 lists of physicians attending Medical Meeting at Hohenlychen." Gives the names of the 324 physicians who attended the meeting and lists the billets assigned to them.

SELECTED ARCHIVAL SOURCES

NATIONAL ARCHIVES AND RECORDS SERVICE

Combined Intelligence Objectives Subcommittee (CIOS) monthly status reports, RG 226.

IRR name and subject dossiers, RG 319.

JIOA administrative files (1945–52), RG 330.

JIOA post-1952 administrative files (1952–70), RG 330.

JIOA dossiers (1945–52), RG 330.

P and O 091.714 TS, sec. 1, case 1 (Finnish soldiers), RG 319.

Scholarly Resources microfilm of State-War-Navy Coordinating Committee, SWNCC 257 series, "Exploitation of German and Austrian Scientists" (policy), RG 353.

U.S. State Department, "Consultation Among the American Republics With Respect to the Argentine Situation," February 1946, known as the "Blue Book," a State-FBI investigation of Argentina's wartime collaboration with Nazis, RG 59.

U.S. State Department, "Operation Paperclip" microfiche (Samuel Klaus memos, CIA memos, and other correspondence), RG 59.

WASHINGTON NATIONAL RECORDS CENTER

ACSI Paperclip post-1952 administrative files (1952–64), RG 319.

ACSI Paperclip "Top Secret" files (1952–57), RG 319.

ACSI Paperclip dossiers, post-1952, RG 319.

G-2 Paperclip administrative files (1945–52), RG 319.

G-2 Paperclip "Top Secret" files to 1952, RG 319.

G-2 Paperclip dossiers (1945–53), RG 319.

G-2 miscellaneous name and subject dossiers, RG 319.

Greenhouse files, including names, correspondence, denazification results, OMGUS Public Safety Branch, RG 260.

Lieutenant Walter Jessel, "Evidence of a Conspiracy Among Leading German 'Overcast' Personnel," with attachments, 12 June 1945, OMGUS FIAT files, RG 260.

Office of Director of Intelligence name and subject files, RG 260.

OMGUS IA and C Division to Chief of Staff, "Political Clearance of German Scientists Presently in the U.S.," staff study, August 1947, OMGUS, Civil Affairs Division files, RG 260.

OMGUS IA and C Division to Chief of Staff, "Denazification of Scientists Desired for Operation Paperclip," with supporting documents, 6 February 1947, OMGUS AG files, RG 260.

U.S. AIR FORCE

Interview with Major General Harry G. Armstrong, USAF, Medical Corps, by John W. Bullard and T. A. Glasgow, Maxwell Air Force Base, April 1976.

Department of the Air Force, *History of AAF Participation in Project Paperclip, May 1945–March 1947* (Wright Field, Ohio: Air Materiel Command, 1948). The appendix contains numerous documents relating to Wright Field, Randolph Field, and the AAF Aero Center in Heidelberg. See especially AAF Aero Medical Center, "Monthly Status Report No. 6," 31 March 1946, for research conducted by Ruff, Becker-Freyseng, and Schaefer for the AAF under Project Paperclip.

U.S. Air Force Historical Division, *History of the Air Research and Development Command*, 1954. (Classified except for chap. 9, "The Command and Project 'Paperclip,' " declassified per author's FOIA request, Bolling Air Force Base.)

U.S. ARMY INTELLIGENCE AND SECURITY COMMAND

Name dossiers listed in notes were declassified per author's FOIA requests and can be obtained by sending a request to INSCOM with the name and birthdate of the individual.

Subject dossiers of special interest include:

"Chemical Warfare Scientists"—a report on scientists' work on chemical warfare.

"CIC With the Alsos Mission," history of the Counter Intelligence Corps, December 1959.

Operation MESA—an investigation of Soviet recruiting of German scientists.

Project Derby Hat—a report on U.S. intelligence experiments with psychochemicals.

U.S. ARMY MATERIEL COMMAND

Edgewood Arsenal documents obtained under the FOIA include:

Office of the Chief of Chemical Corps, EUCOM, "The History of Captured Enemy Toxic Munitions in the American Zone, European Theater, May 1945 to June 1947."

Project Black Magic (use of CN and Mace).

Quarterly Reports, Medical Division, 1945–60.

Quarterly Reports, Chemical and Radiological Lab, 1945–60.

S. D. Silver, "Gassing Chamber for Human Tests: Construction and Operation," Chemical Warfare Service report, 25 October 1944.

J. H. Wills and I. A. DeArmon, *Medical Laboratory Special Report No. 54*, November 1954.

U.S. DEPARTMENT OF THE ARMY

Reports obtained under the FOIA include:

Lieutenant Colonel David McFarling, "LSD Follow-up Study Report," U.S. Army Medical Department, 1980.

Colonel James Taylor and Major William Johnson, "Research Report Concerning the Use of Volunteers in Chemical Agent Research," Department of the Army, 21 July 1975.

U.S. Army Inspector General, "Inquiry Into the Facts and Circumstances Surrounding the Death of Mr. Harold Blauer at the New York State Psychiatric Institute and Subsequent Claims Actions," 28 October 1975.

U.S. DEPARTMENT OF JUSTICE

FBI

Walter Dornberger FBI dossier.
Arthur Rudolph FBI dossier.
Wernher von Braun FBI dossier.

Office of Special Investigations

"Agreement Between Arthur Louis Hugo Rudolph and the U.S. Department of Justice," 28 November 1983, obtained under the FOIA for "Nazi Coverup," the CNN series that first aired in March 1986.

"Order of Mittelwerk Factory Management," 22 August 1944.

Hubertus Strughold OSI dossier.

Interview with Dieter Grau by Frederick Ordway and David Christensen, 1971 (tape obtained under the FOIA).

"OSI interrogation of Arthur Rudolph," 13 October 1982 and 4 February 1983.

"Transcript of Conference of May 6, 1944 in the Office of Director General Rickhey," 6 May 1944.

MISCELLANEOUS ARCHIVES AND LIBRARIES

CIA report to President Harry S. Truman: "German Scientists at Sukhumi, USSR," 31 October 1949, Harry S. Truman Library.

Correspondence between President Harry S. Truman and Dr. Vannevar Bush regarding importing German scientists, January 1946, in Paul G. Hoffman papers, Harry S. Truman Library.

John Marks files, at the National Security Archives, Washington, D.C., contain CIA project files on psychochemical experiments, MK-ULTRA, Artichoke, Bluebird, and a 1951 CIA Inspector General Report.

Inter-American Defense Board annual yearbooks cited in the notes are available at the National War College Library.

CIOS report: "Investigation of Chemical Warfare Installations in the Munsterlager Area, including Raubkammer," National Institutes of Health Library.

John McArthur Harris diary and memoir, March–June 1945, in Parry family collection, U.S. Army Military History Institute, Carlisle Barracks, Pa.

Ralph Osborne, "History of the Field Information Agency, Technical (FIAT)," Ralph Osborne file, U.S. Army Military History Institute, Carlisle Barracks, Pa.

Records of the Portland German Bund and German War Veterans on microfilm, Oregon Historical Society.

INDEX